D0687608

Statesmen and Politicians of the Stuart Age

Statesmen and Politicians of the Stuart Age

EDITED BY
TIMOTHY EUSTACE

St. Martin's Press   New York

LC

Introduction, editorial matter and Chapters 6, 7, 8 and 9
© Timothy Eustace 1985; Chapters 1, 4 and 5 © Jonathan Watts,
1985; Chapter 2 © Donald Wilkinson 1985; Chapter 3 © Jeremy
Ward 1985; Chapter 10 © Rod Martin 1985

ISBN 0–312–75729–8

Library of Congress Cataloging in Publication Data
Main entry under title:
Statesmen and politicians of the Stuart age.
Bibliography: p.
Includes index.
1. Statesmen—Great Britain—Biography—Addresses,
essays, lectures.   2. Great Britain—History—Stuarts,
1603–1714—Biography—Addresses, essays, lectures.
I. Eustace, Timothy.
DA307.S72   1985   941.06′092′2   84–18223
ISBN 0–312–75729–8

Contents

List of Plates

Preface

THIS collection of essays results from the dissatisfaction expressed by
many involved in teaching seventeenth-century British history at the
dearth of accessible and up-to-date biographies of those statesmen
and politicians who dominate any study of the period. There are few
studies of a length suited to the pressures on most students. There are
indeed excellent studies of Buckingham, Shaftesbury and Sunderland, and a new biography of Clarendon, but the standard works on
men such as Cranfield, Laud and Pym need some reinterpretation as
a result of the mass of revisionist work on the first half of the century.
This volume attempts at least a partial solution to this problem by
providing studies of ten significant statesmen and politicians, each
essay aiming to provide relevant and revealing biographical information whilst also examining and explaining the situation in which each
statesman found himself: the problems of the government at that
time; the personal difficulties inherent in the circumstances of Court
life; the specific administrative, financial or religious problems each
was required to solve to achieve any kind of success. Each essay must
of necessity, owing to its brevity, be essentially a synthesis of known
material and interpretation; yet each attempts within such limited
space a clear statement on the motivation, successes or failings, and
significance of its subject. By such emphasis on analysis of the issues
which dominated the century the intention is to create a series of
studies which avoid the limitations of mere potted biography.

There are many difficulties that result from this approach.
Economics have dictated tight curbs on the length of each essay. All
readers, and it is hoped that not only students will find this volume of
interest, will need some prior knowledge of the seventeenth century,
since there is no space to explain every development, especially those
only indirectly connected with the individual subject. Reference to
the notes and bibliographies (themselves only a selection of the more
accessible sources) will be needed by the reader who wishes to

discover more information about the evidence used to adduce the interpretations. Since the bibliographies have been assembled for the student or teacher rather than the professional scholar, I must beg the indulgence of those historians who may recognise their ideas and research behind some of the material, yet who receive no direct recognition.

My own thanks must go first to my fellow contributors for so uncomplainingly accepting the restrictions and demands imposed upon them. I should also like to thank Mr David Maland for his assistance with my initial steps towards arranging publication. Particular appreciation and gratitude is due to Sarah Mahaffy, of Macmillan Press, who has been a most tolerant, sympathetic and helpful adviser and guide, and to Vanessa Peerless for her assistance during the various stages of publication. Finally warm gratitude goes to my wife for her forbearance whilst this volume has been in preparation, and especially for her invaluable assistance in the checking of the typescripts and proofs, a thankless task to which she has devoted many uncomplaining hours.

TIMOTHY EUSTACE

Introduction

TIMOTHY EUSTACE

IT IS always dangerous to compartmentalise history into distinct periods and to elevate a particular period into one of special significance. The process of change is both more gradual and more subtle than such tendencies would allow. Yet the seventeenth century does have some claim both to distinctness and significance in ways which make it of particular interest and value for study by our own age. No historian today could claim that politics suddenly altered course in 1603, or that sixteenth-century harmony abruptly changed into seventeenth-century discord. Yet contemporaries did contrast the apparent failings of Stuart government with the presumed glories of the Elizabethan age: for much of the century and beyond, Elizabeth's accession day (17 November) was celebrated as a national festival. Few doubted that the problems of contemporary government were far more serious and immediate than those faced by their forefathers. There was much to support this view. The nation experienced civil war, eleven years of confused and often frightening republican government, a dramatic if bloodless revolution in 1688, and above all the unique trial and execution of a reigning sovereign in 1649. The sixteenth century had nothing to match this in terms of dramatic turmoil, despite the importance of the events of the 1530s.

Not only tumultuous, the seventeenth century was also of enormous significance in the history of Britain. Every Irishman, of whatever persuasion, remembers all too vividly the actions of Oliver Cromwell and William III. The New Settlers, Protestant immigrants encouraged to settle by the English government, may have started to arrive in the sixteenth century, but the basic land and political pattern of Anglo-Ireland was formed in the seventeenth. Scotland, providing England with a new dynasty in 1603, after at first maintaining its

1

separate identity succumbed to political and economic, if not religious and legal, union in 1707, hence forming the United Kingdom. The British Empire effectively began in the seventeenth century, when the independent settlements, consisting predominantly of fugitives from England's system of law and religion and its social and economic structure, became fully fledged colonies. By mid century they were sufficiently important to persuade the government to oversee their relations with England and with each other, and by 1713 to place colonial and commercial considerations at the forefront of its diplomacy. The Bank of England, the national debt, direct parliamentary control of all taxation, even perhaps the germs of the industrial revolution at Coalbrookdale (by Abraham Darby) and Dudley Castle (by Thomas Newcomen) have all played crucial roles in the development of modern Britain. Many of these and other equally significant developments are perhaps merely witnesses to the presumed phenomenon of historical inevitability, but their characteristics owe much to the circumstances of their birth, and hence bear witness to the significance for modern Britain of the political circumstances of the Stuart age.

In 1603 England was overwhelmingly agrarian; an ineffective imitator of the empires of Spain and Portugal, more successful at raiding others than developing colonies or great trading-companies; a second-rank European power; insular and largely ignorant of the world across the Channel; and bedevilled by financial problems which seemed likely to prevent the nation developing in strength, efficiency or significance. By 1714 (however unsatisfactory such a date may be as a turning-point) Britain was a united kingdom with a substantial, secure and growing empire, the leading commercial power in Europe, and on the verge of leading all others into the industrial age; she possessed the financial machinery which enabled her to become the arbiter of European affairs in 1713, and was about to embark on a period of political stability which would see further economic and military success. If the eighteenth and nineteenth centuries were to be the years of Britain's primacy, virtually all the mechanics necessary for such military, mercantile, financial and economic success were established in the seventeenth – and not the least of these was the establishment of the basis for political stability.

Whig historians have created the impression that the development of parliamentary democracy was virtually the duty of the English nation, a goal consciously striven for. Such a teleological interpretation is not really acceptable today. It has indeed been suggested by Königsberger, commenting on the significance of the Scottish wars,[1] that the ending of the Personal Rule in 1640 was due to one political error, and it is widely accepted that the apparent growth of monarchical power in the 1680s was a logical response to the political problems of the period, as seen in most other European nations, and that again only foreign intervention (by William of Orange, for almost entirely extraneous reasons) altered the steady and relatively stable trend of English government towards entrenched monarchical power. While both arguments tend to oversimplify the explanations of these major events, they do clearly illuminate the significance of immediate political events and in particular the intervention of a handful of political personalities. Whilst it is not easy to envisage the suppression of Parliament, of the gentry's dominance in the counties, of the strength of the common law, indeed of the pride Englishmen took in their rights and independence, it is clear that the power struggle which dominated the seventeenth century – over who should have what powers and what rights, and in what proportion to other groups – was of crucial importance for the course of the nation's history; therefore the men involved in the struggles that punctuated the century played a notable part in shaping the nation.

The role of the individual is a perennial topic of historical debate. Despite Carlyle's claim that 'history is the biography of great men', most historians in recent years have been more influenced by Marx's denial of the significance of the individual. The celebrated 'battle of the gentry' of a generation ago was succeeded by various other attempts to find a single causal explanation of the events of the first half of the seventeenth century, each substantially undermined by ensuing research. If this dialectic has failed to produce the required synthesis, it has led some historians recently to expose the significance of individual response. John Morrill's 'Revolt of the Provinces', many of the local studies relating to this period, and especially the writings of Conrad Russell have illustrated the lack of momentum towards change, the confusion and uncertainty of most of the political nation, and hence have tended to imply that rebellion was indeed the work of a handful. Anthony Fletcher's major study of 1640–2 has to a great extent revived the Clarendonian thesis that the Civil War was largely the consequence of the mutual suspicion of Charles I and John Pym.[2]

Later in the century, can it be presumed that James II's downfall was inevitable? He ascended the throne with greater power – financial, political and military – and with fewer problems to solve, than perhaps any previous monarch. Monmouth's rebellion, apparently the last hope for the Whigs, was a shameful fiasco. Yet by November 1688 James had forfeited all political support. It was not his powers (left largely intact in 1689) but his personality and chosen policies which destroyed him.

To place such emphasis on the choices made by individuals is not to accept that they could override the circumstances of their time. James merely revived the fears and antagonisms already embedded in the political nation. He *chose* to do so, but it was the suspicions of the English, based on their experience and recent history, which ultimately brought about his downfall, albeit with vital foreign assistance.

It is finally this balance of individual initiative with the context of circumstances that remains perhaps the hardest of all historical tasks. To attempt this within the confines of a short chapter is little short of foolhardy. None of the contributors to this volume would claim in these circumstances to be able to provide a definitive interpretation of their subject. What they do believe is that a certain amount of biographical study is an invaluable way to assist in gaining a clearer understanding of many of the problems and conflicts which help to make the seventeenth century so challenging and significant. Each chapter opens up a vista of political life, and attempts to lay out the scenario of choice and obstacle so that the individual's success or failure can be clearly understood and judged. The bibliography attached to each chapter will of course be an essential adjunct for those who wish to study the context in greater depth, but it is hoped that the admittedly concise analysis of each relevant situation will provide a sufficient basis for a reasoned response.

Before examining in more detail the main issues which emerge in this volume, a brief explanation of the choice of subjects is called for. The monarchs and Oliver Cromwell clearly could not be covered adequately in single chapters, and moreover their lives are easily accessible in modern biographies. Robert Cecil, Earl of Salisbury, was omitted, despite his undoubted significance in the reign of James I, because so much of his career, indeed most of the formative influences upon him, would require an examination of Elizabeth's court, distracting from the purposes of this volume. With some disappointment it was also decided not to include chapters on Sidney Godolphin and Robert Harley. These would have required thorough examination of complex administrative history, and the discussion of political issues more relevant to a survey of eighteenth-century British history. The 1690s saw such fundamental changes in the structure of British politics and government that it seemed more practical, given the constraints on the length of each chapter, to end the volume around 1700 rather than 1714. While there are some disadvantages in such a decision, it does mean that all the men covered in this volume were indeed 'men of the seventeenth century'. The Duke of Buckingham, Archbishop Laud, the Earl of Clarendon and the Earl of Danby select themselves as dominant figures at Court and in the government. Thomas Wentworth, while less active in the Court of Charles I, aroused responses which were of paramount importance during the opening months of the Long Parliament, and the survey of his rule in Ireland is important in helping to explain the complex problems of that nation and in illuminating the fears of absolute government so widespread in England at that time. Lionel Cranfield could not be omitted if an examination of the financial problems which dogged the early Stuarts was to be included. The Earl of Sunderland is shown in Dr Martin's chapter to have more significance than many, perhaps too easily impressed by his deviousness and inconsistency, assume. John Pym, while not a major office-holder, was the most important of all opponents of Stuart government, and his career is crucial to any understanding of the outbreak of the Civil War; the Earl of Shaftesbury, less positive and successful, is a key figure in the explanation of the gradual emergence of political parties. The inclusion of Sir Henry Vane the Younger is the least obvious selection. The intention is to provide some understanding of the kind of religious mentality fomented in the middle years of the century and its impact on secular events, and of an Independent who had a substantial impact on events, especially in the area of administration, yet who followed a path distinctly different from that taken by his more illustrious Independent colleague Oliver Cromwell. It is his very separation from Cromwell that makes him a more useful figure in this context than more obvious candidates such as Lambert or Thurloe. Although it will always be possible to think of others who could claim some right to inclusion, it is hoped that this selection does enable the contributors to this volume to concern themselves with most of the major issues facing government during the seventeenth century.

The most prevalent of all problems troubling the Stuart monarchy was that of financial weakness. Despite some uncertain success in the 1630s, it was only in the 1680s that financial viability was achieved. The incautious behaviour of James II ended this rare opportunity for the monarchy to ease itself out of the attenuating pressures of annual deficits and parliamentary harassment, resulting in the accession of William III, whose devotion to the duty of curbing the expansion of French power drew England into a period of major warfare which ensured that traditional finances were overwhelmed, and opened the era of annual parliamentary budgets, continued to the present day. Thus the Stuarts did indeed oversee the demise of the assumption that the 'king should live of his own', and its replacement by the Civil List and the acceptance by Parliament of its obligation to raise the taxes necessary for government. But this revolution, for such it was with enormous political consequences, only occurred in the 1690s consequent on the contrasting personalities of James II and William III.

What emerges from the two chapters which deal most substantially with this issue, those on Cranfield and Danby, is that there were no easy solutions to the financial problem. Both treasurers worked with great energy and considerable skill at managing accounts and searching out waste and corruption. Both indeed made their own fortunes in the course of their duties, but the system of low salaries and high perks and inducements made this unexceptional, and in both cases the government gained far more. Danby had perhaps greater success with Parliament; Cranfield was a more efficient financial operator. Yet their failures also had similar causes. Both were unable to convince their masters of the need for restraint in personal extravagence and generosity; James I seems to have had little understanding of the actual value of money, and Charles II simply spent whatever he received, plus a little more, until the shock of the Exclusion Crisis (or was it merely the onset of advanced years?) enabled Lawrence Hyde to persuade him to become more abstemious. Even Charles I, more cautious than father and son in this respect, spent uncounted sums on the acquisition of his superb art collection. In such situations, any savings achieved were unlikely to provide a permanent solution. Hence the major failing of both treasurers was that neither could formulate new ways to solve this old problem. Neither was original or imaginative, or capable of doing anything other than improve the efficiency of the existing system. Danby if anything reversed the modernising trend of the Treasury Commission of 1667, and Cranfield showed no interest in attempting any such audacious scheme as that formulated by the Earl of Salisbury (who, whatever his failings, at least attempted such a breakthrough with the Great Contract, intended to provide an adequate permanent revenue for the Crown). Only Pym's Excise from 1643, in response to the crisis of war, stands as a successful innovation in this sphere until the financial revolution achieved by the Whig Junto in the 1690s – the Bank of England, the Civil List, and parliamentary control of both taxation and expenditure. In reality, the two overwhelming problems until then were the nature of the Court – the personal pressures on the monarch to be generous: the by-now traditional and accepted forms of financial reward for both ministers and courtiers (be it monopolies, perks, fees or straight cash presents); the natural if unseeing selfishness of all those who feared any substantial alteration likely to reduce their income from the Court and government structure, for so many an essential lifeline, as is often made clear in this volume; and the reluctance of the parliamentary gentry, their interests based firmly in local affairs, to accept a reasonable level of taxation, a situation only overcome when a political party with some organisation and a definite commitment to an active foreign policy found itself in office in the mid 1690s. Until then there was an overwhelming inertia, or rather a positive force resisting change, which meant that reform would be limited, if even attempted. The careers of Cranfield and Danby illustrate well the restraints of circumstances on individual competence.

Yet the scale of the financial problem should not be overstated. Only in 1672 did the Stuart monarch even approach a state of bankruptcy. If the debt rather more than doubled in the reign of James I, within ten years of his death financial solvency was virtually achieved. Charles I proved in the 1630s that revenue could be increased to meet the immediate needs of the government with little effective resistance – Ship Money was perhaps the most efficiently collected of all Stuart taxes. Yet the tax burden he imposed on the nation was well under half that to be imposed during the Interregnum. Charles II, having lost all prerogative means of raising revenue and with a minimal income from Crown lands, was more dependent on parliamentary grants than any previous monarch; yet Professor Chandaman has clearly shown that the early sessions of the Cavalier Parliament were not ungenerous and that MPs were prepared to respond to the needs of the government.[3] Even when the government failings exposed in the second Anglo-Dutch War dissuaded Parliament from being more free with their grants, Charles was rarely in serious financial difficulty. Only between 1640 and 1642, and in 1673, did a Stuart government have to accept major modifications to its domestic policies as a result of financial pressure by Parliament.

It was in the area of foreign policy that the Stuarts found themselves most seriously hampered, but it is quite possible to argue that an active foreign policy was a luxury that they could easily do without, leaving the rest of Europe to exhaust itself in a series of wars which only indirectly affected English interests. Even if most Englishmen did not realise it, wars of religion were things of the past; and the more serious commercial rivalry of the Dutch, and in the latter half of the century the French, did not prevent a steady and increasingly rapid growth of English trade. By the end of the century England was in a position to become the leading commercial and trading nation in Europe, and her financial strength over the French and Dutch during the War of the Spanish Succession illustrates well at least some of the advantages of a century of relative peace.

Despite this analysis made with the benefit of hindsight, few contemporaries doubted that financial weakness was a fundamental problem for all governments (including those of the Interregnum), and only during the 1680s did it appear to them that the problem might be solved. For the last four years of Charles II's reign this was due largely to caution and French subsidies and was unlikely to be permanent. During James II's reign the scenario was radically different. Parliament granted an income sufficient to secure royal finances in any situation short of major war. How could this occur? It would be unwise to assume that Parliament's generosity represented a major trend, or had long-term causes. The Parliament of 1685 was a direct result of the preceding campaign of 'quo warrantos', by which the Crown had packed urban councils and hence ensured a predominance of loyal MPs; this itself was made possible by the hysteria of the Popish plot and the Exclusion Crisis, resulting in a substantial backlash against disturbers of the peace – in effect the Whigs. It remains as yet unexplained precisely why the country gentry so substantially ignored the belief that Parliament's existence and independence was a *sine qua non* of English liberty; after the twenty-one years to 1681, in which Parliament failed to meet in only two calendar years, an unprecedented sequence, the nation showed no concern when the Triennial Act was broken in March 1684, and in 1685 acquiesced in the highest levels of permanent taxation since the Interregnum. The safest assumption must be that stability and good order were preferable to political confrontation (which is what Parliament had predominantly seemed to ensure for many years) and the risk of violence. Charles II from 1681 threatened only the apparent minority of activists; James II promised in 1685 to respond similarly. Parliament and the nation were of course mistaken in their judgement of James in 1685 – perhaps they had been wiser in 1679–81. Yet this very quiescence suggests parallels with what were often rather earlier developments in Europe, in which the promise of security and stability, in admittedly far more dangerous circumstances, seemed preferable to the excitement of individual liberty.

Certainly an examination of the record of Parliament between 1604 and 1681 would seem to suggest to contemporaries that it could claim limited success. Its legislative successes of 1641 had led to civil war; its military success had led to military dictatorship. Its initiative up to 1629 had achieved merely an ineffective Monopolies Act and a provocative and even more ineffective Petition of Right. It had removed ministers (Bacon, Cranfield, Clarendon) when rival Court factions so desired, and had failed to do so (Buckingham) when the King stood firm. Only in the unique circumstances of 1641 had it compelled Charles I to sacrifice Wentworth and Laud. The downfall of Danby occurred admittedly after the political nation's overwhelming rejection of him in 1679, but Louis XIV also played a part and Charles II was anxious to avoid a public confrontation and the exposure of his secret policies. The Exclusion Crisis, when to most observers Parliament seemed to be able to dominate political affairs, resulted in a meagre extension of the Habeas Corpus Act. During the whole period the government had been hampered by inadequate grants from a suspicious and touchy Parliament, ensuring amongst other problems an apparently unsuccessful foreign policy. It is doubtful if such broad generalisations were drawn by the gentry in 1685, but it is undeniable that in the first session of James's Parliament, as during the preceding four years, they showed little inclination to struggle for parliamentary security and significance, and there is no evidence that the rest of the country seriously disagreed. (The second session responded much more positively to the apparent threat of a Papist standing army.) It cannot be claimed that monarchy had established anything like absolutism. Entrenched powers and privileges in the counties ran far too deep, and were to be the force which reacted to and overwhelmed James II. It is an intriguing if unanswerable question whether a wiser monarch than James could have built cautiously on the impressive foundations he inherited. Yet the very extent of those powers illustrates that the Stuart monarchy not only had survived a number of shocks, but also had emerged still well capable of personal government, perhaps more effectively then than half a century earlier.

The mentality of the seventeenth century was inherently conservative. Radicalism won only fragmentary and often illusory support – the failure of the Levellers to sustain enthusiasm for their cause is a notable example of this. At each moment of political struggle, both sides quite genuinely appealed to the past for justification. Antiquarianism was rife in the parliaments of James I, and helped to validate the claims concerning the privileges of the House of Commons which generally emerged as the ultimate issue in any quarrel with the King. Equally in 1689 Parliament responded to the provocations of the past thirty years and predominantly failed to look forward into a new political situation. The result was the necessity for much further legislation (in particular the Act of Settlement of 1701), dependent for royal acceptance on the pressure caused by war and the lack of a clear Protestant succession. Only in 1641–2 and 1646–8 was there some attempt to think into the future, and the process bitterly divided the nation.

The facts of civil war, republicanism, the rise of the Levellers and the numerous radical religious sects, and the fierce political arguments of the period 1640–60 would appear to invalidate this assumption of conservatism. It is of course true that these decades witnessed a ferment of discussion and new, often shocking, ideas; but it needs to be realised that only a small minority were involved. Amongst the gentry it is quite clear that there was at first much apathy about the civil war, and that most people participated, if at all, reluctantly and in a state of some confusion and uncertainty. Even in 1641–2 there were frequent petitions for a settlement, and experience of war merely increased the desire for peace and stability. Despite an acceptance of some of the advantages resulting from Cromwell's

Protectorate, most gentry bitterly resented the interference imposed by essentially military rule, and the unprecedentedly high level of taxation it demanded. The responses of two such divergent personalities as Sir Henry Vane and Anthony Ashley Cooper illustrate this trend. Even staunch republicans were aware that they stood no chance of winning a majority in any parliament elected, on whatever franchise, in anything like a free election (as the chapter on Vane illustrates). There was a section of the community, loosely coming from the lower echelons of the gentry and merchants, who were able to seize the reins of power, largely in the county committees, but they won very little support from their fellows, and few of them seem to have wanted any fundamental change beyond gaining power for themselves, and in some cases imposing more godly standards of behaviour. Even in religious matters, John Morrill has begun to illustrate the surviving strength of Anglicanism, or at least of Anglican practices, during this period.[4] The radical sects made much noise, and did effectively destroy the monopoly of the Church of England for ever, but they won few followers in proportion to the whole nation (and Keith Thomas[5] has warned us against assuming that formal religion was as important as has been widely assumed to be the case – many people were surprisingly ignorant of basic Christian theology, avoided church-going, and preferred alternative sources of comfort and advice). The Levellers have fascinated historians far more than they did their contemporaries. It is intriguing to examine the often amazingly advanced and original ideas produced during this period of ferment, but it would be misleading to suggest that they had anything other than a negative impact on the overwhelming majority of the political nation, as the Restoration period clearly illustrates.

In such a situation the ideas of the leading statesmen were unlikely to be very innovative. All responded almost instinctively to circumstances. The Duke of Buckingham began merely as an attractive weapon used by the Protestant faction to oust the Catholic Howards at James's Court. His emergence as a favourite in his own right was no guarantee that he would become the leading political figure of the 1620s. In his recent biography Roger Lockyer has suggested that only the trip to Madrid inspired ambitions to become a dominant minister in the mould of Olivares – if this was so, how doubly significant that escapade becomes in shaping so disastrously the opening years of Charles I's reign. Wentworth and Laud, famed exponents of

'Thorough', had little concept of government except to make the existing machinery work more effectively, and to deal firmly, indeed viciously, with anyone who dared to oppose or criticise. The chapters covering their careers show clearly the hard and unsympathetic character of their work – admirable in intent but insensitive and unrealistically dogmatic. Wentworth's failure to utilise the divisions in Ireland, and Laud's inability to comprehend the extent to which Puritanism had permeated the English and Scottish nations ensured that men of considerable ability served merely to destroy a system of personal rule which in most other respects was showing notable signs of success (the implications of the tendency of *younger* MPs to support Charles in the Long Parliament may well be significant on this point). Clarendon was above all a traditionalist, who in 1660 pinned his hopes on a balanced relationship between Crown and Parliament that had probably never existed, and which was certainly unworkable in the atmosphere of Restoration England. His ideas on the role of the Privy Council had more valid historical precedent, but again took little account of changed circumstances. Perhaps only the Earl of Sunderland showed sufficient insight and flexibility both to adapt to rapidly changing circumstances and, more creditably, to be able to suggest necessary paths forward, especially in the sphere of party and parliamentary management.

Of those involved in opposition to the Crown, Sir Henry Vane is illuminating on at least one of the radical strands necessary to provide the impetus for attempted rebellion in the middle years of the century; however, his ideas of godly government proved incapable of gaining a lasting hold on the nation. The Earl of Shaftesbury remains something of an enigma: the leader of a great movement which for a time appeared unstoppable, the first effective organiser of a political party, yet a man whose political ideas remained tightly constrained by social conservatism, who seemed willing to sacrifice the political weapon of exclusion if Charles would divorce, remarry, and produce a Protestant heir, a close friend of John Locke yet a politician who formulated a very limited political programme. Even John Pym, the most successful and creative of all seventeenth-century opposition leaders, had no fixed political objective. The so-called Bedford plan of early 1641, which would have enabled him to enter office with a carefully planned programme of revenue reform to restore the Crown's financial viability, was a predominantly traditional solution to a state of executive weakness which caused concern to many. The failure of this scheme, combined with Charles's obduracy and untrustworthiness, compelled Pym to accept more revolutionary methods. But he had as often to curb the extreme demands of some as to persuade others of the need to increase political and then military pressure on the King. The probability must be that he mistrusted Charles rather than resented the monarchy's authority, that his opposition was personal rather than institutional, and that he had at no time after May 1641 a precisely formulated programme. Indeed, apart from a constantly realistic approach to the problem of Crown finances, only on the issues of Arminianism and Catholicism, which he inextricably linked together, was he totally consistent; here his attitude showed an intolerant and traditional suspicion and hostility which was perhaps understandable but cannot be seen as the sound basis for a permanent settlement. He was a great manipulator, organiser and tactical politician, but consistency and far-sightedness were not among his leading virtues.

Pym's underlying anti-Catholicism introduces us to the most obvious feature of seventeenth-century England. The anti-papist phobia, nurtured on Foxe's *Book of Acts and Monuments* (the 'Book of Martyrs') which was almost certainly the most widely read book after the Bible, was fed by a series of real or imagined plots and conspiracies: Mary Tudor's fires at Smithfield and Oxford, the plots surrounding Mary Queen of Scots, the Armada, the Gunpowder Plot, the schemes of Gondomar, the Army Plots and the Irish Rebellion of 1641, the secret Treaty of Dover, the Popish Plot, and ultimately James II's onslaught on the Church of England. Nor should the impact of European events such as the massacre of St Bartholomew's Eve, the assassination of William the Silent, the sack of Magdeburg, and the Revocation of the Edict of Nantes be underestimated. The myth of Papists under every bed was not diminished by the friendly relationship developed by most English Protestants with their pacific and respectable Catholic neighbours. This potent emotion was part cause and part consequence of the development of the distinctively insular brand of patriotism in England. Its impact on political developments was enormous. Between Elizabeth and William III no English monarch escaped suspicion of Papist influence. The securely Protestant James I was damaged by reports of the activities of Gondomar and the Howards, while the passionately Anglican Charles I was linked to the beliefs of Henrietta Maria, Weston and Cottington. Charles II and James II were with rather more validity regarded with suspicion. Since most Englishmen associated Papacy indissolubly with absolutism, religious suspicions had a powerful impact on political developments, and especially on the gulf which, while it widened and narrowed on occasions, never failed to separate the Stuarts from the certain and lasting affections of their subjects. This was most ironic during the reign of James I, who in reality treated the Church of England with considerably more respect and sympathy than Elizabeth had done, and who produced a more stable religious situation than England had experienced since before the Reformation. As is made clear in the essay on Laud, Charles I, later to be regarded as a martyr for the Church of England, managed to alienate nearly all Protestants by supporting the enforcement of the narrow and intolerant view of an Arminian minority on the whole Church, hence fomenting suspicions of Catholicism which were wholly unjustified. The reign of James II of course irrevocably confirmed the belief of most Englishmen that Catholicism and absolutism went hand in hand.

The state of the Church of England is not so easy to define. The ambiguities and uncertainties of the Elizabethan settlement, both on questions of doctrine and structure, had created an undercurrent of discontent which Elizabeth had supressed but not destroyed. This restlessness emerged as a significant strand within the Church with the Millenary Petition of 1603. The apparent failure of the Hampton Court Conference, summoned by James in 1604 to discuss the points of concern raised by Puritan-inclined clergy in the Petition, is misleading. By 1625 the Church of England had been broadened sufficiently to contain most of the demands made in 1604. (The only major exception was the failure to provide a well-paid ministry, which ensured that throughout the century the Church was unable to secure a sufficient body of able and learned clergy to make it the spiritually dominant force in the nation.) The handful of discontented Puritans, such as those separatists given lasting fame by the voyage of the Mayflower to America in 1620, were an isolated and tiny minority, as unacceptable in the tolerant United Provinces as they were in episcopal England. It was Charles I, together with Laud, who was responsible for the division of England into those conflicting religious groupings which at least partly helped to provoke civil war and divide the nation for generations to come into 'Church and Chapel'. Nonconformity resulted from the provocation of the new ideas of Arminianism from around 1626, and Charles and Laud almost alone brought about this development. How unwise and unnecessary this provocation was can be seen by the remarkable survival of Anglicanism during the Interregnum, when services from the Book of Common Prayer were openly read even in London, and by its potent re-emergence in 1660.

The failure of the Church to establish its hegemony during the next few years illustrates another aspect of the role of religion in the seventeenth century – that it was as often used as a political weapon as it was a genuine motivating force. For the Restoration religious settlement was a clear attempt by those who had felt themselves to be penalised between 1642 and 1660 to wreak their revenge on their opponents and persecutors during that period. Just as political and religious Independency, and political and religious Presbyterianism, had become confused terms, so political and religious conformity or dissent became intimately associated until, by 1688, James II shattered the loyalty even of the most committed Anglicans. The traditional attitudes at least partly re-emerged in the party colours of the Whigs and Tories, as the conflicts over the Occasional Conformity bills were later to make clear. It will probably never be possible to separate the religious and political strands which served to form the religious attitudes and loyalties of the seventeenth century, any more than it is possible to define the precise role of religion in the French Wars of Religion or the Thirty Years War. Contemporaries would not have understood the possibility of divorcing religion from politics, and rarely were able to clarify the role played by either in their own motivations.

In conclusion, it would seem that the seventeenth century followed no inevitable pattern; rather that, at several key moments, those in power proved incapable of overcoming the very considerable problems which faced them. A continuous pattern is only formed by the inability or unwillingness of the rulers to respond constructively to those challenges, or even to provide determined and consistent support to those of their ministers attempting to handle them. While each had admirable and valuable characteristics – respectively intelligence, sense of duty, flair and determination – all of the first four Stuarts failed at least in this respect. Some flaw, of indolence or lack of vision, prevented them from emulating the skills of a Henry VII. When such a man of great ability, William III, did come to the throne, his interests were focused primarily on the continent, and, anxious as he was to preserve royal authority, ultimately he would sacrifice parts of the prerogative if this was the only way to secure the support necessary to continue his campaign against Louis XIV.

Hence the century was very much one of inconclusive struggle. The issues of power and responsibility, of central authority and individual, sectional and local liberties, had been thoroughly aired and disputed, even fought over, and certain fundamentals had probably finally been settled. Absolutism on the continental model was no longer conceivable in England after 1700. Parliament had become a regular and effectively permanent part of the process of government, with its stranglehold over the finances of the state. The country squires had secured their monopoly of power in the counties, and no government could contemplate attempting to impose centralised control over their local supremacy. Nonconformity was finally established with a respectable niche in political life, and a perhaps even more significant role to play in the educational pattern of the country.

There was no direct road from 1603 to 1714. At several points divergent paths opened up before those in positions of influence and power, who thus found themselves required, maybe unwittingly, to decide the nation's future. If Parliament rather than the monarchy appeared to have made the greater advances by 1714, this was due quite substantially to the failings of the individual kings, perhaps rather more than to the vision and genius of the leaders of those opposed to them. The failure of the Crown's ministers to bring about financial solvency and successful parliamentary management – a failure so often illustrated in the following essays, and caused as much by the lack of intelligent support from the ministers' royal masters as by their own shortcomings – ensured that the attempts by both Tudor and Stuart dynasties to preserve and maybe extend their initiative and authority were contained and defeated. Parliamentary democracy was eventually to triumph, but not as easily or inevitably as was once believed. These essays are an attempt to give at least a partial explanation of this significant development.

1. Lionel Cranfield, Earl of Middlesex

JONATHAN WATTS

FINANCE was possibly the single most important problem facing the early Stuarts. Conflict with Parliament and within the Council repeatedly came down to money, as with the debates on impositions in 1606 and on the Great Contract four years later, the Cockayne Project in 1614, the problems posed by intervention in the Palatinate in 1621 and all-out war against Spain in 1624 and the subsequent raising of forced loans to pay for the war which Parliament wanted but refused to finance. In the 1630s, the survival of the Personal Rule was threatened by Charles's inability to pay for an army to fight the Scots, and his insolvency provided the occasion if not the cause of the opposition voiced in the Long Parliament. Few political crises between 1603 and 1640 were unrelated to the government's chronic shortage of money and, after 1621, the particular pressure created by war. It is therefore not surprising that repeated efforts were made to improve royal finances under James I and Charles I, by creating new sources of income, exploiting existing ones more effectively, tightening up on administrative procedures and encouraging retrenchment.

Lionel Cranfield hoped to make his mark as the man who made the government solvent. Trained as a merchant and skilled as a financier, profiting from the Crown's financial weakness, he applied the methods of the counting-house to the royal finances with considerable success, in the short-term at least. As part of the reforming regime patronised by Northampton and then, more enthusiastically, by Buckingham, Cranfield tried to remove the worst administrative abuses, introduce proper accounting-techniques, reduce expenditure and squeeze the maximum out of Crown lands, wardship and customs duties. He worked in turn in the customs administration, as Surveyor General, in the Ordnance Office, in the Navy Commission

17

and the Treasury Commission, in the Wardrobe and Household administrations, in the Court of Wards and, finally, as Lord Treasurer. He made a large personal fortune by his activities as a merchant and used service to the Crown as a means of increasing it. By 1624 he was one of the richest men in England. Though some contemporaries accused him of corruption in misusing his office for private gain, there is little evidence to suggest that he ever put his own interests before those of the King, and his eventual willingness to stand against those powerful interests at Court which were to topple him suggest a man who put principle before personal profit. His final reward was condemnation and failure; the 1624 Parliament, encouraged by Buckingham, impeached Cranfield because his policy of retrenchment stood in the way of war against Spain, however expensive it might be. The war ruined what few reforms Cranfield had managed to implement, and lack of money continued to plague the government and circumscribe its actions.

It is the purpose of this chapter to explain the background, opinions, methods and achievements of the one man, after Salisbury, who had a realistic view of the Crown's finances. His failure to institute permanent reform reflects not the inadequacy of his own vision and efforts, but the impossibility, without wholehearted and consistent support from the King and his closest advisers, of working with success against an outmoded system, inadequate to the financial demands of the early seventeenth-century state, but shored up by the self-interest of those who benefitted from this system.

I

Right up to his death, Lionel Cranfield was an able and ambitious businessman, out to increase his own wealth and to keep it intact. The second son of an Eastland Company merchant, he was born in 1575 and educated at St Paul's School to the benefit of at least the impecunious High master, who at a later stage was able to borrow money from his former pupil. In 1590 he was apprenticed to the London merchant Richard Shepherd, from whom he learned the import and export trade while establishing his own business contacts in the main northern European trading-centres, especially Amsterdam, Middelburg and Stade. Cranfield became a member of the

Mercers' Company in 1597 and set up as a trader on his own, specialising in the kersey textile trade. In 1599 he married the daughter of his former master – a tactic previously practised by Cranfield senior. Over the next dozen years he became one of the leading merchants of London and his income grew accordingly: in 1598 he estimated his wealth at £2500; in 1606 at £12,800; in 1611 at £20,000; and in 1613, when he wound up his export interests, he was worth £24,200. Cranfield was fortunate in entering trade at a point propitious for the enterprising individual. Despite a slight depression around 1600, the peaceful state of Europe before the Thirty Years' War was ideal for trade. However, competition from the Dutch was already being felt, and Amsterdam rather than London was now the commercial centre of Europe; moreover, the English share of the cloth market, which had been dominated by heavy cloths, was being eroded by the new light draperies. It is a measure of Cranfield's astuteness that he diverted his commercial interests away from cloth just before the collapse. Though encouraged by such moves as the Cockayne Project, this was predictable by about 1612.

Cranfield's job as a merchant was a complicated one: he had to buy up cloth, sell it, buy foreign goods, reimport them and sell them off in London. He disliked working on credit and his desire for ready cash may well have been behind his purchase in 1605 of the post of Receiver of Crown Revenues in Somerset and Dorset. Lax accounting by the Treasury enabled the holders of such positions to keep the money collected before final payment was made at the end of the quarter.

Cloth export was organised usually by the Merchant Adventurers, though it is interesting that the first evidence for Cranfield's membership of the Adventurers is when he was fined for disobeying their rules in 1602; this is not an isolated example of Cranfield working for his own ends in an unscrupulous way, using an existing system but showing little respect for it. Selling was his forte; in each of the main staple ports he had agents who arranged for the distribution of cloth to the markets of northern Europe. At Stade, a market which was taking over from Hamburg as the gateway to Germany, John Rawstorm organised the sale of cloth and the purchase of luxury goods, especially Italian textiles, for sale at a good profit in London. He collected information on markets throughout Germany, Poland and even Russia, together with details of prices, competitors, bullion movements, rival products, new buyers and potential purchases. Stade had its own bourse and a postal service linked it with London.

Cranfield had other agents working for him in Middleburg and as far away as Danzig. He was a demanding employer, supervising every transaction and insisting on precise accounting. His agents were often exasperated by the unreliable quality of the cloth they were expected to sell and by his expectations that they should respond immediately to any fluctuations in markets since nothing less than maximum profits was satisfactory. Precise supervision, accurate accounting and an obsession with making money, with few moral scruples, were Cranfield's hallmarks as a businessman. He exploited situations to his own advantage by hard work, discipline, meanness, opportunism and, in some cases, the dishonesty classed as good business sense.

Aware of the danger of concentration on a single export, Cranfield diversified his interests by speculative dealing in such products as pepper, saltpetre, starch and the auction of a prizeship. An attempt to corner the market in dye-woods brought him into contact with the Yorkshire political and commercial magnate Sir Arthur Ingram, who, like many successful businessmen, lived on a knife-edge between bankruptcy, respectable business deals and downright criminality. Cranfield's sense asserted itself in not pursuing high-risk speculations with Ingram very far; few of them were of much profit to him and he eventually had to bale Ingram out. What has been described as their 'search for profit and their common lack of scruple'[1] is seen in Cranfield's comment to Ingram that 'we may join together faithfully to raise our fortunes by such casualties as this stirring age may afford'.[2] In a period addicted to borrowing and short of liquid capital, the chief such casualty was the Crown.

The collection of all sources of Crown revenue was insufficient, and fluctuations in trade made income from customs difficult to predict. Largely because of this, the device of 'farming' was increasingly used after the direct collection of customs was abandoned in 1604. The system was simple enough: for a cash payment or annual rent, an individual or financial syndicate was given the right to collect and keep one part of the Crown's revenues. From the King's point of view, it gave him ready money on a regular basis, thereby making budgeting easier; it obviated the need to organise and pay his own collectors and ensured that the dues would be efficiently exacted from those liable to pay. It also linked royal and commercial financial interests and, provided the customs farms were profitable, gave the King a source of patronage which was especially important when he had to rely on the financiers for loans. To the financier, it was a gilt-edged investment; despite efforts to wring the maximum possible out of the farmers, James was in an increasingly vulnerable position and could only play off one tender against another. The obvious loser in this relationship was the outsider, the person paying customs duties, rents on Crown lands, licence fees and the like; taxpayers' resentment was not lessened by the knowledge that much of what was paid was going into private pockets. This rankled even more when such profiteers were 'poor men, by deceit and fraud become rich'.[3]

From about 1606 onwards Cranfield became increasingly involved in profitable dealings with the Crown. His surveyorship for the counties of Somerset and Dorset brought him little financial reward but gave him an insight into the laborious machinery of Crown finance. It also gave Cranfield some of the inside information which helped him profit from the sale of Crown lands organised by Lord Treasurer Dorset from 1605 onwards. In these transactions, as in his later dealings with customs-farming, he normally worked as part of a consortium of London merchants. By 1608 he had tried investment in eight customs farms, including a share of one fortieth in the Great Farm (mainly the wool customs), increased by one sixty-fourth in 1609, and a share in the duties on wines and currants; he also bought up the right to issue licenses to retailers of wine. Increasingly he used his wealth to finance private loans, provide mortgages, discount bills, and generally provide ready cash. If Cranfield seems to have been moving away from direct trade and towards more purely financial business, then this is a sign of his desire for maximum profit from minimum risk, and he avoided the pitfalls which threatened the more adventurous but shorter-sighted Ingram. That this move demanded more contact with the Court is crucial, because it provides the bridge between Cranfield the successful merchant and Cranfield the royal servant. He was also aware that successful service to the Crown could be to his personal profit. By 1611 Cranfield was worth at least £21,000 and bought the Hertfordshire estate of Pishiobury, formerly owned by Sir Walter Mildmay.

Cranfield was a shrewd, hard and meticulous businessman; his strictures to his wife to reduce the level of her spending are totally in keeping with the penny-pinching principles he applied to his business deals. His accounting-methods were clear, accurate and modern, as befits a leading merchant. He knew the world of commerce and finance inside out, and had contacts in every part of it. More specifically, he understood royal finance and could help block the loopholes and opportunities for profit at the expense of the Crown which had provided so much of his own wealth.

II

David Thomas has recently shown that the financial position in 1603 was far from hopeless. The £422,000 debt from Elizabeth contained £122,000 from a forced loan which was not expected to be repaid. A further £355,000 was still to be collected from the subsidies voted by the 1601 Parliament, and James could therefore begin his reign more or less solvent. Peace with Spain meant a reduction in defence spending and a revival of trade with a consequent increase in customs duties. A revision of these duties was long overdue, in the light of the recent inflation, while the lax administration of wardship and Crown lands gave the Crown further scope for profit. Dr Thomas summarises his views thus:

> James had therefore acquired a throne whose income had considerable potential for improvement. If he could have found a way to improve the administration of his customs and his estates, he could have achieved a large increase in his receipts. If he could have restrained his appetite for pleasure and his generosity and if he could have avoided wars, then his receipts might have exceeded his expenses.[4]

But James could not restrain his generosity or extragavance. By 1606 his debts had arisen to £816,000 and, although Salisbury reduced them to £300,000 by 1610, they were up to £500,000 by 1613 and £900,000 by 1618. Despite the present trend among historians for revising their views of the reign of James I, the King's capacity for overspending remains incontrovertible. Admittedly, he had a family to support and needed to build up a core of clients through a system of patronage, but this cannot justify gifts totalling £68,000 between 1603 and 1607, spending on jewels of £185,000 between 1603 and 1612, and the grant of lands worth £30,000 to Buckingham in 1616. In discussing the Crown's increasing reliance on loans from the London money market and financiers such as Cranfield and Ingram, Professor Ashton points out that 'The rise of the debt in Jacobean England indicated that, unlike the situation of the previous reign, heavy royal borrowing was no longer confined to situations of national emergency, though from the financial point of view the very presence of James on the throne was emergency enough in itself.

Cranfield was not the first of James's ministers to attempt reform. Salisbury had tried to settle royal finances by a deal with Parliament in 1610. By this, the Great Contract, wardship was to be abolished in return for Parliament's grant of a lump sum to pay off the King's debts and a regular income afterwards. The scheme was frustrated by mistrust on both sides. Salisbury also increased the revenue from customs by issuing a new Book of Rates, introducing the system of farming and levying Impositions. The administration of Crown lands was tightened up and the income from wardship nearly doubled. Yet the failure of the Great Contract, which effectively ruined Salisbury's career, showed the problems facing a reforming finance minister, problems described by Professor Hurstfield as 'inherent in the faulty administative system of early modern England, made worse by the corrosive extravagance of an unteachable king'.[5] Crucial to this was the inadequate payment received by royal servants for their labours. This resulted in the need to siphon off some of the royal revenue to make service to the Crown worthwhile. Few ministers or officials would have bothered with their job had their only reward been the meagre official stipend. It was not a matter of corruption, but an accepted practice which ensured that royal financial policies were at least put into effect. Some, undoubtedly, did exploit the weakness of the Crown's finances to their own benefit, but there were those, like Cranfield and Salisbury, who while making large fortunes out of government service were willing to risk their jobs, status and wealth by following through their principles. There may have been some truth in Bacon's comment about Salisbury to James I that 'he was not fit counsellor to make your affairs better; but yet he was fit to have kept them from growing worse', but the fault was not Salisbury's. To reform the financial system of the English Crown was to challenge a whole range of interests with influence at Court, in the City and in the counties; could any individual minister take on such opposition without full backing from the King himself?

After Salisbury's death in 1612, the dominance of the Howard faction, through the Earl of Northampton in the Treasury Commission and the Earl of Suffolk as Lord Treasurer from 1614, prevented further reform. While Northampton eventually realised the need for reform and attempted to introduce a policy of half-hearted retrenchment, Suffolk was chiefly concerned with his own fortune and building his palace at Audley End.

It is, though, to Northampton's credit that he was instrumental in 1613 in giving Cranfield his first government post, that of Surveyor of the Customs. As a leading merchant, Cranfield had been consulted by Northampton in 1612 over trade disputes in the Spanish Netherlands and had been invited to arbitrate between the rival syndicates bidding for customs farms. It was as an economic adviser that his services were sought. In return Cranfield received commercial concessions such as the management of the battery-and-brass customs farm, shares in the sweet-wine farm and the opportunity for speculation in Irish customs. The start of his career at Court coincides with a marked increase in his income and the purchase of more lands; when his righteous denunciation of graft and corruption are recalled, his own capacity for profiteering from the Court should not be forgotten.

In the search for new financial expedients the Howard regime looked to trade, and the disaster of the Cockayne Project is well-known; that of Ingram's scheme for the nationalisation of alum supplies (alum being an important part of cloth production) is less famous but equally unfortunate. Both showed that liaisons between the Court and the world of business did not necessarily end to the financial advantage of the government. As Surveyor-General and therefore the link between royal finance and trade, Cranfield offered advice, but it was listened to only in the post-mortem inquiries on the projects and even then it was hardly acted on. His views show the combination of conventional commercial wisdom and business experience to be expected; the cause of poverty in the country and the decline of trade was not royal indulgence or overtaxation but 'that which impoverishes the people is their excess not only in diet, but in wines, tobacco, fruits, silks and such like foreign commodities'.[6] Simple protectionism was the answer: stop the export of bullion, put heavy tariffs on imports of luxuries, exempt exports from impositions, and the balance of trade would swing back in England's favour. The only novelty in Cranfield's view was his attempt to back up all his argument with data and statistics; the precision of the businessman was to be applied to national policy. Despite recommendations along these lines from a committee set up under Cranfield to consider tariff reform, no changes were made; the Crown was unwilling to give up lucrative impositions on cloth and other commodities for an unproven theory. Reform on the domestic front was more pressing and the dominance of the Howards at Court was slipping away with the rapid rise of George Villiers as the agent of their enemies.

None the less Cranfield had shown his ability as a potential reformer with a clear financial sense, a taste for accurate information and a capacity for ruthless organisation. When in 1616 he was made Master of Requests it seemed that he was in line to work for reform on a more fundamental level then hitherto.

III

As early as 1615 Cranfield had been developing links with Bucking-ham, acting as his 'agent and adviser', a role he continued to play into the 1620s. The favourite showed little financial acumen and, despite the King's generosity, was constantly in debt. In 1619 Cranfield was asked 'to take a view of his own private estate and to give our advice how to settle and order his affairs'.[7] The rise of Buckingham inaugurated a period of reform in reaction to the alleged incompetence of the Howards and their replacement by a new faction at Court with the favourite at its head. Roger Lockyer has suggested that Buckingham saw long-term financial reform as a means of repaying the King for his generosity and favour, and Cranfield was seen as the man best fitted to execute this policy. Once reform was underway, Cranfield outlined the nature of the relationship with his patron:

> I have called some men to account who have not accounted these seven years. I doubt some will make their addresses to His Majesty or to your Lordship. I pray let their answer be, His Majesty hath referred the trust and ordering of his estate to me. The pains and envy shall be mine; the honour and thanks, your Lordship's.[8]

James in turn said of Cranfield,

> He was an instrument under Buckingham for reformation of the Household, the Navy and the Exchequer . . . He himself many a time protested unto me that he had not been able to do me any service in the ministerial part if Buckingham had not backed him in it.[9]

Buckingham's advocacy of reform was genuine enough, as James observed: 'I never saw a young courtier that was so careful for the king's profit without any respect as Buckingham was'. The King's opinion of Cranfield was similar in that he 'made so many projects for my profit that Buckingham fell in liking with him . . . and brought him to my service . . . He found this man so studious for my profit that he backed him against great personages and mean, without sparing of any man'.[10]

Cranfield was prepared to cultivate and flatter Buckingham in order to get his support for financial reform. His reforms in the Admiralty were, he argued, to enable Buckingham to pursue a glorious naval career. When faced with a block to his plans, Cranfield urged Buckingham 'not to despair . . . for the more desparate the King's estate is presented, the more honour will be to rectify it and the more shall your Lordship merit of his Majesty to be that happy instrument that do it'.[11]

Cranfield believed in Buckingham's enthusiasm for reform yet must have been aware of the paradox inherent in the favourite's receipt of unwarrantably lavish gifts from the King at a time of retrenchment. Buckingham's patronage provided rewards for Cranfield. His baronetcy, earldom and appointment as Lord Treasurer were all due to Buckingham. His second wife, Anne Brett, was a cousin of the Countess of Buckingham, and the favourite acted as godfather to their son in 1621. Only when Buckingham's ambitions began to threaten Cranfield's financial achievements and intentions did the relationship deteriorate.

Cranfield's view of royal finance was as straightforward as his diagnosis of trading-ills: 'the true ground and cause of the King's want hath proceeded from the misgoverning of his Majesty's revenue as well in receipt as in payment'. Other financial grievances were merely the result of this: 'for all men well affected to their King and country grieve that the King should be deceived by his own, and thereby constrained, for support on his royal estate, to make supply upon his subjects by projects etc'.[12] The remedy was obvious: in order to ensure that the Crown got its full income, reform of the financial administration was crucial; and, if the crown was to live off even this increased income, then rigorous economy was necessary. Reform and retrenchment were the keys to Cranfield's policy; new sources of income were of little importance and his unenthusiastic view of parliamentary taxation as a source of revenue other than in time of war supports the view that parliaments were more trouble and probably more expensive than they were worth. At best he saw them as providing a supplement to the King's non-parliamentary income, and he certainly did not view the Commons as holding the keys to royal solvency or bankruptcy. It also seems clear that the search for an adequate independent income for the King had ample support among MPs as well as at Court; a poor king meant heavier taxation and bad government. There was no hint of sarcasm when in the 1621 Parliament Cranfield said 'I will not speak for money. I see everyone is so free as that no spur need be added.'[13] Pym in the 1620s saw that the failure of Parliament to vote subsidies could lead to its extinction, reflecting in effect Cranfield's view.

In each area of royal finance in which he was given the task of reform, Cranfield adopted the same methods. A precise survey of the offending institution was made and changes in organisation recommended. For Cranfield, the main obstacle to reform was the financial interests of royal servants, as seen in his comment that 'the officers' gain had hitherto been made by His Majesty's loss'. Any attack on vested interests was bound to create enemies. Similarly, retrenchment demanded lower spending by the King and lower incomes for those he chose to favour. Aware of this block to reform, Cranfield wrote in 1620, 'My intendment is to deal clearly with your Majesty by showing you the truth of your estate, that being left to yourself you may take care of yourself and not by pitying and relieving other men's necessities bring yourself into an extremity.'[14]

The first sign of a genuine reforming spirit in the Privy Council was when in 1617 a sub-commission was set up to investigate the royal Household. Cranfield with his ruthless business sense was well suited to lead it. The criticisms made by the Commission were predictable: the Household had too many officers, was wasteful and lavish, lacked efficient management and could be pruned to save anything up to £20,000 a year by reducing personnel and exercising economy in the provision of food, drink and – as an example of the detail of the financial survey undertaken – by burning candles until they were completely finished. Cranfield's dominance was recognised by his appointment as Master of the Wardrobe in 1618, after he had offered to run the Household at £20,000 a year instead of the estimated £42,000 of the previous regime – with the proviso that he would keep any extra savings for himself. The new economy was achieved quickly by effective and accurate budgeting and accounting, by bringing in

Cranfield's own administrators and by cutting out those officers whose peculation reduced revenue so effectively. However, this achievement should be seen in the context of the administration which Cranfield inherited from his predecessor. Under Hay it had reached an all-time low in graft, inefficiency and corruption, and Cranfield had no problem in making an annual profit of around £7000 from the Wardrobe deal.

A similar sub-commission under Cranfield, this time on the navy, revealed a similar network of inefficiency, corruption and waste. Cranfield's view was clear; 'The two royal ships at Woolwich, fit for nothing but firewood.'[15] A five-year programme of repair and ship-building was proposed with a reform of naval administration; senior officials were dismissed and Buckingham was put in control of the reinvigorated fleet.

Appointed Master of the Court of Wards in 1619, Cranfield increased revenues by 25 per cent through greater centralised control and supervision of provincial agents, but his mercantile background was less fitted to estate management than to other areas of finance. New instructions were issued for the management of the Court after the customary report revealed its weaknesses. Once again the primary block was the interest of its officers, especially in the provinces where their discretionary powers were enormous. The wholesale challenge to so many vested interests and the need for complete institutional reform were beyond even Cranfield's capabilities, and best avoided. Clarendon attributed much of the opposition to the Personal Rule to Cottington's exploitation of wardship in the 1630s.

On a larger scale, the problem of Treasury reform showed Cranfield's inability to rise above the need for immediate stringency and piecemeal retrenchment. With the fall of Suffolk in 1618, the Treasury was put into commission and, as one observer ominously said, 'The King is now preparing an exact examination and censure of the abuses in the Exchequer which in all men's opinions is likely to prove very foul.'[16] The demand for reform was widespread, with the expectation that income would rise once the old system was purged of its worst abuses. However, the Commission got no further than collecting detailed information on the state of the Treasury, and showed little initiative either in the work of reform or in promoting new sources of royal revenue. Cranfield specifically advised against extending impositions, arguing that they were detrimental to trade:

he was anyway reluctant to change the system of customs-farming, from which he had profited so well in the past and which provided such important contacts with the money market.

Whatever limited reform the Commission might have achieved, there was still the problem of the King's perpetual extravagance, and the dubious sincerity of those who had advocated reform as a way of ousting the Howards. It seems clear that Cranfield himself was motivated to some degree by desire for office and personal profit: as Pym mentioned in 1626, 'He is accounted the wisest merchant that gains most so that if such comes to offices and places of trust, he thinks it best to advance his profit.'[17] Yet Cranfield increasingly saw that service to the King and service to himself could go hand-in-hand. Lord Keeper Williams recognised his talents when in 1621 he stated, 'If any man living can improve the King's revenue with skill and diligence, you are the good husband.'[18]

Cranfield's view of Parliament and its role in his schemes for reform is not obvious. He had no faith in subsidies as a reliable source of peacetime income, yet in the first session of 1621 he was clearly trying to cultivate parliamentary support. 'Sir Lionel Cranfield hath got great commendation for divers good and honest speeches',[19] wrote Chamberlain, and the text of his speeches shows a full programme of fiscal, administrative and commercial reform. Cranfield was acting for his patrons at Court as their spokesman in the Commons, with the task of selling the policy of reform to MPs in the hope that they would vote the necessary subsidies to finance the imminent war in the Palatinate. Unenthusiastic about parliaments in general, he was uneasy in his role and became increasingly tetchy with the unco-operativeness of the House. A good performance would, however, strengthen his position at Court and win him allies in Parliament and in the country at large. His speeches in the Commons are therefore more a reflection of Court policy than his personal views, and the part he played in the attack on Bacon may well have been an attempt to deflect the criticism of the House from Buckingham.

The scapegoat for the old system was to be Bacon – unfairly so, since the Lord Chancellor had been a mild advocate of reform. Yet Bacon was increasingly isolated at Court by his contempt for Cranfield with his lowly origins, by his distaste for Buckingham and by his intellectual and social reaction against the King. The personal animosity of Coke, who was developing an influential following in the Commons, also contributed to his downfall. Without the initiative of

Coke and Cranfield, both of them seen by MPs as courtiers, Bacon would not have been impeached and his fall is one of many examples of Court faction and personal vindictiveness spilling over into Parliament. The issue of monopolies, on which the condemnation of Bacon was founded, was one which Cranfield viewed with economic detachment; he had at times advocated the extension of monopolies as an elastic source of revenue, but seems to have arrived at the view that, if damage to popular opinion and trade was to be the result, then this particular expedient could be dropped. There was, though, a strong element of opportunism in his attitude, and the disposal of Bacon, who had nothing but contempt for Cranfield, seems to have been at the forefront of his mind. It also deflected the attention of MPs away from Buckingham's possible involvement with monopolies. Bacon's fall left Coke rather than Cranfield in charge of the Commons.

Having initiated talk of reform, the Court found it difficult to control debate; as criticism of financial mismanagement and burdensome taxation and the demands for a more aggresive foreign policy increased, so Cranfield's disillusionment with Parliament grew, along with a reaction to the criticisms levelled against him personally. He was also moving to the position which in 1624 was to be his downfall: that of blocking demands for extensive foreign involvement on the grounds of expense; he found it difficult to sublimate his own views to those of the Court. By the end of the session Cranfield, the apologist of reform, was being shouted down by MPs wanting more drastic measures. They increasingly identified him not with the cause of reform he advocated but as a representative of the unreformed system with which the government was saddled. By temperament, Cranfield was not prepared to conciliate with a House of Commons unwilling passively to accept the leadership of a court spokesman.

One of his repeated weaknesses was his inability to understand the full complexity of interests in Jacobean politics, and his unwillingness, after the fall of Bacon, to play the political games of the Court or of Parliament. Reform was becoming less popular at Court: those very individuals who had risen on the tide of reform now saw it as a block to their own power, prestige and policies. Cranfield was indeed looking for sources of income to finance an expedition to the Palatinate, though not the full-scale war against Spain some MPs wanted. It was a positive gesture none the less and explains his concern to secure subsidies. Like many parliamentary managers, however, he was caught in the crossfire between a House of Commons urged to aggression by Coke and Sir Edwin Sandys and a Court increasingly prone to disregard an apparently irresponsible Commons. Sandys, a rival in the tobacco trade, saw the challenge to Cranfield as part of his personal vendetta against him. Trade therefore became a major issue, with Sandys demanding greater freedom from customs duties and government interference while Cranfield's view was that the expansion of trade was the best means of extending government income. It is to Sandys's credit that he carried most of the House with him, while Cranfield found his ties of allegiance to the Court too strong to allow support for radical opinion in the Commons. This was his own choice, however. Coke was a courtier, yet able to voice strong opposition to court policies. Cranfield had chosen to work as a link between King and Commons and such a role presented problems when economics, national and international politics combined with personal ambitions, interests and rivalries to produce bitter tensions. By the end of the session Cranfield's hold over MPs was negligible; a man of greater tact and political insight might have achieved more co-operation.

IV

On being raised to the peerage and made Lord Treasurer, Cranfield embarked with customary energy on the work of financial reform: 'I will spare no person nor forbear any course that is just and honourable to make our great and gracious master to subsist of his own',[20] and his proven methods were to be applied to the whole structure of royal finance. 'The first thing to be done', he wrote, 'is to know the true causes of his Majesty's want. That known, the supplying of them will be effected without great difficulty.'[21]

In many ways, Cranfield reached the top too late to provide effective change. There was a substantial trade depression which had produced much of the hostility to his policies in the 1621 Parliament, and the 'want of money' was felt throughout the country. The commitment to the Palatinate was expensive enough, without considering extending the war against Spain, and Parliament had not yet voted any subsidies. By the end of 1620 there was a debt of £900,000; interest payments were not being met and further credit was difficult to obtain; pensions were eating up about one sixth of the revenue, while James and Buckingham pursued lifestyles of expensive ostentation. Cranfield's estimates suggested that since the days of Elizabeth income from lands was down by a third and from other sources by a half, while general expenditure had risen two-and-a-half times. He thought that at least an extra £162,000 would be needed in 1621 alone. To remedy this new sources of income were sought and a commission set up to inquire into the Irish revenues, which were a perpetual drain on English governmental resources. Customs duties were pushed to their limits and the harshness of impositions was to figure prominently in the parliamentary attack on Cranfield in 1624. There were also attempts to farm the customs at terms more favourable to the Crown, but only desperate straits could make Cranfield suggest that the farmers should give up their rents for one year. Convinced that income could not be increased sufficiently and apparently unwilling to undertake wholesale financial reorganisation, Cranfield turned his attention to Court expenditure and especially that on pensions. Suggestions ranged from a reduction in existing pensions and a block on new grants to an immediate stop on all pension payments and their eventual abolition.

When in 1622 Cranfield reached the summit of his social advancement by assuming the title of Earl of Middlesex, his influence at Court was already being seriously eroded. Opposition to Cranfield was always present at James's Court: aristocratic resentment against a base-born Lord Treasurer found support among those who saw their livelihood threatened by the reductions in royal generosity demanded by Cranfield's programme; various commercial interests, notably the Virginia Company in which the Earl of Southampton and Sir Edwin Sandys were included, had been opposed by Cranfield; there were strong objections to the increase in customs and impositions and all these factors encouraged the increase of opposition.

Yet Cranfield was not totally isolated at Court. In the committee-council set up during the King's illness in November 1623, he had an ally in Arundel in promoting a policy of peace, and during Buckingham's absence in Madrid Cranfield moved closer to James in an attempt to impress on him the need for continued financial restraint. While there was no formal rift with Buckingham, there were rumours that Cranfield was intriguing against him, and he may well have doubted the favourite's capacity for political survival. By April 1624 the Venetian ambassador could write, 'The Lord Treasurer is almost openly trying to oust Buckingham, assisted secretly by the Earl of Arundel. The method is by bringing forward a young kinsman of the Treasurer.'[22] The boy in question was Arthur Brett, who was intended to supplant Buckingham.

How far Cranfield saw Buckingham himself as a block to reform it is difficult to judge. The campaign against pensions would obviously hit Buckingham and his powers of patronage, yet he seemed willing to act on Cranfield's advice and allow the Treasurer to vet new pensions. However, the two seem to have drifted apart in 1623, and Buckingham's increasing support for an all-out European war was probably behind this cooling of relations. However effective Cranfield's financial reforms were, they could not support the vast costs of further military commitments.

It is worth making clear Cranfield's precise attitude towards foreign policy. In 1621 he seems to have been behind the Court's plan for limited involvement in Europe to help the Elector Palatine and his English wife, but against the wider involvement demanded by Parliament because it would cost too much. MPs therefore branded him an opponent of a really Protestant foreign policy. In supporting the Spanish match, Cranfield was concerned only with the money it would bring in and the fact that it would help avoid a European war. Religion played no part in his calculations, something which sets him apart from many of his contemporaries. While the Spanish-match negotiations continued, Cranfield could live in hope of a substantial dowry and the maintenance of peace. But with the return from Madrid of Buckingham and Charles convinced that continued impartiality was impractical, and that England's role was as a Protestant leader on the European stage, all schemes for retrenchment fell apart. Even though in 1624 royal income was up by about £80,000, there was a deficit of over £100,000 for that year, and the prospect of large military expenditure in future. In 1618–19, ordinary expenditure by the Crown had been £310,459; in 1620–1, £385,135; and in 1621–2, £431,941. Against this, Cranfield could boast in 1621 of savings in the Household of £18,000, in the Navy of £25,000, and in the Ordnance of £20,000; but this was the high point of success.

The conclusion to be drawn from this is inevitable: as Lord Treasurer Cranfield made virtually no headway in ensuring Crown solvency, in changing the system by which money was raised or in preventing increases in expenditure, though it is only fair to add that without the total backing of the king no individual could have done much better. James followed the advice of his chosen intimates, rather than that of his bank-manager.

With the meeting of the 1624 Parliament, Cranfield and retrenchment were both lost causes. He had chosen to stand by his policies and now paid the price of opposing Buckingham. As Conrad Russell has recently shown, Parliament could be used by anyone with an acceptable programme to put before it: just as Bacon's impeachment in 1621 had been the result of personal animosity and Court faction, so Cranfield's fall was engineered by Buckingham and his clients at Court. Their aim was to remove the one possible obstacle to war, while simultaneously cultivating the desire of MPs for a Protestant foreign policy. Beginning with Sandys's condemnations of new impositions in the Committee for Trade in April 1624, and the implied criticism of their chief supporter, the Lord Treasurer, the impeachment proper started in May with various charges of corruption and mismanagement in the Court of Wards, Ordnance Office and Wardrobe. James showed support for Cranfield and told the Lords, 'I was deceived if he were not a good officer',[23] yet it says much for the strength of Buckingham's influence and the reversionary interest around Charles that the King's view was ignored.

The various charges were easily proven, given the atmosphere of both houses and Cranfield's predeliction for personal gain from public office. The 1624 Parliament was prepared to throw financial caution to the wind in a spirit of military solidarity with the defeated forces of European Protestantism; the tetchy obstructionism of Cranfield's financial realism provided an ideal focus for MPs, encouraged as they were by those at Court who stood to gain from the removal of a reforming and penny-pinching Treasurer. Cranfield was sentenced to imprisonment, a fine of £50,000 and perpetual exclusion from office. He was released from the Tower shortly after the dissolution of the Parliament, and his fine was reduced to £20,000. The reappearance at Court of Arthur Brett made Cranfield's return to favour a brief possibility.

The very activities which had made him so vulnerable to charges of corruption ensured that his retirement was comfortable. His years as Lord Treasurer saw no reduction in his personal business deals and he acquired several estates during that time. By 1625 his property was valued at around £100,000, while his annual income was estimated at £25,000. However, he increasingly got into debt and various parts of his estates were sold off to relieve the pressure from his creditors and pay his fine. By 1635 his income was reckoned at a mere £5000 a year. It is important to recognise that, while office might be a gateway to wealth, the loss of office involved equivalent financial loss; and it is to Cranfield's credit that he took this risk by his stand in 1624. Cranfield continued to observe political events from the sidelines, and contacts with Lord Treasurer Weston in the 1630s suggest that a return to office was not impossible. But this was not to be, and he died on 5 April 1645, an almost impartial spectator of events which had overtaken his own political experience.

To the end, he was out to clear his name of the accusations of bribery and corruption which had led to his downfall. In a period when peculation was accepted as the reward of office, the criticisms of Cranfield might seem harsh. Yet his substantial gains were hard to accept from one so keen to limit the profits of others in the interests of royal efficiency. His policy of retrenchment may have been greeted with some scepticism by those who doubted Cranfield's own total commitment to reform, given the way in which his own fortune had been amassed. However, Lockyer's comment on Suffolk's fall could equally well be applied to Cranfield: 'It was only when political and factional considerations made his removal necessary that the charge of corruption was laid against him: moral indignation was in this case, as in so many others, the language of political conspiracy.'[24]

V

So complete was Cranfield's final failure that it is easy to overlook his achievements. The skills of the merchant which he introduced into the financial departments of state were eventually to stick and make accounting more accurate and efficient. His assessments of trade and economic problems impressed contemporaries. His understanding of the financial predicament of the Crown was masterful. Why, then, did he fail to achieve any permanent solution to the Crown's financial problems? How far was he personally to blame for failure, or was he just the victim of a financial system incapable of responding to the pressures now being put on it, but equally incapable of being changed without injuring influential vested interests?

Undoubtedly, Cranfield's personality did not make his task easier. He was an irascible, condescending, intolerant and demanding man,

eager to overcome the middle-class origins so often held against him—
qualities which may have been fitting for a merchant, but were not
part of a successful politician. His own profit-making activities made
him an ambivalent advocate of reform. He had little time for Court
politics, despite the importance of factions in determining policy, and
failed to build up any body of support either at Court or in the country
at large, relying on the support of Buckingham and James alone. His
view of finance was essentially one of piecemeal reform and retrenchment and he lacked the vision required to innovate and provide new
and effective sources of revenue. The success of Ship Money a decade
later showed that with some imagination financial change could be
introduced, and that efficiency of administration was attainable.

Yet, despite all these criticisms, two factors stand out as blocks in
Cranfield's path to success: the King and the financial system in need
of reform. Try as he might, Cranfield could not convince the King of
the necessity of personal economy and the need to back the campaign
for retrenchment against those who sought to increase royal spending. Any reform of finance was bound to alienate all those who
benefited from the old system, above all the royal officers who
depended on it for their income. However, most European governments in the early seventeenth century found themselves trapped
between inadequate resources and vested interests, often the very
classes which kept the Crown in power; very few rulers had the
courage to challenge these interests by sweeping reforms. The
eventual outcome of the Personal Rule in England, the alienation of
the political classes by attempts to tighten up administrative and
financial inefficiency, showed the real problem of governmental
reform. A study of French royal finance in the early seventeenth
century reveals exactly the same tension between inadequate revenue
and the impracticality of reform.

Like Salisbury, Cranfield tried to change the system of English
government finance: both were willing to sacrifice their careers rather
than see the King reduced to poverty; and both were defeated by the
system. As James I observed, 'All Treasurers if they do good service to
their master must be generally hated.'[25]

2. George Villiers, Duke of Buckingham

DONALD WILKINSON

BUCKINGHAM'S career was frequently compared by contemporaries to the progress of a comet across the sky. Their comparison was justified. In the period between 1614 and 1628, he travelled from obscurity to become the most powerful, and the most hated, man of his time. He amassed a considerable fortune which was spent in especially conspicuous consumption. He dominated and ultimately controlled the patronage network at the Courts of James I and Charles I. He was, in effect, the chief minister of both kings, although there were important differences between the extent of his control of decision-making under James and under Charles.

Brief though it was, Buckingham's career has been the subject of virtually unanimous condemnation by historians. S. R. Gardiner concluded that Buckingham 'must rank amongst the most incapable ministers of this or any other country'.[1] Twentieth-century historians have been equally censorious. H. R. Trevor-Roper remarked that Buckingham had 'a political megalomania which was a political disaster'.[2] Clayton Roberts, an American historian, produced as damning a verdict on the Duke as it is possible to construct in a few sentences;

> Governed by pride and passion, swept by unreasonable hope and unreal dreams, devoid of wisdom and prudence, he rushed from one disaster to another . . . His follies were not trivial, occasional or of a kind that can be explained away. They were continual, gross and palpable.[3]

Until quite recently, few historians would have dissented at all from such sentiments. However, Buckingham has been accorded more

37

sympathetic treatment by some of the so-called 'revisionist' historians of early-seventeenth-century England. Conrad Russell, for instance, has argued that Buckingham 'showed more sagacity than he has been given credit for' in attempting to deal with the problems he faced.[4] But the most sympathetic reappraisal is to be found in Roger Lockyer's biography of the Duke. In this a picture of Buckingham emerges which would be impossible to imagine from the collective disapprobation of Gardiner, Trevor-Roper, Roberts and their ilk. Buckingham is presented as an intelligent, sensitive man who used the political power he acquired in what he considered to be England's best interests. In domestic affairs, the Duke frequently took on the role of the trimmer, attempting to achieve compromise so that the King's government and administration could proceed as efficiently and effectively as possible. Roger Lockyer also argues that, after his visit to Madrid in 1623, Buckingham pursued a coherent foreign policy designed to counter the threat of a Habsburg-dominated Europe.

It is the aim of this chapter to try to reconcile these contrasting views of the Duke, by examining some of the major aspects of his career against the background of the times in which he lived.

I

There was little about Buckingham's early life to suggest the career he was to have. George Villiers was born at Brooksby Hall, Leicestershire, on 28 August 1592, the third child of his father's second marriage. The Villiers family had lived in Leicestershire since the thirteenth century, but by the time of George's birth the family was typical of many county gentry families, neither particularly illustrious nor completely obscure. Although his father was by no means poor, George Villiers could not expect to inherit much wealth. Most of the family property went to the eldest son of his father's first marriage. However, after George's father died in 1606, his mother remarried twice, and her third husband, Sir Thomas Compton, was able to provide her and her children with greater financial security. More importantly, Compton also had contact with the Court. He was the son of a peer, and brother of the future Earl of Northampton.

George Villiers displayed little academic promise, and his education was not extensive. When he was sixteen he went to France, and, although he gained an understanding of the language, he could speak it only with difficulty and hardly write it at all. His stay in France was more important in teaching him social skills, such as horse-riding, fencing and dancing. When he returned to England in 1612 or 1613, he and his family decided that he should seek his fortune at Court. There was probably not much else open to him.

Villiers's acquisition of favour and fortune revolved upon his relationship with James I. James had always had a predilection for handsome young men. Esmé Stuart, James Hay and Robert Carr had all owed their high estimation in James's eyes, at least in part, to their looks. Clarendon believed that no one had ever achieved such greatness as Villiers did, 'upon no other advantage or recommendation than of the beauty and gracefulness and becomingness of his person'.[5] Even Sir Simonds D'Ewes, a rather dour commentator, 'saw everything in him full of delicacy and handsome features'.[6]

James I probably saw Villiers for the first time in 1614. While he seems to have liked him immediately, it was not until the following year that Villiers's fortunes really began to rise, when Villiers was used as a weapon in the faction fighting prevalent at Court. For some time, and especially since the failure of the Earl of Salisbury to negotiate the Great Contract in 1610, James had listened increasingly to the advice of the Howard family. This gave the Howards a large amount of influence over the destination of royal patronage, and allowed them the opportunity to persuade James to follow a pro-Spanish foreign policy. This policy, manifest in attempts to negotiate a marriage between James's son and the Spanish Infanta, was James's own policy anyway. However, it was interpreted as a pro-Catholic policy opposed to the true interests of Protestantism by a rival faction at Court, in which the Archbishop of Canterbury, George Abbot, and the earls of Pembroke and Southampton were the leading figures. The Abbot–Pembroke–Southampton group thought that they would be better able to win James round to their point of view if they could establish somebody dependent upon them close to James. It was particularly important that they acted quickly, for the dominance of the Howards had appeared to be secured when Frances Howard, the daughter of the Earl of Suffolk, the Lord Treasurer, had married the King's favourite, Robert Carr, Earl of Somerset, in December 1613.

However, there were signs by 1615 that James's relationship with Somerset was under some strain. Somerset had begun to act increasingly high-handedly towards James, and now that he was married he found James's affections tiresome. He was also alarmed by the opposition which his marriage into the Howard family had aroused in some sections of the Court. When Somerset saw James's liking for Villiers he tried to stop Villiers's advancement. At first he had some success. In November 1614 James acceded to Somerset's request not to appoint Villiers to a post in the Bed-chamber. Instead, Villiers had to make do with an inferior position as a cupbearer.

Villiers's advancement was not to be held up for long. In April 1615 Archbishop Abbot was able to persuade the Queen to recommend Villiers's promotion to James. James insisted that his favourites should first have his wife's recommendation so that he could use this in his, and their, defence if she ever complained about their behaviour. Queen Anne, according to Abbot's account of the incident written twelve years later, consented reluctantly, warning Abbot that one favourite was like another, and that he was only preparing a scourge for himself. But Abbot was insistent 'that the change would be for the better'.[7] Despite opposition from Somerset, James knighted Villiers and made him a Gentleman of the Bedchamber.

It is not absolutely certain that James intended to replace Somerset with Villiers, for he seems to have hoped that Somerset would have shared his delight in honouring Villiers. It was unlikely that Somerset would ever have been reconciled to such an idea, but his wishes in the matter became immaterial when he was committed for trial in October 1615 for his part in the Overbury affair. Frances Howard, Somerset's wife, had formerly been married to the Earl of Essex. She had managed to obtain a divorce from Essex to enable her to marry Somerset. Her divorce had only been recommended by a majority of seven to five by the commission set up to consider it. The commission granted the divorce on the dubious grounds that Frances Howard had remained a virgin because of, and despite, Essex's failure to consummate their marriage. Sir Thomas Overbury had been a friend of Somerset. He was alarmed by his loss of influence over Somerset after Somerset's affair with Frances Howard began. Somerset, tired of Overbury's attentions, tried to have him sent abroad on a minor diplomatic mission. Overbury refused to go and was sent to the Tower. It was here that he was murdered, certainly through the instigation of Frances Howard, and possibly with Somerset's conni-vance, because it was feared that he possessed evidence which could

have prevented Frances's divorce. In 1616 Frances Howard and
Somerset were tried and found guilty of the murder. Although they
were spared execution, they were effectively removed from Court life.
Somerset's rapid fall was an object lesson that favour in James's reign
was far from fixed or guaranteed.

Villiers, therefore, had won the King's attention through his
handsomeness, and, in a few months, because of the workings of
Court faction and the disgrace of James's former favourite, established himself as the King's favourite. His relationship with James
became very close. That is evident in their letters, where James clearly
regarded Steenie, his pet name for Villiers (apparently after his
likeness to a painting of St Stephen which James possessed), as
virtually his son. Villiers, in his turn, referred to James as his 'Dear
Dad and Gossip', or his master, and himself as the master's dog.
There was also another element in Villiers's rapid and firm establishment in James's affections. It seems almost certain that Buckingham and James had, at least for a time, a physical homosexual
relationship. Circumstantial evidence of this is plentiful, for James
was noted for the attention he paid his favourite. Direct evidence is,
by the nature of the matter, less easy to find. However, writing some
years later, Buckingham referred to an occasion in the summer of
1615 at Farnham Castle when 'the bed's head could not be found
between the master and his dog.'[8] If Buckingham did go to bed with
James, that perhaps also helps to explain Somerset's fall from favour,
because he appeared to be uninterested in any physical relationship
with the King.

II

James was quite open about his fondness of Buckingham. A speech to
the Privy Council in 1617 provided clear evidence of his feelings:

> I, James, am neither a god nor an angel, but a man like any other.
> Therefore I act like a man, and confess to loving those dear to me
> more than other men. You may be sure that I love the Earl of
> Buckingham more than anyone else, and more than you who are
> here assembled. I wish to speak in my own behalf, and not to have it
> thought to be a defect, for Jesus Christ did the same and therefore I
> cannot be blamed. Christ had his John and I have my George.[9]

However, this close relationship did not mean that Buckingham's position was entirely secure.

It was only in 1618 that his rivals, the Howards, were disgraced and removed from their offices. Buckingham had to face competition from potential rival favourites. The Howard faction tried to groom William Monson to captivate James and thereby arrest the decline in their fortunes in 1618. In 1622 Lionel Cranfield was linked with the emergence of Arthur Brett at court. Brett, another good-looking young man, was appointed a Gentleman of the Bedchamber and there were rumours that James showed him unusual favour. Buckingham, however, was not displaced in the King's affections, but he took the precaution of having Brett sent on a minor diplomatic mission before he went to Madrid. The journey to Madrid, by taking Buckingham away from the source of his power, gave him many anxious moments as his correspondents related how his influence could be seen to be declining at Court. It was even rumoured in the last few months of James's life that he was planning to reduce Buckingham's influence. In 1624 James seems to have taken seriously Spanish allegations that Buckingham had been involved in plots against him. At any rate, he made all his Privy Councillors swear that they had not conspired against him.

On the other hand, it would be equally wrong to see Buckingham as merely James's 'plaything', as Roger Lockyer comes close to suggesting in his biography of the Duke. Buckingham certainly profited greatly from the King's generosity and favour, as if James were merely a sugar daddy to the favourite. As Clarendon remarked, Villiers's 'ascent was so quick that it seemed rather a flight than a growth'.[10] Offices, titles, wealth and influence all accrued to him. On 4 January 1616 he was appointed Master of the Horse. It was a sign of Villiers's favour that Somerset had never managed to acquire the office despite considerable attempts to do so. In April 1616 Villiers became a knight of the Order of the Garter, while in July he became Viscount Villiers. In January 1617 he was elevated to the title of Earl of Buckingham. A month later he was appointed to the Privy Council, and at the beginning of 1618 was made Marquis of Buckingham. Thereafter, his acquisition of titles and offices was a little more restrained. He became Lord High Admiral in January 1619, in succession to the Earl of Nottingham. While he was in Madrid in 1623 he became the Duke of Buckingham, England's first duke of non-royal blood for nearly a century. In the following year Buckingham purchased the Lord Wardenship of the Cinque Ports from its previous incumbent, Lord Zouch.

Titles and offices alone did not provide their holders with much wealth. For instance, the official fee of the Master of the Horse was only £66-13s-4d per annum. However, the office could produce for its holders about £1500 annually when its perquisites were exploited, and the Master of the Horse could also keep horses he judged no longer fit for the King's stables.

Gifts of land were especially important in improving Buckingham's financial position. In 1616 and 1617 he was given about £30,000 worth of lands by James. Large gifts were given to him at other times, especially in 1623 when James tried to help him escape from his burgeoning debts. Sales of titles also produced income for Buckingham. Between 1615 and 1628, about £350,000 was made from sales of peerages. The Crown obtained about £150,000 of this sum; much of the rest went to Buckingham. Exact calculation of Buckingham's income is impossible, but by 1620, and for the rest of his life, it cannot have been less than £20,000 annually. Buckingham's financial gain was not unusual by the standards of the early seventeenth century. Robert Cecil, Lionel Cranfield and Thomas Wentworth all made similar, if not greater, profits from their service to the Crown. Despite his high income, Buckingham had considerable debts because of his even higher expenditure. As a great man at Court, he was under considerable pressure to act the part. This involved generosity towards his family and friends, and a high degree of conspicuous consumption, in terms of entertainment, dress and the decoration of his houses. Buckingham also used his own income in the service of the Crown. Debts led to borrowing, which produced interest charges. Therefore Buckingham's income, like the Crown's, was inadequate for his needs.

Buckingham was exceptionally keen to see that his family was well provided for. His mother and brothers acquired titles. Close and distant relatives were provided with marriage partners of high social status. Buckingham himself married Katherine Manners, the daughter of the Earl of Rutland, and an heiress of considerable wealth. His sister, Susan, married the Earl of Denbigh. A cousin, Anne Brett, of no fortune and little beauty, was made the price of Lionel Cranfield's further political promotion. But marriage-broking was not without its problems. John Villiers, Buckingham's half-witted brother, was married to Frances Coke, the daughter of Sir Edward Coke, despite

Frances's and her mother's objections to the match. Frances later had an adulterous relationship which produced a child, a case before the Court of High Commission, and much embarrassment for the Duke of Buckingham, and, no doubt, poor John Villiers.

As the King's favourite, Buckingham was a key figure in the patronage network at Court. This meant that he was an important political figure almost from the time he began to acquire offices at Court. Certainly as early as 1617 there was considerable opposition and discontent expressed at the way in which Buckingham tried to prevent Sir Henry Yelverton becoming Attorney General because he had not courted him for the office. Buckingham deliberately used his position to create a patronage network dependent upon him alone. Most important offices went to his clients, especially after the fall of the Howards in 1618. Sir Francis Bacon, an early adviser of Buckingham on the ways of the Court and politics, became Lord Keeper in 1617. Sir Robert Naunton, a Buckingham client, became Secretary of State in 1618. Montagu and Cranfield owed their promotions to the Lord Treasureship in 1620 and 1621, at least in part, to Buckingham. Buckingham's patronage network has not yet been thoroughly analysed, but it seems that he had a tendency to favour men who were ordinarily outside the usual circle of clients finding favour at Court. This was probably a reflection of his own position as an outsider amongst those who felt they should be the recipients of the Crown's favour, especially aristocrats of old families, such as the earls of Arundel and Pembroke. However, Buckingham was in many ways in an unenviable position. Given that the favours he and the Crown could distribute were limited, resentment was bound to occur. A monarch's favourites were often unpopular with some people. Elizabeth's favourites, the Earl of Leicester and the Earl of Essex, had had to endure similar dislike. More importantly, Buckingham promoted men who were often purely creatures of the Court. This meant that the Crown was failing to use its best device for securing loyalty in the counties.

However, Buckingham did not have total control of patronage while James was King. James still made appointments and decisions against his wishes. For instance, Sir Walter Ralegh's execution went ahead despite Buckingham's intercession on his behalf. In 1621 John Williams was appointed Lord Keeper according to James's personal wishes. Sir Robert Naunton was removed as Secretary of State because he had offended James. The great aristocrats of the Court were not excluded from the King's presence. This was very important in enabling the Court to maintain a heterogeneous structure. It was still a place where diverse opinions existed, so that it was possible to feel that redress could be had there. The Court was not as narrow and exclusive under James as it was to become in the later 1630s. There was, moreover, the prospect that Buckingham's influence would end with James's reign. Besides, Buckingham possessed many qualities that made him an attractive figure.

He was noted for his charm and courtesy. Contemporaries commented on his intelligence. Bishop Goodman, for instance, wrote that 'truly his [Buckingham's] intellectuals were very great; he had a sound judgement and was of quick apprehension'.[11] Clarendon remarked upon Buckingham's understanding of 'the arts and artifices of the court'.[12] It is this side of the Duke which helps to explain how he was able to establish himself as a successful Court politician. And, as the Earl of Kellie remarked in a very interesting view of Buckingham in 1622, his faults were to some, understandable and excusable:

> and this much I may out of my own observation say, that he has a great deal more wit than men would believe, and that which most men complain of him is his doing so much for his friends. If it be an error it is a pardonable one, and I could wish myself so fortunate as to be one of them, for I could never have the good hope to be so well beloved with any that has been yet in favour . . . .[13]

III

Buckingham's first impact on the direction of what we would now call government policy came with his emergence as the patron of reform of the Crown's finances. James's financial situation had worsened steadily since his accession to the throne. Expenditure frequently exceeded an anachronistic income. Reform of the Crown's financial situation through Parliament had proved impossible and, as the Crown's resources were inadequate to pay its servants, the exploitation of office and the increased competition for it had increased the venality of offices and made allegations by outsiders of corruption against officers and courtiers more frequent. Buckingham's patronage of reform was also a reaction against the notorious inadequacies of the attempts of the Howards to run royal administration. Reform had its greatest successes when Lionel Cranfield reduced Household and Wardrobe expenditure. However, reform of the whole structure of government finance was impossible, because of the entrenchment of vested interests in the prevailing system. It was impossible to increase the Crown's income without affecting adversely gentry, aristocratic, commercial and financial interests. The Crown depended on these groups for the government of the counties, taxation and loans, so that it was unable to offend them without creating dangerous political problems, as Charles I was to discover. Moreover, desire for reform was tempered by those favoured by royal largesse because it would have meant an end to such generosity. Buckingham's own position was a classic example of the problem.

Buckingham had a genuine interest in reform, as he clearly demonstrated as Lord High Admiral. He exercised close supervision over all departments of the Navy. He was neither incompetent nor neglectful. Indeed, he was probably the first Lord Admiral to take his administrative responsibilities seriously. Much of his work was concerned with the deployment of ships and men. His correspondence with Pennington shows how seriously he took this aspect of his position. But Buckingham also tried to improve the conditions of the sailors by his concern with wages, clothing and even the availability of medicines for the treatment of the sick and wounded.

Lockyer has argued that the years between 1618 and 1621 saw Buckingham emerge from his position of favourite to that of statesman. This occurred largely because of the pressures caused by the beginnings of the Thirty Years War and the way in which Buckingham, as the figure closest to James, was courted by those with interests in the fate of the Palatinate, such as the Spanish ambassador, Gondomar, and Elizabeth of Bohemia's representative, Count Dohna. There is much truth in this, but there is not much sign that Buckingham had emerged as a 'policy-maker' in his own right until after his return from Madrid in 1623.

In the first session of the Parliament of 1621, Buckingham was largely on the defensive as he tried to avoid the Commons' wrath against monopolies. After the successful prosecutions of Mompesson and Bacon, he was forced to defend himself in the Lords against the accusations of Sir Henry Yelverton that he was entirely responsible for monopolies. Yelverton had been implicated in the enforcement of the gold-and-silver-thread patent and thought that an attack on Buckingham would be his best line of defence. However, he pressed his case too hard when he compared James and his favourite to Edward II and Hugh Despenser. Buckingham defended himself skilfully against the charges and Yelverton was fined heavily for his behaviour. Buckingham probably never had any idea of just how unpopular he was in this session of Parliament. His success in avoiding prosecution and diverting the attack against monopolies from the monopolists to the lawyers who had approved the patents in the first place perhaps gave him the idea that he could, if he wished, manipulate Parliament to his advantage. At any rate, one contemporary observer noted that Buckingham was delighted to have discovered himself 'Parliament proof'.[14]

If Buckingham thought that Parliament was easy to manipulate, the second session of the 1621 Parliament probably made him warier. The session began in the expectation that the King was going to declare open war on the Habsburgs, in a rather belated attempt to help the Elector Palatine. Most MPs, however, were more concerned with domestic affairs because of the current economic depression. Support for the idea of war was at first limited and confined largely to those associated with particularly apocalyptic views on the Protestant cause. The Crown did not help by its failure to give any lead through its spokesmen in the House. Against this background Sir George Goring introduced a motion in the Commons on 28 November that, if the King of Spain did not agree terms about the Palatinate, then England should go to war in its defence. It seems that MPs assumed that this was a sign of the King's wishes. Goring was well known as a client of Buckingham, who, at this time, was at Newmarket with the King. It seems very likely that Buckingham was here following the King's instructions and that his intervention was not his own initiative. However, Parliament responded too enthusiastically. Not only did it endorse Goring's motion, but it also suggested, in its petition of 3 December, that Prince Charles should marry a Protestant and that the recusancy laws should be strictly enforced. James had probably wanted Parliament to make some positive commitment towards war so that he could use this as a bargaining-factor with Spain over the fate of the Palatinate. It has been suggested that Charles was particularly upset by Parliament's interference, as he saw it, in his marriage plans. Moreover, James learned shortly afterwards that the Spanish had been dealing with him more fairly than he had previously thought. The resulting misunderstanding produced the famous debates about the Commons' right of freedom of speech and its Protestation of 21 December, and resulted in the dissolution of the Parliament. The affair, however, did much to increase distrust of Buckingham and made his task of winning support in future parliaments more difficult.

The next few months saw Buckingham concentrate on affairs at Court. Negotiations for a marriage between Charles and the Infanta of Spain continued. At the beginning of 1623 Endymion Porter returned to England from Spain with the view that negotiations for the marriage were almost complete. It was probably Porter's news that decided Charles to go to Spain to collect his bride-to-be. The journey to Madrid has long been portrayed as a scheme by Buckingham to insinuate himself into Charles's favour. It certainly was an extremely hazardous venture. Buckingham and Charles went in disguise from England, through France and Spain to Madrid. The journey itself could have exposed Charles and Buckingham to the dangers of accident and robbery. Once in Spain, Charles's presence offended the very strong sense of protocol at the Spanish Court, and it also provided the Spanish with all the advantages in negotiating the exact terms of the marriage agreement. However, as Lockyer has pointed out, there is no reason to believe that the plan was Buckingham's. In fact, Buckingham had much to lose from a trip to Spain which would take him away from Court for several months. His absence would give his enemies a chance to ingratiate themselves with the King. He was already very friendly with Charles, so he had no need to secure a reversionary interest in this way, and he was probably also aware of the diplomatic problems which the trip posed.

The journey to Spain did not fulfil its aims. Charles obtained neither his bride nor any concessions over the Palatinate. However, it does seem to have led to profound changes in the character of Buckingham's political career. When he returned, he desired a much more active part in government than he had done hitherto. He became a strong supporter of war against Spain and was instrumental in having Parliament called in 1624 so that attempts could be made to persuade it to support a war effort. When Parliament was in session, Buckingham was very active in trying to persuade MPs to provide the taxation necessary for war preparations to begin. The House of Lords was eager enough for the commencement of war. Men such as Pembroke and Abbot shared the apocalyptic view of Protestantism and were always ready to support war against Spain. Pembroke was suspicious of Buckingham, but his suspicions seem to have been overcome by Prince Charles's support for the war. In the Commons there was plenty of anti-Spanish feeling but little effective support for the practicalities of war. It was Buckingham, therefore, who suggested the device of appropriation of supply to try to get the Commons to vote the King subsidies. The Commons did vote the King three subsidies and three fifteenths, which raised about £278,000, an amount well short of the five subsidies and ten fifteenths James thought he would need. Buckingham did not confine his activities merely to starting the war. He also managed the impeachment of Cranfield, and was influential in the negotiations for a French marriage, which were completed in December 1624. Buckingham hoped that the marriage treaty would also provide a military alliance with France against Spain. His relative success in his dealings with Parliament certainly made him feel that he would be able to work in partnership with Parliament in the future. His failure to understand Parliament's reluctance to pay for the war was to cause many of his problems in the next reign.

What caused Buckingham to play this much more active role in the making of policy? It is possible that he was influenced by Olivares in Spain and that when he returned to England he decided that he wanted to emulate his power. Certainly he and Olivares became personal enemies while Buckingham was in Madrid, and Buckingham might have been motivated by a desire for revenge and for satisfaction of his and the Prince's honour after their disappointment in the Spanish marriage business. Lockyer has argued that Buckingham's visit to Spain convinced him of the danger that the Habsburgs posed to non-Habsburgs Europe. This again is a possibility, but it is not something that Buckingham's actual conduct of foreign policy in Charles I's reign makes that easy to defend. Buckingham was alarmed by the precariousness of his position at court while he was away in 1623. He received numerous warnings about how his influence was being challenged, and so his attempt to put into effect an anti-Spanish foreign policy was perhaps an attempt to make his position more secure by following a policy which would win him wide popularity.

However, his attempt to push James into a war was not successful. There was never any formal declaration of war against Spain and there was no direct military action against Spain in James's reign. The only military expedition mounted by James after the 1624 Parliament was Mansfeld's, which succumbed to the weather and disease in the first months of 1625 in Flanders. In fact, Buckingham's attempts to dictate policy in the last few months of James's reign show both the strengths and weaknesses of his position. Buckingham could engineer the fall of servants of the Crown whom James was prepared to see fall, but he could not force James to courses of action he did not want. Ill though he undoubtedly was, James was not so senile that Buckingham could disregard him. Buckingham was much more than a 'plaything' as James I's favourite, but he could not emulate the power of Olivares as the *valido* of Philip IV.

IV

The accession of Charles I inaugurated a new style of kingship. James's style had been casual and familiar, and, even when a faction had enjoyed a large share of the King's favour, access to the King had not been denied to other factions. Thus neither Robert Cecil, Robert Carr, the Howards, nor Buckingham had entirely monopolised James's attention. There had always been a possibility of change in the factional line-up against James, as the careers of Cecil, Carr and the Earl of Suffolk demonstrated. Moreover, many hoped that James's death would see a reversal of the trend of Buckingham's increasing dominance at Court. Their hopes were not to materialise. Charles's friendship with the Duke was closer than Buckingham's relationship with James had been, although it lacked the latter's homosexual character. Buckingham fulfilled the role of dominant elder brother and adviser which Charles's character required, and of which Charles had been deprived by the death of Prince Henry in 1612. Charles's preference for formality and elaborate ceremonial cut him off from his subjects, and elevated Buckingham's position still further. Charles disliked the business of government much more even than James had done, and this too gave Buckingham the opportunity to enhance his ascendancy by taking the principal lead in the direction of government and diplomacy.

Buckingham's success in transferring his power as favourite from one King to the next represented a very considerable personal achievement. However, it created great problems for the English state in the first years of Charles's reign. Buckingham now clearly monopolised patronage, and was going to do so for the foreseeable future. The potential threat of a rival patronage network centred around the Queen was not allowed to become a reality. Many of her French associates were expelled from court in 1626, and Buckingham was quite successful at making himself and members of his own family influential with Henrietta Maria. Therefore, it mattered a great deal more that he had frequently bestowed his patronage on men who were either purely courtiers and who lacked estates and influence in the localities, or who were excluded from the usual circles of preferment at Court. This meant that the Crown would not receive the sort of support it usually did at Court or in the country. The consequences of this were especially serious at a time of war, and Buckingham used the influence he had gained over the conduct of government and diplomacy to involve England in foreign wars against two of the most powerful states of Europe.

It is very difficult to discern what Buckingham was trying to achieve in his foreign policy. Even Lockyer is contradictory about Buckingham's aims. At one point in his biography he argues that Buckingham was trying to organise a crusade against the possibility of Habsburg domination of Europe; at another, he contends that Buckingham merely wanted to recover the Palatinate for the Elector, and that he would have been prepared to do this by negotiation. It is quite likely that Buckingham at different times considered both these aims appropriate and feasible. However, Buckingham's foreign policy appears not to have been so coolly calculated. Personal pique seems to have played its part, both against Olivares and, later, against Richelieu, in the wars with Spain and France. Buckingham, too, no doubt would have liked the glory military success could have brought. The famous equestrian portrait of Buckingham by Rubens was an indication of the image Buckingham hoped to create for himself by his military adventures.

Without the caution of James to temper their enthusiasm, Buckingham and Charles decided to press ahead with an offensive action against Spain. They were probably spurred on by rumours that the Spanish were planning to invade England. Their offensive took the form of the expedition to Cadiz, commanded by Sir Edward Cecil, who was created Viscount Wimbledon shortly before the fleet set out in October 1625. It returned in December. Lack of adequate preparation, military and naval incompetence, drunkenness and disease all played their parts in ensuring the failure of the expedition, in the preparations for which Buckingham had been very closely involved. About £500,000 was spent on it, but it was still short of arms, clothing and victuals. England's absence from foreign war for so long made it difficult for the administration to cope with the demands of preparation, especially when the House of Commons refused to vote adequate supply for the war effort. Besides, joint military and naval expeditions of this type were notoriously difficult to accomplish successfully; Drake's expedition against Lisbon in 1589 had been an unmitigated disaster. Moreover, it seems that successful warfare in the early seventeenth century was generally defensive in nature. Buckingham's partial responsibility for the failure of the Cadiz expedition cannot be ignored, but at the same time it must be recognised that he was labouring against a vast number of institutional difficulties.

Buckingham seems to have decided that a successful war against Spain could be conducted only with French assistance. He had hoped that the French marriage treaty would produce a formal military alliance. When this did not happen, he seems to have pinned his hopes on persuading the French to join the Treaty of the Hague, which he negotiated with Denmark and the United Provinces in December 1625. Far from being the origins of a great anti-Habsburg alliance, this proved to be a desperate attempt to keep together the major Protestant nations of Europe in a united front against Spain. It also committed England to continuing to pay substantial subsidies to Denmark and the United Provinces. Neither Denmark nor the United Provinces was able to reverse the general trend of Habsburg success in the next three years.

In the eighteen months after the Treaty of the Hague, England drifted into war with France. The reasons behind this development are very complicated, and only the briefest outline of them is possible here. The attempts by the English to stop French ships from carrying Spanish goods classed as contraband led to numerous disputes with the French over the extent of English rights in this matter. As French ships were confiscated for carrying contraband, the French retaliated by confiscating English ships. The wine trade with France was particularly hard hit in these series of measures and counter-measures. The motivation toward war was further strengthened by a desire to help the Protestants of La Rochelle against the French Crown. Since September 1625 the Duke of Soubise, a Huguenot nobleman, had been given refuge in England after his fleet had been defeated by the French navy off the Ile de Ré. Although the Huguenots of La Rochelle had made peace with the French King early in 1626, Soubise continued to assure anyone who would listen to him that the Rochellois wanted to fight against Louis XIII to preserve their position. Buckingham's own reason for wanting to fight against France appears to have been to engineer the downfall of Cardinal Richelieu, whom he blamed for the failure of the French to fight against Spain. Here Buckingham seems to have failed to realise the precariousness of Richelieu's position at the French Court, which meant that the Cardinal had to pick his way very carefully between the different factions there and so had little freedom of manoeuvre. The fact is that there had never been any evidence to suggest that Louis, naturally reluctant to commit himself to an alliance with a Protestant country, would even have contemplated fighting alongside England against Spain. If Buckingham had paid more attention to the reports of the resident English ambassador in Paris, Sir Edward Herbert, he would have realised this. Instead he was more credulous of the naïve reports of his own representative in Paris, Viscount Kensington, who seems to have provided Buckingham with what he wanted to hear rather than with an objective account of attitudes in Paris. Moreover, Louis XIII was not enamoured of Buckingham after Buckingham's misconduct with the Queen, Anne of Austria, during his visit to France to accompany Henrietta Maria back to England in 1625. Although Anne's virtue remained unbesmirched, Buckingham's dalliance with her went beyond the bounds of propriety.

More flattering interpretations can be placed on Buckingham's decision to involve England in war with France. It can be suggested that Buckingham was planning a pre-emptive strike against a Franco-Spanish attack on England, which the Treaty of Monçon of May 1626, settling Franco-Spanish differences over the Val Telline, and other diplomatic agreements of 1627 made a possibility. Buckingham might have been planning to nip French commercial expansion in the bud. Richelieu was certainly trying to encourage commercial development on France's Atlantic coast at this time. However, such interpretations seem unrealistic in the extreme. Buckingham, as Lord High Admiral, could not even protect English shipping in the Channel from the depradations of pirates. The Cadiz expedition, and the expedition under Willoughby against the Spanish treasure fleet in the autumn of 1626, defeated by the weather in the Bay of Biscay, illustrate the impracticality of Buckingham's schemes. The whole direction of his foreign policy seems to have been dominated by an inability to appreciate the realities of the situation in which England was placed in the first decade of the Thirty Years War. He expected too much from his allies. He failed to realise the weakness of English military and naval preparedness. It is hard to avoid the conclusion that Buckingham was hopelessly out of his depth in competing with the likes of Richelieu and Olivares. It was the height of folly to commit England to war with France at the same time that she was at war with Spain.

War with France resulted in the expedition to the Ile de Ré in the summer of 1627. Buckingham commanded this in person and invested much of his own money in it. Although he acquitted himself bravely and luck did not run kindly for him, the campaign itself was another sorry tale of incompetence and inadequate preparations. When the fleet first arrived off La Rochelle, the Rochellois were at first extremely reluctant to admit Soubise and Buckingham. In fact, the townspeople only declared themselves in rebellion against the French king on 10 September, two months after Buckingham first arrived. Most of the fighting was concentrated on the citadel of St Martin on the Ile de Ré. The siege went badly. Guns were positioned wrongly and trenches dug incorrectly. Disease took its toll of the men, and reinforcements failed to arrive from England. A final attempt to storm the citadel proved suicidal, and Buckingham returned home in October amidst general grief. But, as D'Ewes remarked, 'his coming safe home occasioned almost as much sorrow as the slaughter and perishing of all the rest'.[15]

Buckingham immediately decided to mount another expedition to relieve La Rochelle in the following year. Yet again, he devoted considerable time and energy to trying to prepare it. Lack of money and administrative inertia meant that it was as ill-equipped as the previous one. Buckingham, however, did not lead it. He was assassinated shortly before the expedition left. It was commanded by the Earl of Lindsey, and achieved nothing.

V

Buckingham's foreign policy contributed considerably to the political instability of England in the first years of Charles's reign. Not only was defeat unpopular, but the costs of war placed a burden on the English administrative system which it could not tolerate. The failure to finance the war adequately was, as Lockyer has remarked, a failure of political will. Vast sums of money were raised in England in the 1640s and the 1650s to pay for war, so it was not the case that England simply could not afford war. Buckingham and Charles could not find support for their war efforts because they had alienated most of the English political nation by Charles's style of kingship and because of Buckingham's domination of patronage. The men who should have been drumming up support and finance in the counties for the King's wars were frequently involved in trying to remove the King's favourite from his position. The men who disagreed with Buckingham were denied access to the king to present their differing points of view. They could not use the Court as 'a point of contact'. They could not gain advancement without kowtowing to Buckingham. They had to use other methods, therefore, to try to get a hearing for their ideas. Opposition to Buckingham had to be transferred away from Court. Most obviously, all these difficulties were reflected in Parliament.

All Charles's parliaments during Buckingham's ascendancy were summoned because he needed money for the conduct of the wars against Spain and France. All were dissolved or prorogued against a background of acrimony. Charles obtained seven subsidies (about £425,000) from these parliaments: two from the Parliament of 1625, and five from the Parliament of 1628. But Charles's needs were running at well over £1 million per annum. In 1625 alone, he required over £700,000 just to pay subsidies to his allies, before he even contemplated action himself, or his domestic needs.

In his dealings with Parliament Buckingham was confident that he could manage it to the King's advantage. Even when hostility towards Buckingham was quite patent, his confidence remained undiminished. In 1625, despite advice to the contrary from Sir John Eliot and others, he insisted that Parliament should meet for a second session at Oxford only three weeks after the end of the session at Westminster. He was correct in thinking the war effort could not proceed effectively without greater aid from Parliament, but he completely misread, or perhaps just disregarded, the mood of most MPs. In 1626, as he faced the prospect of impeachment, Buckingham wanted Parliament to be allowed to continue so that his innocence could be established, and the King's business could then be prosecuted more vigorously. He admitted that his youth and inexperience might have led him into error, but he hoped that 'his love and duty to his country, have restrained him and preserved him

. . . from running into heinous and high misdemeanours and crimes'.[16] Similarly, in June 1628, when, shortly after the King had accepted the Petition of Right, the Commons passed a resolution that 'the excessive power of the Duke of Buckingham, and the abuse of that power' were the chief causes of the problems and dangers facing the kingdom, Buckingham was prepared to justify his actions to the Commons in the hope that he could establish harmony with it.[17]

Was Buckingham, then, as Lockyer has suggested, a trimmer who devoted much time and energy to finding compromise solutions to his disputes with Parliament? It cannot be doubted that Buckingham wanted political harmony in England, and wanted to prosecute the King's business as effectively as possible. However, he chose to do this by disregarding many of the political realities of his time. Repeatedly, he tried to circumvent the traditions and conventions of English government. Such a course of action can be defended by the argument that warfare produces extraordinary demands which require extraordinary measures. But Buckingham's demands were so far out of step with the ordinary rules of political behaviour that he was bound to create disharmony in a political system which was not able to meet the demands of foreign war.

Buckingham's control of patronage meant that he was not without supporters. Members of the House of Lords were wary of falling out with Buckingham. In 1625 Pembroke and Arundel were prepared to offer Buckingham guarded support because they feared the consequences of disfavour, and because Pembroke hoped to see the war against Spain develop successfully. In 1626, the Lords refused the Commons' demands to imprison Buckingham while his impeachment trial proceeded, and they allowed him to speak in his defence. In the debates over the Petition of Right the Lords were, on the whole, supportive towards Buckingham in his opposition to the Commons' demands that the King should renounce completely his right to imprison without stating a cause. The House of Lords was, of course, easier to manipulate. Its smaller numbers made it more open to persuasion. Buckingham had a considerable number of proxies in his control: in 1626 he held thirteen. Troublesome members could be kept away, as the Earl of Bristol was in 1625, and the Earl of Arundel in 1626. Moreover, there were considerable pressures on many lords to remain on good terms with the King and, therefore, Buckingham. The Earl of Pembroke is perhaps the best example of this. He hated Buckingham, but he usually allowed his hatred of Spain to overcome this. Besides, he was motivated by strong notions of honour and service to the Crown. Thus, while Pembroke clearly encouraged the impeachment of Buckingham, he was able to contemplate a marriage alliance with the Duke, so that shortly after the 1626 Parliament was dissolved his seven-year-old nephew became betrothed to Buckingham's four-year-old daughter. Moreover, the complexity of family relationships should not be ignored. Pembroke's brother, the Earl of Montgomery, seems to have been friendly with Buckingham for much of the 1620s.

Buckingham also had supporters in the House of Commons. The tenuous alliance he made with some leading MPs, such as Sir Robert Phelips, in the 1624 Parliament was short-lived. But the extent of his patronage held others' loyalty. For instance, in 1626 about one hundred MPs voted against the motion to ask the Lords to imprison him. However, Buckingham seems not to have made the best use of the opportunities for managing Parliament which his offices gave him. As Lord Warden of the Cinque Ports between 1624 and 1628, he had fewer of his clients elected for those boroughs than any previous Lord Warden. His high-handedness and determination to bring in outsiders seem to have accounted for his failure. Patronage, of course, could also be a two-edged weapon. Sir John Eliot remained loyal to the Duke in the Parliament of 1625. In the next Parliament he emerged as one of the Duke's bitterest enemies. Criticism of Buckingham's policies partly accounted for his volte-face. But Eliot's disappointment at his failure to rise as high as Sir John Coke, another Buckingham client, in the naval administration also contributed to his hostility.

In all his dealings with Parliament, Buckingham failed to acknowledge the main concerns of the members. Of course, Charles also has to share the blame for this. His refusal to accept criticism and the authoritarian way in which he stated his demands made Buckingham's task as a manager of Parliament all the more difficult.

Derek Hirst has shown how Parliament became 'the representative of the people' in the 1620s. MPs, aware of their accountability to their constituents, were wary of granting taxation to finance wars which did not happen, as occurred in 1624, or were massively unsuccessful. The pressures of war led to disruption of life in the counties. Increased militia-training, martial law, billeting and free quarter all threatened the gentry's control of the counties and the sanctity of private property. The war forced the Crown to use extra-parliamentary methods of taxation. Tonnage and Poundage was collected without statutory authority. The King had recourse to a forced loan because of Parliament's reluctance to grant subsidies. Men who refused to pay the loan were imprisoned without cause being shown. Moreover, the Crown then tried to manipulate the evidence in the Five Knights' Case to its own advantage.

Buckingham's record on religion did not win him any support. He had close connections with Catholicism. His wife was converted to Protestantism only just before their marriage. His mother became a Catholic. Buckingham had been closely associated with the Spanish marriage policy. He was the main instigator of Charles's marriage with the Catholic Henrietta Maria. It was widely thought that Buckingham had offered English ships to Louis XIII for use against the rebels of La Rochelle in 1625, although this had, in fact, been James I's own decision. In Charles's reign, Buckingham was increasingly associated with the Arminians. His friendship with William Laud had become progressively closer since the early 1620s. The York House Conference of 1626, of which Buckingham was chairman, made it clear that no official action was going to be taken against the growing influence of the Arminians.

Buckingham, therefore, came to represent 'the grievance of grievances' to MPs. As Sir John Eliot declared in his impassioned concluding speech to the Commons' indictment of the Duke in 1626, 'In reference to the King, he must be styled the Canker in his Treasure; in reference to the State, the Moth of all Goodness.'[18] It was this hostility to the Duke which underlay the activities of the parliaments of 1626 and 1628. That the Commons put aside its hostility to Buckingham in 1628 while it sought the Petition of Right from the King did not mean that they considered Buckingham less of a threat. Rather, in 1628 they sought protection in legal terms from the methods of government associated with Buckingham. Their grievance remained the same. Indeed much of their delight when the King finally agreed to accept the Petition of Right with the form of words usually reserved for statutes was engendered by the thought that the King was at last going to dismiss Buckingham. When this did not transpire their dismay quickly turned to another open attack on Buckingham. Charles prorogued Parliament to protect his friend.

It was possible that Charles and Buckingham were contemplating changes in policy at the time of Buckingham's death. Sir Richard Weston had recently been made Lord Treasurer. He was not particularly close to Buckingham, and he was a supporter of peace with Spain. Overtures towards peace had been made to the rulers of the Spanish Netherlands in the previous few months. Buckingham and Charles were perhaps beginning to face reality at last.

Buckingham's assassin, John Felton, acted alone. He was aggrieved by his failure to win promotion in the Army and by his arrears of pay. He also carried a justification of his action, sewn into the lining of his hat, because he thought he would be killed immediately. He had been convinced by the remonstrance of the Commons that 'by . . . killing the Duke he should do his country great service'.[19] Many agreed with him. Although Felton was executed for the murder of the Duke, he had a great deal of popular sympathy. Few mourned Buckingham, probably none with the intensity of Charles I. He seems never to have forgotten his people's reactions to the death of his friend on 23 August 1628.

VI

Until 1623, it would appear that Buckingham's career followed a fairly conventional course. He came to prominence as an instrument of faction. He then used the King's favour to create his own faction. It was after his return from Madrid that he seems to have tried to alter the nature of his power. By the death of James I he had established a virtual monopoly of patronage, although James did not surrender to him the direction of government. Charles I gave Buckingham the chance to become the director of government. Assured of Charles's support and affection, Buckingham's monopoly of patronage was untrammelled; Charles's government was Buckingham's government. The King allowed Buckingham to decide on all major courses that the government followed. Buckingham was in a very real sense Charles's chief minister, or *valido*.

To what extent does Buckingham deserve the more favourable interpretations placed on his career by Russell and Lockyer? It has to be admitted that England faced severe institutional problems in the 1620s. There was, in G. E. Aylmer's revealing phrase, a 'functional break-down' in England's administrative institutions. War especially exacerbated this situation. Moreover, Buckingham was a victim of the philosophical poverty of the English political mind of the time, as J. P. Cooper has succinctly pointed out: 'The claim that the constitution rightly understood must produce harmony, though clearly untrue historically, exacerbated political feeling; when disharmony and deadlock manifestly prevailed, scapegoats had to be found.'[20] Buckingham was the scapegoat of the fiction that the King could do no wrong. Buckingham, too, was a victim of Charles's dislike of administrative business. He had to make up for Charles's sins of omission.

But the factors which mitigate the verdict against Buckingham have to be balanced against his own failings. It is not easy to see much sagacity in the Duke's direction of English diplomacy. His attempts to win support in Parliament and at Court are constantly marred by his unwillingness to appreciate the worries of those who disagreed with his methods. Buckingham could certainly be charming and sensitive. He could inspire great loyalty. Laud referred to Buckingham's death as 'the saddest news that ever I heard in my life'.[21] But Buckingham was also arrogant, high-handed and, in the eyes of many, a mere arriviste. Even his art-collecting, which saw him gather one of the finest collections ever assembled of Venetian paintings, and many other works of art from all over Europe, excited hostility amongst other collectors. This was, of course, partly jealousy. It was also indicative of the way in which Buckingham aroused enmity by his constant desire to be regarded as pre-eminent in all he did. As Buckingham observed during the impeachment proceedings against him in 1626, 'the King's liberality cannot be imputed as a crime to the Duke'.[22] However, the use the Duke made of the opportunities presented by royal generosity appeared virtually criminal to many of his critics. His failures in diplomacy, in administration and in managing men, and his vain self-confidence, if not exactly crimes, revealed dangerous inadequacies in a man with so much power. Buckingham was partly a victim of circumstances, but he also helped to create the circumstances which have led so many historians to be critical of him.

3. William Laud, Archbishop of Canterbury

JEREMY WARD

The want of Thorough in a time of opportunity is cause of all.

Laud to Wentworth, 1638

WILLIAM Laud played a crucial role during the 'personal' rule of Charles I. First as Bishop of London, then as Archbishop of Canterbury, he was responsible for formulating the religious policies of the period. These policies reversed the previous tendency of a measure of at least tacit toleration for those who did not follow the King's own beliefs. Under Charles I and Laud, deviation from a fairly carefully defined set of religious beliefs and practices frequently resulted in heavy fines and sometimes far harsher punishment. The extension of this more stringent policy to Scotland led to the 'Bishops' Wars' and then the calling of the parliaments of 1640. This in turn secured Laud's downfall as well as leading to Civil War and the eventual destruction of the monarchy. But Laud was not only concerned with religion. Along with Thomas Wentworth he enjoined the King to practise an efficient and uncorrupt style of government which they termed 'Thorough'; but, while Wentworth spent the bulk of his time in the north of England and in Ireland, Laud was at the very centre of political life with frequent access to the King, so that there were few aspects of policy which were not influenced by him in the 1630s. Indeed Laud was one of the most influential ministers during the Personal Rule and consequently much of the blame for the government's failings has fallen on him. He was frequently cited as one of the King's 'evil councillors' and most of his biographers have found it difficult to praise him beyond a certain admiration for his

61

single-minded industry in carrying out his stated policies. The object of this chapter is to assess his contribution to the early Stuart age and in particular to discover whether his contribution to Charles I's reign was indeed 'evil' or whether his policies can be defended in practical terms.

I

In choosing the Church for his career, Laud, as Wolsey had done before him, selected one of the few routes by which a man of his background might reach an eminent position in the service of the King. According to William Prynne, Laud was 'a little, low, red-faced man' of relatively poor social origin. But Prynne had little reason to love Laud and exaggerated the poverty of his upbringing if not Laud's diminutive stature and florid complexion. Born in Reading in 1573, he was the son of a cloth merchant. The family lived in a respectable house and Laud's uncle became Lord Mayor of London in 1591. It was through his local grammar school, which had connections with St John's College, Oxford, that Laud earned his chance to appreciate a wider world. He gained a Commoner's place at St John's and entered Oxford in 1589. From then on the College played a major role in his life and it might be argued that one of his most lasting contributions to English life is still to be found there in the elegant form of the Canterbury Quad. Certainly his times at Oxford seem to have been his happiest. He soon won a College scholarship and settled down to making a career for himself within the University. Something of his character emerges at this time. He was not altogether popular, leading a somewhat lonely life although at one stage sharing a room with one John Jones, who was later to return to England as a Papal agent bearing the more exotic title of Dom Leander a Sancto Martino.

Laud himself gained a reputation for Popish views, so much so that he was apparently frequently cut in the streets by those whom such views offended.[1] But Laud was never afraid of unpopularity and contented himself by keeping physically fit with some indoor exercises until he ruptured himself swinging a heavy book in his bedroom. He also undertook the responsibility of University Proctor, which was conferred on him in 1603. He was much concerned with the low standards of morality, the trendy modes of dress and the long hairstyles which the students of his time affected.

It was during these early years at Oxford that Laud formulated a set of religious views that were to remain with him virtually unaltered until his death. St John's, founded by a Catholic a few years before Laud's arrival, became a centre for anti-Puritan or 'Arminian' views. English 'Arminians' looked to Bishop Lancelot Andrewes for inspiration. The Elizabethan Church Settlement had left the Church of England as a strange amalgam of Protestant theology and Catholic liturgy and it was this latter aspect that the Arminians favoured. Whilst denying any loyalty to the Pope, they none the less emphasized the Catholic nature of the Church, much to the annoyance of the dominant Protestant groups of both clergy and laity. During Elizabeth's reign and especially at the time of the war with Spain, Catholicism was inevitably associated with treachery and Arminians ran the risk of considerable unpopularity, but, with the accession of James I and the end of the war, conditions became more favourable for Andrewes and his followers. The King had a natural interest in theology and greatly enjoyed acting as judge between disputatious divines of both Puritan and Arminian leaning.

Yet Laud's first contact with the King was hardly auspicious. In 1603 he left Oxford to become chaplain to the Earl of Devonshire. He was soon embroiled in the Earl's marital problems. The King strongly disapproved of a marriage performed by Laud between the Earl and the divorced wife of Lord Rich. Laud admitted that his 'conscience cried out against it' at the time, and it was a rare blunder on his part, for he normally remained true above all to his moral and theological principles.

His lesson learned, Laud returned to the safety of Oxford and by 1610 had become President of St John's after what one historian has termed 'a notoriously corrupt campaign'.[2] In the same year he acquired a royal chaplaincy through the influence of Richard Neile, who with Andrewes was the most influential of the Arminian bishops. Laud's career then developed smoothly enough with a succession of promotions and the occasional opportunity to preach before the King and thus repair the damage to his reputation which the Devonshire affair had caused. He was largely successful in that James allowed Laud to accompany him to Scotland in 1617. The task of the royal party was to bring the Church in Scotland into conformity with that of England. The fierce opposition of the Scottish Calvinists prevented any significant change. Laud might well have remembered this lesson when he embarked on a similar road twenty years later.

The culmination of this early part of his career was Laud's elevation to the Bench as Bishop of St David's in 1621. This promotion owed much to a new and significant influence in his life – George Villiers, Marquis (later Duke) of Buckingham. It was pressure from the royal favourite that persuaded James reluctantly to promote Laud. From then to his assassination in 1628 Buckingham played an important part in Laud's life, so much so that on one occasion the Bishop dreamt that the King's handsome favourite had climbed into bed with him! Even the King began to think more favourably of Laud when he acquitted himself well in a debate with the Jesuit, Father Fisher, in 1622 which had been arranged in an attempt to dissuade Buckingham's mother from converting to Rome. By 1625 Laud was providing the favourite with lists of Arminian clergy deemed suitable for promotion. Clearly he too was becoming a power in the land.

It was the death of James and the accession of his son, Charles, in 1625 that probably ensured Laud's future more than any other factor. The new King shared not only Laud's strong Arminian views but also his abiding hostility to Puritanism.[3] Both men supported the fashionable theory of the 'Divine Right of Kings' and saw the bishops as enjoying similar authority in the Church. This coincidence of religious and political views cemented a close working-relationship between them. Over the next fifteen years Charles put a great deal of trust in Laud, especially where religious matters were concerned, yet their relationship generally remained a businesslike one and Laud often expressed anxiety that he might lose royal favour. The two men had met through Buckingham, and Laud soon found himself preaching the opening sermon of the first parliament of the new reign, officiating at Charles's coronation and then, in June 1626, receiving promotion to the wealthy bishopric of Bath and Wells. It was at this point in his career that Laud began to play a significant role in politics. Appointed a Privy Councillor in 1627, he soon began to urge support for Buckingham's unpopular war with France and attracted unfavourable comment from Parliament, which attacked him and other Arminians for their 'unsound opinions'. If anything, this was a recommendation to Charles, whose own struggles with Parliament culminated in 1629 in its passing of the Three Resolutions, one of which condemned Arminianism.

Laud had already provided Charles, in the Declaration prefixed to the Thirty-nine Articles issued in 1628, with a new instruction forbidding further discussion of dogma. It was clear that the King listened to few others in preference to Laud where Church matters were concerned. It was therefore logical to promote him if not to Canterbury, which was currently occupied by Geroge Abbot, then to London, which was second only to Canterbury in terms of power and prestige. It was from the diocese of London, therefore, that Laud launched his great campaign to reform the Church of England by reducing Puritan influence within it and enforcing a uniformity hardly envisaged by previous regimes.

II

From his appointment as Bishop of London in 1628, Laud lost no time in establishing his authority over the Church. With the backing of the king he issued in 1629 his 'Instructions' to other bishops to 'consolidate' their dioceses and to destroy Puritanism within their borders. The 'Instructions' reflected Laud's view that there were two principal reasons why the Church of England was weak and divided at that time. Since the Reformation the Church had suffered from poverty. Short of land and other resources, it paid its clergy badly and as a result many were below the standard of education and dedication deemed desirable. Laud urged his fellow bishops to attempt to consolidate their landholdings and to press for more generous support from their laity in order to produce a better paid and motivated clergy. The second problem encompassed the theological divisions within the Church. By 1629 Puritanism was deeply entrenched within the Church of England. Archbishop Abbot and several other bishops were sympathetically inclined to the movement; there were many Puritan clergy and where there were none, local groups of Puritan laity would hire lecturers[4] to preach Puritan sermons to their communities.

Yet, to Laud some Puritan practices were an affront to the dignity of the Church as he understood it. It encouraged an individual approach to religion, placing less emphasis on the traditional authority of the bishops within the Church. Puritan services were simple and, to Laud, undignified affairs which placed little emphasis on the sacraments and rather too much on the preaching of sermons, which all too often seemed to imply criticism of any authority except that of the Scriptures. Laud's Instructions of 1629 therefore required bishops to reside permanently within their dioceses and forbade them to sell off or lease out any lands belonging to them. Those bishoprics, such as Oxford and Bristol, which lacked accommodation for their incumbents were provided for as soon as possible. The remainder of the Instructions dealt with the problem of the Puritan lecturers. Laud was unable to suppress them completely because the acute shortage of beneficed clergy meant that large tracts of the country had no minister at all without the lecturers. The Instructions did, however, require lecturers to read divine service in hood and surplice and to agree to accept a local benefice as soon as one should be offered. Further, Laud instructed his fellow bishops to suppress afternoon sermons, replacing them with a simple but orthodox catechism. The two problems which the Instructions attempted to solve were interrelated. The continuing poverty of the Church ensured that there was a continuing need for lecturers to fill gaps where there were no beneficed clergy, while the groups of Puritan business men who might have provided more benefices preferred to spend their money on hiring Puritan lecturers rather than give generously to an Arminian bishop.

Perhaps Laud's most notable achievement here concerned his suppression of a body known generally as the Feoffees for Impropriations. A group of London-based Puritans had decided to buy up Church livings already in lay hands and to dispense them to suitable Puritan ministers. When they offered their plans to Laud for inspection he was suspicious, and, when in 1632 clear evidence reached him that the Feoffees were opposing his policy of uniformity by encouraging a growing Puritan ministry within the Church, he denounced them in his diary as 'the main instruments for the Puritan faction to undo the Church', brought them before the Exchequer Court, had them dissolved and confiscated their funds. Even so the Puritan lectureships continued to thrive, mainly because of the shortage of suitably qualified alternatives. In London alone there were still eighty-eight known lecturers in 1638, although this did mark a decline from the high point of 121 in 1628.[5]

Laud's destruction of the Feoffees was the most celebrated incident in his more general campaign to regain clerical control over the Church. Wherever possible lay authority over benefices or land which Laud considered should belong to the Church was challenged, often in the courts. Since the targets of these attacks were gentry families or wealthy City merchants, it was inevitable that Laud alienated some of the most influential people of the kingdom. Had he been successful in his efforts to reform the Church and to impose uniformity perhaps it would not have been too high a price to pay, but taken with other aspects of his policies and put in the wider context of the unpopularity of other aspects of the Personal Rule, such as taxation, it was a risky policy which made Laud increasingly unpopular with the most important social classes in England.

In the long term Laud did fail to reform the Church and even in the short term success was limited. In almost everything he attempted, Laud encountered opposition. There was overt resistance from his Puritan enemies and from personal enemies on the Bishops' Bench, such as John Williams of Lincoln. Even more frustrating for Laud was the inertia which afflicted so many of the clergy who were not basically unsympathetic to his ideas. In practical terms Laud was to find himself waging a lonely battle with only a handful of sympathetic fellow bishops, such as Matthew Wren of Norwich, on whom he could rely for full co-operation. It is significant, for example, that even his protégé William Juxon, who succeeded him at London when he finally replaced Abbot at Canterbury, offended the Puritans so little that he survived the Interregnum unscathed to become the first Restoration Archbishop of Canterbury.

Yet what Laud lacked in support, he made up for by his own sterling efforts. First from London and then on becoming Archbishop in 1633, he authorised and personally supervised a programme of visitations to ensure that the Church was being run according to his instructions. In 1633 the bishops were ordered to submit a detailed account of their dioceses to Laud and in the same year he extended his visitations to include Oxford and Cambridge universities. He checked the visitors' reports carefully and soon a horrifying tale of neglect and unorthodoxy emerged.

The standards which Laud wished to see applied to the Anglican Church derived from his view that the Reformation, which should have stripped away the excrescences of Rome and restored the orthodoxy of the early Christian centuries, had instead turned out to be a 'Deformation', largely owing to the rise of Puritan practices which were just as inimical to the Church as Popery. It was therefore Laud's task to reform the Church properly, for 'all I laboured for was that the external worship of God in Church might be kept up in uniformity and decency and in some beauty of holiness'. The visitations provided a different picture. It was reported that the public used St Paul's Cathedral as a meeting-place, so that little of a service could be heard, owing to the general buzz of conversation. One man, prosecuted by the Court of High Commission for urinating in the Cathedral, maintained that he did not even know that it was a church. Archbishop Neile's visitation to Manchester in 1633 resulted in twenty-seven puritans being charged with failing to kneel at Communion, fifty-three for not kneeling during the prayers and sixteen for keeping their hats on in church. William Bourne, a Fellow of the Collegiate Church of Manchester, was persuaded to use the Prayer Book for the first time in thirty years while taking Divine Service but still refused to wear a surplice and so was suspended. Laud personally reported to the King after his visit to Norwich that 'the whole Diocese is much out of order'.

From all over the country came reports of resistance to the uniformity that Laud demanded. He had ordered that the Communion table should be removed from the centre of the church to the east end, where, termed an 'altar', it should be fenced off with rails at which communicants were to kneel.[6] Organs and choirs were to be installed where possible, and dogs and other animals were to be kept out of churches during services. The campaign met with limited success. In London, where Laud had most control, Sir Nathaniel Brent congratulated him on his success: 'It is generally believed in the Diocese by the better sort that by your Grace's strong persuasion and vigour mixed with mildness, much reformation hath been wrought.' But elsewhere a grim story emerged of altar rails ripped out, of Communion tables being returned to the centre of churches and of vandalism to organs and stained-glass windows. The enforcement of uniformity was to prove most difficult, for by 1628, when Laud as Bishop of London launched his great crusade, Puritans had embedded themselves deeply in the religious structure of the kingdom. Laud therefore determined to root out the leading offenders and the result was a campaign of prosecutions in the Prerogative Courts.[7] Some trials were for failure to observe the ground rules laid down for the taking of services – not using the Prayer Book, not wearing a surplice, and so on; others were for offences committed during a service, such as not kneeling at the appropriate moment; but the most significant trials were for those accused of offensive use of the written word.

Laud had great faith in the power of the written word. He assumed that merely by issuing instructions they would at once be implemented and equally he feared that anything written contrary to the doctrines of the true Church as he conceived them would have a powerful effect in nullifying his orders. As a result he found himself engaged in a running battle with some doughty Puritan pamphleteers, whose works he did his utmost to suppress. Censorship was based on the Licensing Act, which Laud used against those who advocated Puritan ideas. Some spectacular cases resulted. Only extreme Puritans had much sympathy for Alexander Leighton, a fanatical Scot who dedicated his *Sion's Pleas against Prelacy* to the Parliament of 1628. The book was libellous by any standards and his arrest was no surprise. In 1630 the Star Chamber inflicted a severe punishment – a £10,000 fine, the pillory, and his ears to be cut off, his nose slit and his cheeks branded. The Scot was, however, daringly rescued from the Fleet prison before the more violent aspects of the punishment could be inflicted. It would probably have suited the government to let the matter drop, but Laud insisted on tracking him down and on administering the rest of the sentence. Not surprisingly he gained a national reputation for the harshness of his judgements, for when sitting in the Star Chamber or the High Commission he usually voted to apply the toughest sentences allowed.

Many other Puritans passed before him and seven years later another case was to cause widespread outrage. William Prynne, John Bastwick and Henry Burton, a lawyer, a doctor and a clergyman respectively, were brought before the Star Chamber each charged with writing Puritan propaganda. Prynne had long been a thorn in Laud's side. His pen emitted a steady stream of political and theological polemics mainly attacking Arminians and their beliefs. His vast *Histriomastix* attempted to prove that stage plays were mortally sinful, just as Queen Henrietta Maria was about to appear in one at Somerset House. Prynne described actresses as 'notorious whores' and 'lewd, lascivious strumpets'. It is not surprising that in 1632 he was bundled off to the Tower and incarcerated there for a year. As a result of his trial he was heavily fined, imprisoned for life, and was to have both ears cropped, although on this occasion only the tips were removed. Laud busied himself with impounding and destroying all remaining copies of Prynne's book. The Archbishop must have been surprised shortly afterwards to receive a lengthy letter from Prynne clearly indicating that the Puritan was unrepentant. This led to a further session in the Star Chamber and a clear example of Laud's better nature. The Attorney General, William Noy, wished to deprive Prynne of all reading- and writing-materials, but Laud persuaded his fellow judges to relent, for 'My Lords,' he said, 'he hath undergone a heavy punishment. I am heartily sorry for him.' There is no reason to doubt Laud's sincerity but his patience was ill rewarded, for the pamphleteer used the pens and paper supplied by Laud to launch further attacks on Church and state. He wrote against Ship Money in 1635 and a spate of six pamphlets followed in the next year, including *News from Ipswich*, an unusually brief and therefore much read document which attacked Bishop Wren of Norwich for his vigorous imposition of Arminianism on his diocese and in particular for his banishment of the highly esteemed Puritan lecturer Samuel Ward from his work in Ipswich. The pamphlet rapidly ran to three editions. At first Laud ascribed it to Henry Burton, the puritan rector of a London church, who was quickly arrested and sent to the Tower. Then he and Prynne were joined by John Bastwick, a Puritan physician who had lambasted the Arminians with a series of vituperative pamphlets. As long before as 1628 all three men had attracted Laud's anger by accusing Bishop Goodman of Gloucester of Popery (correctly as it was to turn out). Thus by 1637 Laud had all three under lock and key and decided to end their opposition forever. Their case was heard in June and was to cause a furious public outcry, which Laud certainly did not expect or desire. Popular opinion did not believe that Laud had played little role in the trial, although, in fact, the accused's sentence of a heavy fine, loss of their ears in the pillory and permanent imprisonment was proposed by Lord Cottington, and it was Lord Chief Justice Finch who added that Prynne's cheeks should be branded with the letters 'SL' for 'Seditious Libeller', a misfortune which the resourceful Prynne turned to his own advantage later by claiming that the letters stood for 'Stigmata Laudis'.

The results of the trial were to prove disastrous for Laud and for the government he represented. His efforts to impose censorship, whilst not in any way slackening – for he now turned his attention to presses all over the country and even abroad, in France and Holland – were to fail as there was a steady increase in the amount of Puritan literature imported, especially from the United Provinces. Worse still, public sympathy, which had been stifled for some years, now broke out violently in favour of the three sentenced men. Much was made of their genteel status, for tradition dictated that only members of the lower orders should be subjected to public corporal punishment, but the mob who cheered the three men in the pillory, who mopped up blood from their severed ears, who held lengthy services on their behalf and who feted them on their progresses to remote provincial prisons was really criticising Laud and his programme of reform and censorship. Unfortunately Laud was quite unable to comprehend that this method of dealing with opponents was counterproductive. Ironically, in his lengthy summing up of his own position after the trial, he had rhetorically asked the King, 'What safety can you expect if you lose the hearts of your people?' It was Laud who by 1637 had done more than any other to lose the hearts of the people for Charles I. A spate of hostile posters and pamphlets appeared, especially in London, attacking Laud and referring to him as, among other things, the 'Archwolf of Canterbury'.

In the aftermath of the trial, Laud went to great lengths to punish those who had demonstrated in favour of the condemned men. The cities of Coventry and Chester, which had welcomed Prynne, were fined, the money to be paid into the St Paul's rebuilding-fund. For a time Prynne, incarcerated on the isle of Jersey, was silent, but others continued to defy the Archbishop. A few months later John Lilburne, the future Leveller leader, was facing the Star Chamber for printing Puritan books in Rotterdam, and Bishop John Williams was at last called to account. The Bishop of Lincoln had long been a leading opponent of Laud. They had been rivals for James I's and Buckingham's support and, although Laud had eventually emerged as the favourite, Williams maintained close contact with the Court through a friendship with Queen Henrietta Maria and her supporters. In religious terms Williams was no Puritan, but nor was he an Arminian. His vast and wealthy diocese was run to his rather than Laud's specifications. Laud recognised that Williams was a formidable enemy, and so, when a pro-Puritan pamphlet entitled *Holy Table, Name and Thing* appeared attacking Laud's instructions regarding the position of the altar, the Archbishop tracked it down to Lincoln and rightly detected in it the hand of his rival. The Star Chamber had first tried Williams in 1635 but his influence at Court had saved him then. Now in 1637 he was back and Laud made no mistake in cornering him on a charge of perjury. The hapless bishop was heavily fined, deprived of the revenue from his wealthy diocese and subsequently confined to the Tower for the remainder of the Personal Rule.

The sheer scope of Laud's religious activities was remarkable. In spite of the time-consuming effort which he put into crushing his chief enemies, such as Prynne and Williams, he was constantly extending his influence to deal with other threats to uniformity both at home and abroad. As early as 1627 he had become concerned at the threat posed to orthodox Anglicanism by the activities of the English churches in Holland, where there was a substantial English merchant, military and emigrant community. He subsequently employed agents to drive out puritan ministers and replace them with nominations acceptable to himself. His greatest triumph was the removal of John Davenport, one of the original Feoffees for Impropriations, who had fled to Holland in 1633, fearing that Laud would prosecute him in the High Commission. He became a pastor at the English Church in Amsterdam, but Laud and his agents managed to convince the Dutch authorities that he was thoroughly undesirable. Soon both he and another English Puritan, Hugh Peter, later to be Cromwell's chaplain, were on their way to America. Although Laud was not entirely successful in suppressing Puritans who ministered to the English community in Holland, it was not for want of effort. He collected a detailed dossier on Puritans operating there, employing amongst others the English ambassador at the Hague, Sir William Boswell, as his spy. Yet one or two sturdy opponents outlasted Laud's persecution, most notably Samuel Balmford, pastor at the Hague from 1630 to 1650, who, in spite of threats, bribes and being arrested when he returned briefly to England to visit his elderly mother, continued to minister to his flock.

On one occasion Laud referred to English Puritans abroad as 'swarmes of waspes'. His long arm tried to destroy them not only in Europe but also in America. He planned to appoint a bishop to bring the colonies into orthodoxy and was a member of the powerful Privy Council committee set up for their regulation. In practical terms, however, the government had no effective power across the Atlantic and, try as he might, Laud failed to exert any influence there. He met with considerably more success in Ireland, mainly through the active support of his friend Thomas Wentworth, whose military and economic control over the Irish gave him considerable religious authority as well. Since he was happy to go along with Laud's ideas on Church reform after his appointment as Lord Deputy in 1633, Wentworth embarked on a policy of restoring churches and of punishing recalcitrant bishops and clergy through the Irish Court of High Commission, which he had quickly established. Wentworth's ferocious methods worked well for a time and no doubt pleased Laud too, but nearer to home the Archbishop faced a much more formidable challenge in the form of the growing power of Roman Catholic influence, especially at Court.

One of the most frequent misunderstandings concerning Laud both amongst his contemporaries and by subsequent generations of students was that in some way he was sympathetic to the Roman Catholic Church. Certainly many Puritans assumed that he was in league with the large Catholic contingent at Charles I's Court and was part of the 'plot' to return England to the clutches of the Vatican. Nothing was further from the truth. The Archbishop was an outspoken critic of Roman Catholicism and repeatedly warned the Privy Council of the danger that it represented to the established Church in England. He had some reason to be afraid. Henrietta Maria and her entourage of priests and Catholic servants were a growing influence at Court in the wake of Buckingham's death and the growth of a close and loving relationship between the King and his wife. The Queen's private chapel was widely and openly used by many. Three of the King's leading ministers – Weston, Cottington and Windebank – were themselves crypto-Catholics and there was a steady increase in Papal representation at Court. In 1633 Laud's old room-mate from St John's College, John Jones, the Benedictine Prior of Douai, now calling himself Dom Leander a Sancto Martino, arrived in England and proposed links between Charles I and the Vatican. A book was then produced by a Franciscan, Christopher Davenport, brother of the Puritan John Davenport whom Laud was busy persecuting in Holland. It attempted to show that the differences between the Roman and Anglican churches were minimal. The following year Gregorio Panzani arrived from the Vatican and spent time at Court sounding out the prospects for further steps to union, and in 1636 relations between the two powers were formally restored with the appointment of George Con, a Scot, as official legate of the Vatican to the English Court. To Laud all these developments were alarming and he opposed them as best he could. But he was skating on thin ice. Whilst the Court was only too happy to see him chasing Puritans, the Queen and her friends could not approve of his anti-Catholic stance and it is clear that Charles was not prepared to favour his Archbishop at the expense of offending his wife. The result was something of a stalemate. Panzani admitted that Laud had successfully blocked his path and that, while the rest of the Privy Council could have been bought for 20,000 crowns, Laud was incorruptible. Laud managed to suppress some Catholic literature and closed down St Winifred's Well, a popular Catholic shrine in the diocese of St Asaph. He also ensured that recusants were heavily fined when caught and was able to report to the King in 1636 that 'the number [of Catholics] is much decreased', but at Court he became increasingly unpopular with the Queen and her circle. 'Of all the royal ministers, Laud was the least sympathetic to religious freedom for the Catholics', writes a recent historian of Catholicism in England.[8] Only his pen friend Wentworth seemed to sympathise, so it was to him that Laud wrote trenchantly that 'the Papists are the most dangerous subjects of the Kingdom . . . they will grind the Protestants to powder'. On one occasion he recorded in his diary that he awoke in a cold sweat from a dream that he had been converted to Rome! Clearly his two refusals of a cardinal's hat were to be expected; the only surprise is that they should have been offered. Laud's antagonism to Catholicism was not, however, the reason for its failure to make significant headway in England. Charles I was himself a loyal Anglican and did not seriously consider a rapprochement with Rome, especially as his sister, Elizabeth of Bohemia, remained the victim of a Catholic invasion of the Palatinate. It was above all the Vatican's inability to resolve that matter that accounted for the lack of Catholic advance. Thus, just as Laud's ferocious opposition to Puritanism made him widely unpopular with an increasingly Puritan-minded public in the English provinces as well as in London, so his refusal to countenance the advance of Rome left him largely isolated and unpopular at Court. By 1637 he had few friends left.

III

Unpopular though he had become, at least Laud could claim to have made considerable progress in his policy of reforming the Church in England. Given time, his efficient and uncorrupt methods might well have had a lasting impact, just as Wentworth's even more forceful style was to have in Ireland. But, ironically, Laud's great efforts in England were soon to be destroyed by the results of his policy for Scotland. It had long been his intention to bring the Scottish Church into line with the English, and two visits north of the border with his royal masters in 1617 and 1633 had failed to teach him the intractable nature of Scottish Presbyterianism. Since 1629 he had urged Charles I to introduce uniformity into Scotland along Anglican lines. In

theory the King himself was solely responsible as Head of the Scottish
Church for any changes made there, and certainly the aging
Archbishop of St Andrew's, John Spottiswoode, had little influence.
It is also clear that Laud, although without any official jurisdiction
over Scotland, was one of the prime architects of Church policy there.
With his agent, John Maxwell, Bishop of Ross, he planned to
introduce a revised Canon Law followed by a prayer book almost
identical to the one used in England. When this was done in 1636 and
1637 the results were predictable, albeit surprising to Laud. The
celebrated riot in St Giles' Cathedral upon the first use of the new
Prayer Book was merely a symptom of an almost universal rejection of
the new religious policy. Laud had completely failed to comprehend
the nature of Scottish religion, which consisted of a potent mixture of
Calvinism and nationalism. It was as insulting to the Scots that the
canons and Prayer Book emanated from England as that they were
tainted with Catholic liturgy and theology. The results are well
known. The Kirk and the Scottish nobility, previously estranged,
came together with the mass of the people in a formidable alliance and
drove the Scottish bishops and their supporters out of the country.
Unhappily, Charles and Laud still showed no appreciation of the
situation and, as the Venetian Ambassador reported, 'the Archbishop of Canterbury, on whose advice his Majesty alone decides in
these matters, pertinaciously upholds his regulations and will not
listen to anything different'.[9]

The result was the 'Bishops' Wars', a term coined by Laud to
promote the image of a holy crusade. The military fiasco which
followed was not Laud's fault: indeed, but for his fund-raising efforts
demanding contributions from the clergy there would have been no
military campaign at all. As it turned out for both King and
Archbishop, these events were to lead to their ultimate destruction.
By misreading the depth of Scottish opposition to their religious
policy they occasioned a military conflict which had no support in
England. Thus they were unable to contain the united and better-led
Scots and were forced themselves into calling a parliament as a
last-ditch method of avoiding disaster. In consequence the whole
basis of the Personal Rule and Laud's part in it was destroyed and
both the King and the Archbishop were eventually sent to their
deaths. It is possible to understand and even sympathise with Laud's
policies in England, but his part in the Scottish affair, although
perhaps predictable, was quite the most unfortunate of his career. Yet

again it had demonstrated his curious belief in the written word, for he had naïvely imagined that, by issuing his canons directing the introduction of a new prayer book, the Scottish Calvinists would meekly obey. When they did not, he showed no capacity for compromise but merely insisted that, if necessary, military force must be used to impose his policy. As so often, the King was of the same mind and thus the tragedy unfolded.

By 1640 Laud seemed to have lost much of his drive and confidence. Wentworth, who had returned from Ireland, became increasingly influential at Court, while the Archbishop confined himself mainly to Church matters. Unlike Wentworth he did not look forward to the calling of Parliament and even protested at the continuation of Convocation after the Short Parliament had been dissolved in May 1640. Yet, on being assured that its sessions were constitutional, he did more damage to his declining reputation by enshrining his policies of the previous decade in the canons of 1640. The law now upheld his rulings on controversial matters such as the position of the altar, but it was the notorious 'Etcetera Oath' that did most harm to Laud. One of the new canons required laymen in responsible positions, such as lawyers, teachers, and doctors, to take an oath promising to respect Church government as laid down by 'archbishops, bishops, deans and archdeacons etc.'. There was, in fact, nothing sinister in this wording, but the 'etc.' was soon interpreted as a synonym for the powers of Antichrist (Rome) and the canon was attacked by Puritans and some middle of the road Anglicans as yet another example of the Church's ruthless suppression of the individual's rights.

The summer of 1640 saw further serious reverses for the English forces against the Scots in the Second Bishops' War and at the same time a mounting public outcry against Laud, who was widely regarded as the author of the policies that had led to the present situation. It was certainly true that Laud had not confined himself to religious policy, for throughout Charles's reign he had a hand in the social, economic, financial and foreign policies of the King.

IV

Two principles dominated Laud's approach to secular affairs. The first was that every government policy should as far as possible advance the position of the Church and the second that government should be as efficient and uncorrupt as possible. These policies were reflected in the Archbishop's approach to economic and social matters. The absence of Parliament meant that throughout the Personal Rule the government had to use every possible expedient to raise money. Laud played a key role in supporting the resulting tax and fund raising schemes. Until 1635 Richard Weston, Earl of Portland and Lord Treasurer, was mainly responsible for financial policy. On the whole he did remarkably well in reducing Charles's financial dependence on Parliament, but Laud continually badgered him to raise more money and to end the corruption at Court which so annoyed him. Distraint of Knighthood was probably Weston's most successful method of raising cash from the gentry, but Laud insisted that even more could be taken. When Weston died in 1635 Laud became head of the Treasury Commission which took over responsibility for the King's finances. Laud pressed hard for increased taxation and instituted the most thorough inquiry into state and royal finance since Cranfield's time. Corrupt officials were punished, and Chief Justice Heath was sacked at Laud's instigation when he failed to impose the harshest penalties against those who opposed royal policies. But Laud did not always get his own way. Francis Lord Cottington was a bitter rival and opponent on the Treasury Commission who stood for most of what Laud disliked. He was a crypto-Catholic with a dashing, articulate manner which went down well at Court, especially with the Queen. He was also corrupt. The case of the soap monopoly highlighted their animosity. Weston had granted a soap monopoly to a group of mainly Catholic producers in return for £20,000 a year for the Treasury and a £2000 rake-off for himself. Laud disapproved of both the favouritism to Catholics and the corruption of Weston. The monopoly came up for renewal when Laud was head of the Treasury Commission and a rival tender offered the Treasury twice as much as the Catholic company. Laud supported it, but Cottington, backed by the Secretary of State, Sir Francis Windebank, argued successfully in favour of the original company. This was a bitter blow to the Archbishop, more especially because Windebank had owed his rise almost entirely to Laud and had now deserted him.

Laud's social policy also brought him into conflict with his fellow ministers. The Archbishop believed that the welfare of ordinary people was intimately bound up with the wellbeing of the Church, for a wealthy Church staffed by enthusiastic and highly qualified clergy would ensure that local communities would be well served. In practice, however, the Church was poor and its clergy often inadequately educated and motivated. Laud acted strenuously to improve the situation and was especially anxious to halt the enclosure movement, which threatened both to reduce the population of many parishes and the value of the Church livings and land that went with them. This brought him into conflict with many landowners and courtiers and on one occasion with the King himself, whom Laud opposed unsuccessfully when Charles attempted to enclose what is now Richmond Park. Laud's support for the 'ordinary man' can also be seen in his opposition to sabbatarianism. Puritans believed in strict observance of Sundays, but for many it was their only opportunity to relax and enjoy themselves, having worked hard for the other six days. Laud favoured a more liberal approach whereby activities such as dancing and archery were permitted, and the reissuing of the Book of Sports in 1631 sanctioned such pursuits. It was over such a matter that Laud came into conflict with Chief Justice Richardson. In 1632 certain Puritan justices of the peace in Somerset petitioned against the practice in that country of 'church ales', local festivals to honour the saint to whom a parish church was dedicated. There can be little doubt that many of the ales ended as drunken orgies, but Laud was not prepared to allow any Puritan magistrate to dictate what the Church should or should not allow. Thus, when Richardson issued an order forbidding further ales, Laud summoned him before the Privy Council and berated him so violently that the unfortunate judge was reduced to tears. It is clear that for Laud it was the Church's prerogative to organise parish life and such a policy was bound to bring him into conflict with a gentry class that was ever growing in social importance in the localities.

Laud also played a role in other spheres of policy. Although he knew little of foreign affairs he none the less found himself head of the King's inner council or 'Junto' for Foreign Affairs in the mid 1630s. Broadly he was suspicious of Spain and the pro-Spanish faction at Court led by his hated rival Cottington. Equally, however, his distrust of the Queen did not allow him to support the cause of France. On the whole he had the most cordial relations with the King's Protestant sister, Elizabeth of Bohemia, but he was never able to devise a scheme whereby her lost lands in Germany could be returned to her. Unfairly his enemies often accused him of Catholic sympathies, but they were certainly not evident in his views on foreign policy, and when Charles appeared to be moving towards some arrangement with Spain in the latter years of the Personal Rule he received no encouragement from Laud.

Although Laud played a significant role as one of the King's chief advisers, his lack of expertise in non-Church matters meant that he contributed relatively little to the actual policies of the period. Yet the very fact that he had fingers in so many political pies meant that he was regarded as the key figure in the administration by those who opposed it. Laud was hated, therefore, not only for the religious policies for which he was responsible but also for the financial, social and foreign policies for which he was not.

Laud's most positive contribution to his age was in the cultural and educational spheres. In spite of his reputation for bad temper, he was a surprisingly generous and kindly man on occasions, creating generous endowments for his home town of Reading and his adopted place of residence, Croydon, where he owned a house. The money was to benefit the poor of those places. On another occasion he stepped in to save what is now Charterhouse School from extinction, and hospitals in Winchester, Edinburgh and Sevenoaks were also indebted to the Archbishop. Admittedly his scheme to diminish unemployment in the Oxford area by setting up an expanding cloth industry failed, but it was in Oxford itself that he made his most lasting impact, for he took his duties as President of St John's and later as Chancellor of the University seriously. The Canterbury Quad at St John's is one achievement of his life that remains today. Arguably the most beautiful in Oxford, it reminds us that Laud did have a genuine concept of architectural splendour to match his spiritual hope for the 'beauty of holiness' in Church services. It is perhaps appropriate that the greatest moment of his life occurred at St John's when in 1636 he entertained the King and Queen at the College to celebrate the completion of the new quadrangle. Laud presided over the junketings with great pride and, the royal party having departed, he checked the silver and was relieved to find only two spoons missing – a small price to pay for an event that confirmed that he still enjoyed Charles's confidence and favour. His other great and lasting contribution to Oxford was the presentation of numerous ancient and valuable manuscripts culled by his agents from all over Europe and the Middle East, and his support for the study and teaching of Arabic was far-sighted.

His greatest project, however, was a failure. He longed for the restoration of the decrepit St Paul's Cathedral so that it would be a fitting bastion of Anglicanism in the capital city. His efforts at fund-raising were indefatigable: fines from High Commission, gifts often extorted from reluctant courtiers (the project had the support of Charles) and levies from Church funds were gathered in, but there was never enough and the rebuilding was never completed.

As the Long Parliament gathered in the autumn of 1640 these achievements were not remembered and instead Laud was regarded as the architect of the hated policies of the past few years. That 'the Archbishop is the root and ground of all our miseries' was the view of one MP, Sir Harbottle Grimstone, and a contemporary pamphlet accused 'cursed Canterbury' of 'trying to make way for popery'. Yet Strafford was the prime target of Parliament, for he was the man they feared more. Laud, then in his late sixties, was almost a broken man and thus it was Strafford who was arrested, impeached, attainted and executed first, all in the space of six months. For Laud the same process was to take over four years. Most of that time he spent in the Tower, harried by his old enemy William Prynne, who thoroughly enjoyed his task as Laud's chief prosecutor. But Laud found dignity in defeat, and at his trial defended himself so effectively that even Prynne grudgingly complimented him. It was to no avail, for the trial was political and his eventual execution certain. As with his royal master four years later, it was on a cold January morning that Laud went to the block in 1645. Needless to say, most of what he had stood for was dismantled by Parliament as bishops, Prayer Book and Church of England were all swept away by the rising tide of radical Puritanism.

Things were never to be quite the same again, for, while Laud would have had much sympathy for the Restoration Settlement – the Act of Uniformity was in line with his own ideas – it was for the first time tacitly recognised that non-Anglicans might legitimately worship in England, and not one of Laud's successors at Canterbury was to hold the degree of political power that he had enjoyed. A more permanent reminder of his work in his London diocese were the numerous churches whose building he had encouraged and which he consecrated, but only a few remain unaltered today.

V

There can be little doubt that Laud was one of the most disliked political figures in English history. Most of his contemporaries would have agreed with Pym's assessment that Laud 'went about to subvert all the laws both of God and men'. By 1640 he had succeeded in alienating most of the groups whose views mattered, for his religious policy had offended not only the large and influential numbers of Puritans but also moderate churchmen, whilst his opposition to Catholicism meant that he could expect little sympathy from a Court where Catholics enjoyed considerable influence. His support for other measures of the Personal Rule tarred him with the unpopularity which issues such as Ship Money, distraint of knighthood and the soap monopoly aroused. His friendship with Wentworth and his patronage of Windebank suggested to many that he was responsible for advancing the careers of the other men most hated and feared at the time, and his use of the courts of Star Chamber and High Commission and abuse of judges such as Richardson and Heath suggested that he bent the law to his own requirements. His harsh treatment of the hundreds who came before him in the courts convinced the masses that he was cruel and wicked. In short, almost every public action of Laud was to lose him popularity and support.

Even so Laud might well have survived, for with the crucial support of the King he more than held his own whenever major decisions were contested. Laud was used to loneliness and unpopularity, for they were a consequence of his personality as well as of his policies. But it was his fatal miscalculation concerning the imposition of the Scottish Prayer Book that sealed his fate and that of his royal master. Christopher Hill has aptly said, 'As soon as Laud's imposing edifice was shaken by the external force of the Scottish armies, its internal weakness made it collapse like a house of cards.'[10] The internal weakness of Laudian England resulted from the fact that 'Thorough' was a fiction. Although Laud and Wentworth dreamed of strong, efficient central government, no serious steps were ever taken to provide the large and uncorrupt civil service needed to sustain such a system. Even in the realm of religious policy, where Laud had most chance of success, he failed. Lack of support from fellow clergy, the poverty of the Church and the indifference of Court and people meant that he had to compromise all too often. As Hugh Trevor-Roper says, 'he frequently had to sacrifice the orthodoxy which he preferred to the moderate Puritanism which was the most he could get'.[11]

Yet, in spite of political and religious failure, Laud is important and he is remembered. He made a major contribution to the causes of the Civil War yet he was admirable in many ways. Clarendon presented a sympathetic evaluation of him as 'a man of great courage and resolution' and in a different age his hard work and resistance to corruption would have been regarded as virtues. Ironically, in the seventeenth century they were to ensure his downfall. Perhaps it is kindest to remember his generosity to charity, his forward-looking endowment of buildings, manuscripts and lectureships at Oxford, and the humility which is evident in the genuine sorrow he felt every time his quick-tempered nature got the better of him. In these respects he was far from the inhuman monster that his opponents painted him.

4. Thomas Wentworth, Earl of Strafford

JONATHAN WATTS

On 16 April 1641 the House of Commons resolved that Thomas Wentworth, first Earl of Strafford, had 'endeavoured to subvert the ancient fundamental laws of these realms of England and Ireland and to introduce an arbitrary and tyrannical government against law'.[1] Five days later an Act of Attainder was passed by the House after its managers had failed to secure an impeachment. On 7 May the Lords endorsed the decision of the Commons. The royal assent was given on the 10th, and within two days Strafford had been executed. The debate which surrounded his trial and death was considerable. Parliament was by no means united in its acceptance of the evidence of legal justification for Strafford's condemnation. The trial became the *cause célèbre* of the parliamentary leaders and an object of macabre entertainment to Londoners and visitors from the provinces. By the end of May 1641 nine pamphlets about Strafford were in circulation. Yet his execution failed to produce the settlement with Charles I for which its proponents had hoped.

Historians since have been caught up in the drama of Strafford's final months, and analysis of his career has tended to be in the black-and-white terms of his trial. Contemporaries saw him either as 'Black Tom Tyrant', or as the faithful servant of the King and first martyr to the royalist cause. At the Restoration the details of his trial were expunged from the Journal of the House of Lords. The nineteenth-century Whig tradition, epitomised by Macaulay, saw him not only as the architect of a hated royal absolutism but also as an apostate from the cause of parliamentary progress. Increasingly Strafford has come to be regarded as the most able of Charles I's ministers, as a man of principle and stature working for effective monarchical government but frustrated by popular opposition and the King's lukewarm support. More recently, a more balanced and less partisan approach has been forthcoming in which Wentworth's career has been seen in its contemporary political perspective and assessed with a realistic view of his personal achievement. While this may have diminished the traditional importance accorded to Strafford as an agent of the Personal Rule and a cause of the conflict which led to Civil War, it is impossible to ignore the fact that in 1640 the leaders of the Long Parliament singled him out as the chief author or exponent of the government they sought to limit, change or destroy. One of the purposes of this chapter is to suggest why Strafford became such a figure of hatred, and why his removal was so important to those who wished to reform the so-called abuses of the Personal Rule.

However, the events of 1640 and 1641 form only a fraction of a long political career, and much of this assessment of Strafford will be concerned with the way in which his ideas and career developed in the light of the pressures on any early Stuart politician. In dealing with each section of Strafford's career, it is tempting to look for evidence illustrating subsequent stages, and this has led historians to endow Strafford with principles, ambitions and a capacity for planning and far-sightedness he did not possess. In the 1620s, for example, Thomas Wentworth was a typical knight of the shire, not a man marked out to become an agent of absolutism. At the time when he was alleged to have changed sides, in 1628, his standing at Court was insignificant and the importance of the event developed only in the light of his later activities. As President of the Council of the North and Lord Deputy of Ireland he was out of the political limelight. His reputed success in Ireland owes as much to the allegations of his accusers in 1641 as to his actual intentions or achievements there. Quite simply, Strafford's career must be seen in the context of contemporary political reality, where concepts such as Court and country, loyalty or opposition to the King, disinterested motives and long-term principles were less important than personal ambition, patronage, county standing, Court faction, rivalries and the immediate reaction to political situations.

I

Thomas Wentworth was born at the house of his maternal grandfather in Chancery Lane, London, on 13 April 1593, the oldest surviving son of Sir William Wentworth of Wentworth Woodhouse in the West Riding of Yorkshire. Sir William was a typical member of an Elizabethan 'rising gentry' family whose general success was capped by the acquisition of a wealthy heiress: Thomas's grandfather had married a Gascoigne, who provided both money and good breeding, a point continually stressed by Thomas, much to the boredom of his acquaintances. Sir William was wealthy and extended his property by purchases from the Talbot estates in Yorkshire. He provided a good, if conventional, education for his son under the Dean of Ripon, then at St John's College, Cambridge, and at the Inner Temple, equipping him with the smattering of theology, law, classics and argumentative skill deemed necessary for the Jacobean gentleman. In 1611 Sir William bought himself a baronetcy, while his son was knighted and married to Margaret Clifford, daughter of the Wentworth's impressive neighbour the Earl of Cumberland. This further enhanced Wentworth prestige and the family's pre-eminence among the Yorkshire gentry. Such were the delights of marriage that Wentworth straightaway undertook a tour of France, returning with his critical views of foreigners reinforced and a marked distaste for what he had seen of Roman Catholicism.

On the death of his father in 1614 Wentworth inherited an annual income of around £4000 but was unable to provide an expensive education for all his eight younger brothers. Personally ambitious and eager to show the importance of his family in Yorkshire society, he was elected MP for Yorkshire in the 1614 Parliament along with Sir John Savile of Howley Park, near Batley. Savile was a much older man whose family, tainted with illegitimacy, had rivalled the Wentworths for political and social dominance of the county community for some time. The Wentworth–Savile rivalry is an excellent example of the way in which local disputes and power struggles could influence politics as far up as the Court. It was one of the chief factors behind Wentworth's career up to 1628, and first emerged when in 1615 Wentworth replaced Savile as Custos Rotulorum (chairman of the bench) for Yorkshire. Savile was at the time under investigation by the Star Chamber for fraud, but by carefully cultivating the rising favourite, George Villiers, he rehabilitated his reputation. Wentworth, having exploited his rival's eclipse, was then subjected to considerable pressure from Villiers to return the post to Savile, but he refused to do so. Villiers, the future Duke of Buckingham, was never one to take refusals lightly, and the antipathy he showed towards Wentworth in the 1620s may date from this early confrontation, compounded by Wentworth's later links with the group at Court opposed to Buckingham's policies and thereby excluded from influence.

Wentworth's ambition meant that he was often at Court. There his contempt for fashion, his tedious conversation, arrogance and concern for his family pride ensured his isolation. Throughout his career, his capacity for alienating individuals was remarkable and he had no idea of the value of tactful and sensitive behaviour. An inveterate southerner might attribute this to Yorkshire bluntness, or to that lack of imagination which makes it impossible to perceive another person's viewpoint. Wentworth's one ally at Court was Archbishop Abbot, a co-trustee of his nephews' estates, but he was less influential than the Howard faction and the rising favourite, Buckingham.

Wentworth's parliamentary career began properly in 1621, when he was given the task of engineering the election of the Court candidate and his patron, Secretary of State Sir George Calvert, as a knight of the shire for Yorkshire. This arrangement neatly illustrates the balance of Court patronage: Wentworth proved himself useful by securing the election and the support of Yorkshire for the Court, thereby recommending himself for further office while raising his own status in the county as a known courtier who could transmit Court patronage to his own clients. In discussing Savile and Wentworth, J. P. Cooper writes, 'Court and country were interdependent factors in their career; standing and influence in the country supported their claims for preferment and influences at court, on which, in turn, their prestige in the country would be nourished.'[2] The only block to electoral success was Sir John Savile, whose strong power base among the West Riding clothiers threatened to prevent Wentworth's victory. In a period when candidates were often unopposed there was frantic electioneering, based not on policy but on the loyalties claimed by the two rival families. Despite the struggle, and despite widespread gentry hostility to the outsider Calvert, Savile failed to prevent the victory of the court duo. Wentworth subsequently adopted a conciliatory approach to parliamentary business, being willing in 1621 to follow the guidance of the King. Two contributions, however, do show some originality of thought: he suggested the innovation of prosecuting patentees, which led to the condemnation of Mitchell and Mompesson, and he expressed concern, on returning to Yorkshire, at having voted subsidies but not passed any legislation, showing a sensitivity to the demands of his gentry constituents while still actively pursuing his ambitions at Court.

The desire for office may in part have been prompted by financial considerations. Although Wentworth had no children of his own, he supported a large inherited family, maintained four houses, made frequent visits to London and purchased land worth £8000 in 1617 alone. Additional income therefore seems to have been necessary. The death of his wife in 1622 provided the time-honoured opportunity for marriage with a rich heiress. Wentworth first approached Mary, the daughter of Sir William Craven, who would have brought with her £25,000, but rumours of Wentworth's impotence and incontinence seem to have frustrated both this match and plans to marry Lady Diana Cecil, co-heir of the Earl of Exeter. After a third attempt, with Lady Anne Clifford, dowager Countess of Dorset, he eventually married Arabella Holles, in February 1625. As the sixteen-year-old daughter of Lord Clare, Arabella brought a dowry of £6000 as well as great beauty and charm into Wentworth's life. She also saved her husband's reputation by producing children.

Profitable office, however, was not as forthcoming as potential wives. Wentworth had hopes of advancement from the links he developed with Lord Treasurer Cranfield, probably by way of Sir George Calvert and his Yorkshire neighbour Sir Arthur Ingram of Temple Newsam, whose shady business deals involved many contemporary politicians, including both Wentworth and Cranfield. Wentworth was made Receiver General for the Crown lands of Yorkshire, but sold the post after a year. This again suggests that he might have been experiencing some financial problems.

The election of 1624 bore witness to the decline in Wentworth's standing in the county community; he did not even bother to contest the prestigious county seat and Sir John Savile got in unopposed. Savile's links with Buckingham, the dominant power at Court, were well known, and the patronage to which this gave him access ensured a clear advantage in the county election. Wentworth, on the other hand, was associated with the group around Cranfield, Calvert and Williams, opposed to Buckingham in the faction struggle which spilled over from Court to Parliament in 1624. Wentworth was reduced to representing the borough of Pontefract and there was even some doubt as to whether it had the right to return an MP at all. By

1625 Wentworth had reasserted himself enough to contest the county seat, but a second election had to be called when Savile protested about Wentworth's victory in the first.

In 1624 Wentworth missed the start of the parliamentary session through a bout of the illness which was to dog his career, and, confused as to how his own career might best be served amid political struggles at Court, he inquired of Calvert and Ingram, his contacts there, 'what I had best do'. Yet on one point of principle he opposed Buckingham strongly: the Spanish war. He was aware of the financial burden a war would impose and saw Spanish friendship as a means of avoiding unnecessary expenditure and of encouraging trade and the consequent increase in customs revenue. His views on this were reflected by a number of northern MPs, aware of the disastrous effect this might have on the wool industry. S. P. Salt has pointed out that a man such as Wentworth, an MP, a landowner and a county administrator, had to respond to the interests of his electorate as well as pursue his own political ambitions, ensure the productivity of his estates and avoid any cause of social disruption in the county.

In the light of the harsh treatment he received from the Court afterwards, Wentworth's contribution to the 1625 session was markedly modest; having in 1624 spoken briefly in defence of Cranfield, a gesture unlikely to win Buckingham's approval, he continued to be mildly critical of the level of expenditure necessitated by the war, showing the dilemma of an MP asked to grant subsidies without passing the legislation his constituents wanted. After Charles requested additional subsidies Wentworth stated, 'This demand, being without all precedent, may be dangerous in the example, that we fear the granting thereof will be esteemed by his subjects no fair acquittal of our duties towards them or return to their trusts reposed in us.'[3] As Russell adds, 'what the king was asking of him was simply more than he could live down when he went home.' Ambitious as Wentworth was, he was unwilling to risk the county basis of his personal power.

What prompted Buckingham to recommend Wentworth's nomination as Sheriff of Yorkshire in 1625 is unclear. Since the Sheriff was returning-officer for the county, he could not return himself as an MP, and so possibly Buckingham's aim was to keep Wentworth out of Parliament in order to reduce opposition to his Spanish war policy. Wentworth could in no way be seen as a leading trouble-making. The move may instead have been a reaction against a speech made at the end of the 1625 session in which Wentworth discouraged the granting of extra subsidies. His association with the anti-war and anti-Buckingham group around Cranfield, Williams and Arundel was, anyway, well known. That he should receive such severe treatment is perhaps explained by the influence Savile and other opponents of Wentworth were able to exert on Buckingham. Aware of this, Wentworth had over the previous year made half-hearted efforts to cultivate the favourite. Unsuccessful in this, he was not only excluded from Parliament and the status which that gave him in the county, but also saddled with an unglamorous and expensive office. Savile, returned unopposed in 1626, was now able to exploit his superiority to the full, showing how important Court patronage could be to county standing and political ambition.

Wentworth's standing in the country was further reduced when he was dismissed from his position as Custos Rotulorum. This again was almost certainly owing to Savile's influence at Court. Their rivalry became even more acute when a tentative request for consideration as a future President of the Council of the North was met with the promotion of Savile to the vice-presidency of the same council. Wentworth's financial position also deteriorated until late 1627, when his debts were at least £6000 and he was trying to sell off land. The only encouragement for a man so keen to pursue family ambition was the birth of a son in 1626.

Much has been made of Wentworth's imprisonment for refusal to pay the forced loan which Charles ordered after the collapse of the 1626 Parliament over the impeachment of Buckingham. Wedgwood, for example, writes, 'Was this the case of integrity and conscience which justified defying the Crown? Apparently it was',[4] and constitutional historians have seen those who refused to pay as martyrs to the cause of liberty in the face of incipient tyranny. Wentworth seems an unlikely martyr. Certainly he was opposed to the war, objected to the overtaxation of the landed interest and had no love for Buckingham, whom he could blame for much of his recent failure. However, his tactic in the past had always been ingratiation rather than opposition to achieve his ambitions and, like nearly all MPs in the 1620s, he believed in co-operation and conciliation with the Crown. There was no long-term constitutional point behind his refusal to pay; his primary motive was that, along with most Yorkshire landowners, he objected to paying large taxes for a policy which seemed pointless and profitless and which was being handled with increasing incompetence.

Secondly, his humiliation at the rejection of all his overtures to Buckingham and the Court pushed him, if only through pride, into the role of opponent and the pursuit of status in the county rather than at Court. Thirdly, by showing personal strength and county support which had been consolidated during his time as Sheriff, Wentworth could hope to force recognition of his abilities and worth on the Court in the hope of future office. His friends were surprised at the strength of his resistance, and there was some fear that his health might not survive the rigours of imprisonment. On his release, on 27 December 1627, he returned to Yorkshire to prepare for the general election. His victory demonstrated the support which his stand had generated among the Yorkshire gentry and heralded the end of Savile's brief dominance. As a Court supporter, Savile had been obliged to organise the collection of the forced loan in Yorkshire, thereby alienating his county supporters and, in his lack of success, his patrons at Court; his customary appeal against Wentworth's election was summarily dismissed.

Wentworth's role in the events leading up to the Petition of Right are well-known, though his subsequent move towards the Court has led some historians to emphasise the radical nature of his parliamentary activity, as though to heighten the drama of sudden political change. His views had not changed since 1625 and he did not see himself as an innovator; he saw only the need to strengthen 'our sober, vital liberties by re-enforcing of the ancient laws made by our ancestors'.[5] He, as much as anyone, was responsible for focusing attention on the issues of illegal taxation, billeting and arbitrary imprisonment – issues which were of practical rather than constitutional significance – yet he saw the need to cultivate more moderate opinion in both Commons and Lords. By his eventual decision to frame the complaint as a petition rather than a bill, he hoped to avoid unbridgeable confrontation with Charles. His role at the forefront of the Commons attack in 1628 was impressive, and his time in the political wilderness had increased his stature. He also saw a forceful performance in Parliament as a further way of demonstrating his abilities to the Court.

There was no hard and fast distinction between Court and Country or Court and Parliament in early seventeenth-century England. As late as 1641, Pym, Bedford, Hampden and other opponents of the Personal Rule seriously considered a scheme by which, having criticised royal policy, they would be taken on as councillors to put the policy to rights. Wentworth had shown that he was a forceful politician with strong local backing and could respond both to ambition and to principle. From the Court's point of view, his recruitment as a Privy Councillor would serve to conciliate a potential opponent and at the same time be a gesture confirming Charles's acceptance of the Petition of Right and the initiation of a policy of reform and retrenchment under the rehabilitated politicians who filled the gap left by Buckingham. For Wentworth, office under the Crown would fulfil many of his ambitions, would strengthen his position in Yorkshire and might allow him to pursue his political principles at a level of real influence. Already, enthusiasm for the Spanish war was waning, while there was disillusionment with the disastrous interventions in France, and the success of Lord Treasurer Weston's recommendation in 1628 that Wentworth be made a peer shows that the peace faction in Court was becoming more influential. Weston, known also by his title of Earl of Portland, had been a patron of Wentworth throughout the 1620s but could only now exercise influence in his client's favour.

In moving from the Commons to the Lords, Wentworth did not have to surrender any principles and was following the conventional path of political promotion. He was a practical politician, not a man interested in long-term constitutional ideas or novelties. He supported peace because war annoyed taxpayers, interfered with traditional liberties and ruined trade. He supported the Petition of Right because it defended existing laws from royal innovation. At the same time he was ambitious and keen to promote the honour of his family by service to the Crown. His early years in Parliament had enabled him to cultivate patrons at Court, but their opposition to Buckingham frustrated Wentworth's hopes. Attempts at a personal reconciliation with Buckingham in 1624 failed, and Wentworth looked then to Yorkshire rather than the Court as the basis of his political power. In 1625 his defence of county interests incurred the wrath of many courtiers. S. P. Salt has shown that, where Wentworth found it difficult to please both King and county, then county interests predominated along with personal convictions, strongly held. Pre-eminence in the county community was ensured by his appointment as a baron in July 1628 and as President of the Council of the North in succession to Lord Scrope in the following December. The dismissal of Savile from his vice-presidency, after a scandal in which he was accused of receiving bribes from Roman Catholics, completed the triumph with an element of personal vindictiveness which Wentworth often found gratifying. As though on probation in the royal service, Wentworth had to wait until November 1629 for his seat on the Privy Council.

Wentworth's political views have been summarised by Dr Cliffe as a belief 'in a strong authoritarian system of government based on the royal prerogative ... responsible and benificent government distinguished by its efficient administration and its care and protection of the poorer members of society'.[6] What Wentworth objected to was the arbitrary use of power and actions which destroyed the unity between government and governed. In his acceptance speech as President, Wentworth outlined political views which few MPs would have challenged:

> Princes are to be indulgent, nursing fathers to their people; their modest liberties, their sober rights, ought to be precious in their eyes; the branches of their government be for shadow, for habitation, the comfort of life, repose, safe and still under the protection of their sceptres. Subjects on the other side ought with solicitous eyes of jealousy to watch over the prerogatives of a crown; the authority of a king is the keystone which closeth up the arch of order and government, which contains each part in due relation to the whole and which, once shaken, infirmed, all the frame falls together into a confused heap of foundation and battlement, of strength and beauty.

As to his own role, Wentworth argued that the servants of the King and his people 'must look equally on both [i.e. King and subjects], weave, twist these two together in all their counsels, study, labour to preserve each ... and ... cut off early all disputes between them'.[7]

Such views remained with Wentworth to the end: in his final defence speech in 1641 he declared, 'The happiness of a kingdom consists in [the] just poise of the king's prerogative and the subject's liberty. ... No, I have and shall ever aim at a fair but a bounded liberty, remembering always that I am a freeman, but a subject; that I have a right, but under a monarch'.[8]

II

The Council of the North, established by Henry VIII to extend effective Privy Council control to the northern counties in the wake of serious unrest among the nobility, had under the early Stuarts become merely an agent of local government, incompetently run by its retiring President, Lord Scrope, and his deputy Sir John Savile. The death of Buckingham deprived Savile of Court protection from accusations of accepting bribes, which led to his dismissal as Vice-president and consequent loss of county status, a situation which Wentworth was quite ready to exploit. Recent presidents had all been political non-entities – a life in York cut off the incumbent from Court and the opportunity to develop political ambitions. If Wentworth did in fact raise the status of the Council, improve its efficiency and correct some of the more glaring faults, then it was owing to his desire to impress his superiors and do a job well, rather than because of any initiative from the Court to tighten up the activities and role of the Council. It was rumoured as early as 1629 that Wentworth was a candidate for the lord treasurership, which suggests that some at Court did respect his political abilities. His appointment to the North, like that to Ireland, may have been an attempt by Weston to exclude possible rivals from Court.

As President, Wentworth saw his role as that of ensuring the good government of the North. The main challenges to this were administrative and judicial inefficiency and the ambitions of various northern landowners (many of them recusant Catholics) no longer powerful enough to undermine royal authority but still able to exert considerable local influence. The judicial power of the Council was similar to that of Star Chamber: it heard cases in a summary way and provided quick remedies, especially against the wealthy and powerful. Wentworth imposed a virtual ban on the recently developed custom of issuing 'prohibitions' by which cases were removed to the common-law courts and hence became more susceptible to magnate influence whilst simultaneously providing endless lucrative employment for the vast body of lawyers in Stuart England. While some of the Yorkshire gentry saw these actions as those of an agent of royal centralisation, Wentworth's only intention was to do his job efficiently.

This policy of 'Thorough' has been described by Dr Cliffe as 'a greater emphasis on state intervention in the social and economic fields, determined efforts to re-assert the authority of the Council of the North and closer supervision of the work of justices of the peace. Inevitably it aroused resentment, and not least among the country gentry whose interests Wentworth had once espoused.' His attitude to the North was similar to that he showed towards Ireland, and in one of his conflicts with the Yorkshire gentry he stated, 'Humour and Liberty I find reign in these parts of observing a superior command no farther than they like themselves and of questioning any profit of the crown called upon by his majesty's ministers which might enable it to subsist of itself.'[9] This concern for the Crown's finances led him into frequent conflict with members of the gentry class, many of whom resented the promotion to President of a fellow landowner no better than they and one prone to personal vindictiveness. On taking up his post Wentworth had immediately given jobs to a number of his supporters, either on the Council itself or as deputy-lieutenants or justices of the peace, specifically excluding known clients of Savile. An attempt to increase the income from the fines on recusant Catholics alienated the strong landed but Catholic interest in the North Riding of Yorkshire, and, while their legal position remained secure, their income was more effectively tapped. Opposition to the scheme for Distraint of Knighthood was organised by Sir David Foulis, whom Wentworth saw as a symbol of gentry opposition to his aims. His inability to see how any of his actions or methods could be misunderstood by his critics was one of his major problems and, while he did reduce corruption, improve the level of justice, increase the government's revenue and challenge local landed interests very effectively, much of his time was spent attacking various individuals with local support and contacts at Court. Corrupt as these people might have been, many felt that Wentworth was motivated in his actions as much by personal spite as by the desire for efficiency.

It is surprising for a man so typical of the English landed classes that Wentworth totally failed to realise the importance of cultivating personal support, either of influential individuals or of dominant groups in society. His capacity for alienating almost everyone with whom he dealt is extraordinary and goes a long way to explain the unanimity of opposition towards him in 1640. Three examples of personal harassment gained notoriety. Henry Bellasis, with whom Wentworth had once been elected knight of the shire, was punished by the Council for insulting its President. When Bellasis's father, Lord Fauconburg, complained to the Privy Council he received a blunt reprimand. Sir David Foulis became involved in a series of wrangles when he was accused of embezzling about £5000 from the Royal Household; counter-accusations on Wentworth's own financial dealings, which were not beyond reproof, pushed the matter as far as the Star Chamber, which awarded Wentworth £3000 damages and fined Foulis a further £5000. Sir Thomas Gower challenged the competence of the Council in judicial matters and, when his case was remitted to the Privy Council, judgement was again given in favour of Wentworth and Gower returned to the north and four months imprisonment. A further conflict illustrates Wentworth's predicament as President, a position in which class, political and personal pressures were often hard felt. It arose when the Savile family and Cornelius Vermuyden put forward a scheme for the draining of Hatfield Chase. Wentworth took the part of the displaced smallholders, some of whom were completely flooded out. To defend the rights of the underdog was perhaps morally correct but politically unrealistic when politics and society were dominated by the landed interest. In taking such a stance Wentworth was open to accusations of pursuing his personal vendetta against the Saviles. Apart from this episode there is not much to suggest that Wentworth's presidency saw any general improvement in lower-class living standards. His opinion carried little weight when he acted as a Poor Law commissioner after 1631, and the effectiveness of the New Book of Orders issued as a result of the Commision was minimal, its main impact being the arousal of hostility from those who had to undertake the onerous duties it imposed.

In pursuing his personal wealth, Wentworth also showed a blindness to public opinion: he believed that, provided the net result of any transaction was improved efficiency and a greater income for the Crown, then his personal profit was irrelevant; contemporaries whom he challenged for their own corruption inevitably saw things differently. As soon as he became President, Wentworth's creditworthiness improved and, having been in financial straits in 1627, he was able to spend up to £10,000 on new lands in 1628. A great deal of government money passed through his hands, largely from two sources – Distraint of Knighthood fines and recusancy fines. One of Wentworth's many conflicts with Lord Treasurer Portland was over his refusal to hand over cash until the last minute, suggesting that it was being used as speculative capital. Conventional as such behaviour was among Court officials, it did not look good when practised by one advocating new standards of honesty and efficiency.

Yet he could still condemn his business associate Ingram with the words, 'I know well his avarice . . . a man of no virtue or ability.'[10] In 1631 Wentworth also hoped to capitalise out of a shortage of corn in London by shipping in supplies from Yorkshire and acting in defiance of Privy Council directives. His failure to make more than £80 profit out of the deal is evidence only of a lack of business acumen.

Despite all the criticism which can be made of Wentworth as Lord President, despite his apparent exclusion from Court and his failure to cultivate support there, his appointment as Lord Deputy of Ireland in 1632 shows that some people were impressed by him. If Portland felt threatened by his continued presence in England, then this suggests that Wentworth had made his mark and made it where it was most important – with the King. Charles backed him, and, while his opponents at Court grew in number, until 1639 the King never failed to support him in the face of attack, even if the support was sometimes grudgingly given. To Charles, Wentworth was an able and efficient public servant who was further recommended by his friendship with Laud.

The two royal servants became acquainted in the early 1630s, sharing a similar view of the desirability of efficient government and the need to challenge the interests which prevented it. This was the oft-quoted concept of 'Thorough', a system of administration based on increased efficiency, tight control, attack on corruption, accurate information, uniformity of practice and centralised authority. Their views were simplistic and took little account of the nature and problems of English (and Scottish) society and politics, neither of which were suited to the sudden imposition of centralised uniformity. As to religion, Wentworth had little personal commitment above the traditional piety and anti-Catholicism of his class; he shared Laud's ideas not out of any doctrinal conviction, but in the belief that a uniform state Church was an essential part of a politically stable regime. He accepted the lord deputyship as a promotion for good service in the North from a king who appreciated his efficiency but had little regard for him as a person. He kept his presidency of the Council of the North, and continued to supervise its business through his deputy Sir Edward Osborne.

III

In 1633 Wentworth wrote,

> I find myself in the society of a strange people. . . . Great cures to be
> wrought, but where the medicines or the persons faithful to apply
> them are to be found, I know not. I find this kingdom abandoned
> for these late years to every man that could please himself to
> purchase what best liked him for his money, and consequently all
> the crown revenue reduced . . . there is little left either to befit the
> king's servants or to improve his own revenues by.[11]

He was writing shortly after his arrival in Ireland, and a more acute
politician might have observed in this statement a similarity with
problems in England.

Ireland has traditionally been the politicians' graveyard, but it has
not been any easier territory for the historian. Social, economic,
religious, political and racial divisions preclude any simple explanation or understanding of Irish politics, whether in the seventeenth or
in the twentieth century, though a student today is in a better position
to sympathise with the complexities than twenty or thirty years ago.
As recently as 1959, the foremost historian of Wentworth in Ireland
expressed surprise that Wentworth viewed his Irish opponents in
religious terms: 'I see plainly that, so long as this kingdom continues
popish, they are not a people for the crown of England to be confident
of.'[12] Much has been written of English anti-Catholic sentiment in the
seventeenth century, and fear of Catholicism was a fundamental
cause of political feeling in the years before the Civil War. Despite the
fact that Wentworth was attached to a Court tarred with the brush of
Popery and was himself accused of trying to introduce an arbitrary
government by means of a Catholic army, he shared the popular
revulsion to Catholicism and held the majority of the Irish population
in contempt. Religion was not in itself a strong force behind
Wentworth's actions, but what there was of it was in keeping with his
class, background and nationality.

However, Irish society was not to be seen just in terms of
Protestants and Catholics. There were in effect four divisions, and it is
to Wentworth's dubious credit that he managed to alienate all four
groups during his period in office. At the bottom of the social scale
were the Gaelic Irish, Catholic peasants whose habitual resentment

to any overlord was heightened by differences in race or religion. Of comparable origin, though with a protected and arguably overexalted status, were the Calvinist Scottish settlers or planters who had been encouraged to colonise areas confiscated from rebellious landowners. They had established a firm foothold after the defeat of the Ulster rebellion in 1601 and the flight abroad of its leaders, O'Neill and O'Donnell, some years later. The two dominant landed and politically strong classes were the Old English or Anglo-Irish aristocracy and the New English planters. Ever since the twelfth century, the use of Ireland as an enemy base had been of concern to the English Crown, and many of the Old English claimed descent from English aristocratic settlers in the Middle Ages. Their chief source of power lay in massive estates outside the area of direct English control around Dublin, and their leaders, men such as the Earls of Clanrickarde, Westmeath or Fingal, were among the wealthiest men in Ireland. They were mostly Roman Catholic and were occasionally subjected to persecution or recusancy fines, though their leader, Clanrickarde, had permanent exception. While they were excluded from government they had some say in the Irish Parliament, and many had contacts with the English Court; Clanrickarde himself was a viscount in the English peerage.

The only area of complete English control in Ireland was 'the Pale' around Dublin, where the New English predominated. This group consisted of wealthy, often aristocratic landowners who had exploited the Crown's need for a reliable landowning and administrative class in a strategically important area and as a result had amassed large estates and gained complete control of Irish government. Richard Boyle, the Earl of Cork and Lord Treasurer of Ireland, is the most well known of the New English, with an annual income from rents alone of £20,000. Others at the forefront of this group were Sir William Parsons, in charge of wardship, Viscount Ranelagh, Viscount Mountnorris, the Loftus family and Charles Wilmot. They controlled the Irish Privy Council and, by the English Crown's creation of new seats and peerages, the Irish Parliament. They were Protestant and supported the Protestant ascendancy, not out of any intense religious conviction but because it was in their financial interests to do so. After all, the basis of their wealth was the government's belief that the loyalty of a Roman Catholic enclave could not be taken for granted. Some were absentee landlords; most had contact with or relations in the English peerage; and, until Wentworth's appointment, the government of Ireland had been with their co-operation and consent.

None the less, the New English were in a minority and the pressures of the continental war in the 1620s had given the Old English aristocracy an opportunity to demand a confirmation of their status, which was in continual danger of erosion by a centralising, English administration. Their specific complaint was the threat to their estates from a government intent on further schemes for plantation. The 'Matter of Grace and Bounty' consisted of twenty-eight clauses designed to meet Old English grievances – notably their title to land, their exclusion from posts in law and in the government, and their general harassment. Though they failed to become statute law, the Graces seem to have been accepted by Wentworth's predecessor, Lord Falkland, and in 1632 there was an atmosphere of potential co-operation between the Old English and the government. A split in the Irish Privy Council which polarised round the two figures of Cork and Mountnorris gave further opportunities for a tactful Lord Deputy to cultivate support and harness to his own cause the very divisions which complicated the political situation.

Wentworth's aims were clear. As part of the Arundel–Cottington–Laud group which emerged after the death of Buckingham, he was associated with the policies of retrenchment, reform and greater efficiency immediately expressed in the ending of the Spanish war. His role in Ireland was to increase royal revenue and get for the King all that was rightly his. If he needed to adapt old or introduce new methods of government, then it was solely as a means to the efficient exploitation of Ireland as a source of royal revenue and, later, military strength. If Wentworth's government of Ireland has been open to the accusation of arbitrariness, then it was because Wentworth saw this as the best way of doing his job; he had no long-term plans for absolutism nor abstract concepts of centralised government. Even his religious policy was primarily concerned with Church revenue rather than matters of doctrine or practice. His arguments with individuals and confrontations with Parliament almost all resulted from attempts to pursue sources of income to their limit and were characterised by an inflexibility of action and thought which failed to recognise the need to win support and the resentment which injured self-interest could cause.

In 1632 Ireland was a financial liability to England. Ordinary income – from recusancy fines, royal lands, wardship and customs – stood at £40,000 a year, and expenditure at £60,000. The shortfall had been made up since 1628 by three subsidies granted by the Irish Parliament as payment for the conversion of the Graces into law. Before leaving England, Wentworth had already negotiated with the Old English leaders for an extension of this subsidy, thus alleviating the immediate crisis. He had also taken the advice of the Mountnorris faction of the Privy Council to base future financial improvements on a reformed customs system involving a new book of rates and increased contributions from the farmers. This option was preferred to Cork's suggestion of capitalising on recusancy fines, since the New English would obviously be exempt from these; Cork had, anyway, already aroused some indignation by prematurely putting his scheme into operation. The grant of further subsidies and the refusal to penalise Catholics encouraged friendship between the Lord Deputy and the Old English, still eager for the confirmation of the Graces. On arriving in Ireland in July 1633, Wentworth showed a rare capacity for tact and political sense. Cork's faction might feel ousted, though even they were aware of how much they might gain or lose by Court favour, but the support of Mountnorris and the Old English nobility was something on which Wentworth could base his government and showed that Old and New English were not necessarily in a state of natural hostility.

Nevertheless, given Wentworth's methods, objectives and personality, conflict was bound to arise. Any recognition of the Graces involved giving up royal claims to many areas of Ireland under Old English control, and Wentworth would not agree to this. Any reform of administrative and financial procedures would alienate the New English administators, yet it was Wentworth's aim to create a new group of professional 'intendants' to do the work of government, taking it out of the hands of the New English leaders, whom he saw as corrupt and self-interested. Any unity between the Old and New English was jeopardised by the recent remodelling of Parliament to reflect an unreal Protestant dominance; and faction disputes within the Privy Council were likely to transfer themselves into the open in the Parliament Wentworth called for July 1634.

The first session was peaceful enough and resulted in the voting of four subsidies and the preparation of a bill on the Graces, but by the second session Wentworth perceived a 'strange and insolent forwardness' when it became clear that he had no intention of accepting the more important of the Graces, especially those confirming tenure of land. In this many of the planters had cause for fear as well, being as susceptible to royal counter-claims as the Old English nobility. Opposition to Wentworth from the Old English continued to grow through the later months of 1634 until the dissolution of the Parliament in April 1635. It was probably encouraged by Cork's faction of councillors and took the form of a refusal to pass several pieces of minor legislation, such as bills on sodomy and houses of correction. Despite this, the permanent Protestant majority and the large number of proxy votes at Wentworth's disposal, owing to absentee MPs and peers, ensured that government policy prevailed as far as the Graces were concerned. The Deputy, moreover, showed some understanding of the Irish situation in attributing the opposition to Papists and the influence of 'Jesuits and friars', thereby encouraging a split on religious lines and obscuring the real issue, which was that of a royal attack on the landed interest. When Parliament was dissolved, Wentworth and the Old English were enemies, and their leader, Clanrickarde, organised a campaign against the Deputy in Ireland and London.

Loss of parliamentary support sent Wentworth in search of other means of extending royal revenue: the increase or resumption of Crown lands, greater financial efficiency, and an expansion of economic life with its consequent boost to the customs all helped to improve Crown finances. The blocks to such a policy were those individuals whose interests would be most affected by financial change, and Wentworth was not one to treat such men with caution. His methods and their results are best illustrated by his attempts to take over Connacht in the west of Ireland as an area for future plantation. A plan for this had been prepared in the early 1620s and specific opposition to it had appeared in the Graces (clauses 24 and 25). None the less, the Deputy went ahead with the scheme and a royal title to all the land in the counties of Mayo, Sligo and Roscommon was quickly found; the only stumbling-block was in the one remaining county, Galway, dominated by the Earl of Clanrickarde. A campaign to establish a royal title to that county in the latter months of 1635 failed, and the Earl and his agents appealed to the English Privy Council. Clanrickarde's death in England provided Wentworth's opponents with further propaganda and they accused him of hastening the Earl's demise, even though he was seventy-two. (It says something for Wentworth's public image that such allegations were credible: some years earlier, rumour had suggested a blow from Wentworth as the cause of his wife's death.) The King backed Wentworth, and Clanrickarde's agents were sent back to Ireland and imprisoned. The jury who had failed to find the royal title to Galway and the sheriff who had selected them were all gaoled and fined £4000 each. Under such pressure, the new Earl conceded defeat and the jury found for the King, providing what Kearney has described as 'a complete but pointless victory'. Wentworth's estimate of £20,000 as the value of the Connacht lands was a gross exaggeration; if he had dropped the claim to Galway he would still have had most of the area, and there were, anyway, few people willing to come and settle in the province. The Puritans who had so willingly taken over Ulster were, in the 1630s, the very people who were contemplating emigration to the New World as a result of disillusionment with royal religious policies; they were unlikely to show enthusiasm for a new royal plantation in Ireland. In the end Galway was barely touched, yet the leading Old English landowners had been totally alienated and the whole of the Irish landed interest felt threatened. A later campaign to take over the area of County Wicklow known as the Birnes Country had a similar effect.

Wentworth tended to identify causes with individuals and often attacked the individual more successfully than the problem he symbolised. In the same way as Clanrickarde became a martyr to the resumption of Crown lands, so Mountnorris was sacrified to the cause of greater efficiency. As Vice-treasurer, he was undoubtedly corrupt and less than competent, yet a series of moves culminating in a court martial and sentence of death for a trivial personal slight to the Lord Deputy seemed excessive. Following the Galway fiasco it merely served to confirm the view that Wentworth's approach was somewhat heavy-handed. The sentence was intended only to frighten Mount-norris and show a change of government policy and personnel, but it did nothing to ingratiate the political nation with Wentworth's regime or improve his reputation in England. Indeed, in 1636 many in Ireland thought Wentworth had overplayed his hand and would be recalled. In fact, although Charles refused to give him an earldom as a formal mark of approval and a bolster to his status, he supported the Deputy in every case which was taken to England. Wentworth therefore resumed his duties.

The purge of personnel was matched by the development of reinvigorated instruments of royal government: the three courts –

High Commission, Wards and Livery, and Castle Chamber – and the Commission for Defective Titles. The last-mentioned was created to provide firm title to disputed land and had three main uses: first, it provided a theoretical answer to the demand in the Graces for security of tenure; secondly, it was a means by which alienated Crown lands could be restored; and, thirdly, if it could confirm titles on the right terms, it could provide further sources of feudal income for the Crown. This was in line with the expansion of the Court of Wards under Parsons to exploit to the full the Crown's feudal income. By a Statute of Uses, those in actual possession of land had to pay all taxes to the Crown, which thus incurred the hostility of many planters as well as the older landowners, who, along with the Gaelic Irish, were suffering burdensome new systems of subsidy assessment. The Court of Castle Chamber was the Irish equivalent of Star Chamber and was the judicial arm of the Privy Council. By excluding Cork and later Mountnorris, Wentworth brought it completely under his own control, providing him with a quick and efficient weapon against opponents. The Castle Chamber also provided the bonus of an income from the large cash fines it imposed. High Commission, which is discussed below, played a similar role in the enforcement of the Lord Deputy's religious policy.

The Irish economy in the early seventeenth century was not a flourishing one; with few natural resources, the perpetual competition with England and a European depression, Irish producers and merchants were not in a strong position. Among exports were wool, fish, butter, linen and hides, and the trade with England predominated. Reference to the merchant community in the Graces suggests that it was of some importance, but its success was stultified by English protectionism, especially in the wool industry, which was rigorously regulated and licensed to prevent undercutting the home market. Any interest Wentworth had in the economy was purely financial, his main objective being to raise Crown income by increased customs or selling licenses. His close supervision of the wool industry shows not a mercantilist concern for industrial growth but the operation of English protectionist policies towards Ireland at a time of economic stagnation. He attempted to establish an Irish linen-manufacturing industry in a scheme by which linen yarn, hitherto exported to Lancashire, would be woven in Ireland. Wentworth himself lost £3000 in the failure of the venture and it reduced the demand for Irish linen yarn overall, as the Lancashire weavers found supplies elsewhere. In dealing with customs duties, Wentworth was more successful. Cranfield in the 1620s had considered the Irish customs a useful source of income, yet a decade later their value was greater to the syndicate which farmed their collection than to the Crown, even after the issue of a new Book of Rates in 1632. The farmers, who included Sir Arthur Ingram and Lord Mountnorris, were making profits of up to £20,000 a year and provided a real financial threat to the power of the Deputy. In 1636 Wentworth worked out a new deal by which five eighths of the profits went to the King, a quarter to Wentworth and one eighth to his close friend Radcliffe, thereby excluding the former profiteers. Improved administration, a clamp-down on smuggling and the consolidation of control over a very complex system increased customs revenue to about £57,000 by 1638.

In this, as in all his financial schemes, Wentworth was simply exploiting an existing system and not creating anything new. In the past justification for such a cautious policy was that any new scheme would benefit those who benefited from the old. It is nevertheless difficult to see how Wentworth could have created more hostility than he actually did from those who had influence in Ireland and support in England. To arouse such hostility could only be justified if the financial results were remarkable, and they were not. None the less, Ireland was no longer a drain on the English Treasury, and the failure of Wentworth's economic schemes was in part at least owing to the lack of natural resources and the lack of capitalist enterprise within the landowning class. There *was* enough money to raise an army in 1640, but not enough to give it any substance.

The complexities and tensions of Irish society were reflected in its religious life. Of the four main social groups, the Old English and Gaelic Irish were still predominantly Roman Catholic. The influx of missionaries and increasingly close contact with continental religious centres that had developed since the Counter-Reformation tended to encourage the two groups to take a rather more aggressive attitude towards their Catholicism. There were Irish seminaries at Douai and Salamanca and close contacts with Lille, Paris and Bordeaux. This revival of Catholicism was further encouraged when, in an attempt to win the support of the Old English aristocracy during the wars of the 1620s, the recusancy laws were only laxly enforced. By 1629 most dioceses had their own Roman Catholic bishop. The planters, on the other hand, were rigorously Protestant. The Ulster Scots shared the

Calvinism of their fellow countrymen, giving to it an intensity seen in other areas when Puritans lived close to Catholic communities. They were also aware that their status as immigrant landowners depended on maintaining the religious difference, and this encouraged the great planter landowners to adopt a similar attitude. Archbishop Ussher was a strong Calvinist sympathiser and the 1615 Articles of the Irish Church reflect his views. As far as the structure of the Church was concerned, several dioceses had only recently been incorporated into the Church of Ireland and the role of bishops was inferior to that of the lay landlords who had taken over control of most of the Church lands and taxation. To all sections of Irish society, a weak Church was desirable: for the Catholics it meant that persecution was unlikely; for the Ulster Scots it enabled the Calvinist congregation to decide its own path to salvation without the unwanted direction of bishops and priests; to the planter landlords, any attempt to strengthen the Church would involve their surrender of lands and of control over the Church.

Nowhere was the introduction of Laudian reform more likely to provoke hostility. Laud's aims were simple enough: to raise the standard of the clergy by providing them with an adequate income; to purge the church of Puritanism; and to raise the status of the Church and churchmen in society. In Wentworth he had an overzealous agent who saw control of the Church as another means of exerting control over the blocks to administrative efficiency – in this case, the New English community. Laudianism was quickly introduced. Laud himself became Chancellor of the previously Puritan Trinity College, Dublin; the Thirty-nine Articles were promulgated; and under Bramhall, Bishop of Derry and Wentworth's chaplain, Laudians were appointed to vacant bishoprics, often in opposition to Ussher. Puritan opposition was summarily crushed by the Court of High Commission, set up in 1634, and recalcitrant ministers were ejected. In a society where Catholicism was the traditional enemy, a purge of Puritans seemed unnecessary, foolhardy and insulting to the majority of Protestants. It was positively dangerous when it was combined with a threat to the owners of Church lands and tithes.

Throughout Ireland, the lands of the Church and the right to collect tithes and appoint vicars to do the work of a priest was almost entirely in lay hands and the chief cause of clerical and episcopal poverty. Laud's hope of a voluntary surrender met with little success and there was not enough capital available to buy out those who held these impropriations. The only area where income was substantially increased was in the diocese of Connor and Down in Ulster, one of the wealthier and most strongly Presbyterian parts of Ireland – and there Presbyterians resented the financial demands of effective tithe collection to support a brand of Protestantism they disliked intensely.

Wentworth decided on a campaign against the lay impropriators, beginning with the Earl of Cork, who controlled the dioceses of Lismore–Waterford and Cloyne–Cork in the very south of Ireland. Cork actually lived in the Bishop's Palace at Lismore, and the bishops of both sees were related to him, giving him almost complete control over the lands and tithes of the dioceses. Confrontation with Cork had begun before Wentworth's arrival in Ireland and there had already been a heated exchange over the siting of the Earl's family tomb in Dublin Cathedral, which Cork took as an insult to his family. Wentworth's campaign against the estates Cork had impropriated from the Church centred on the College of Youghal in south-east Cork and its substantial income. A long and involved case in which Cork tried an appeal to the English Privy Council, legal chicanery and outright bribery ended with a £15,000 fine, a regrant of the estates at a higher rent and a compromise over diocesan control. As with so much of Wentworth's activity in Ireland, the result was neither a victory, a statement of principle nor a matter of great financial profit. On the other hand, it ruined the already deteriorating relations with the foremost New English aristocrat and made his fellow landowners feel threatened. Only the Catholics had any cause for celebration over Wentworth's handling of the Church, and they had already been alienated by his politics.

Never one to miss an opportunity for personal profit, Wentworth had by 1640 acquired some 34,000 acres in Ireland, showing that at least *he* had confidence in the future. Much of this investment was speculative and he lost a good deal of money in high-risk ventures such as tobacco, iron and linen. His most dubious deal was probably that concerning the Irish customs farm after 1635, by which, on the grounds of the increased revenue for the Crown, he got a substantial share of the profits, even though he had to borrow £40,000 from the English Treasury to finance the deal. By 1639 his income from Irish lands was around £13,000 a year, that from his Yorkshire estates £6000, and he was one of the richest men in England, though his large-scale purchases of land and his speculative investments overstretched him into debt in 1640. The house he built at Jigginstown, near Naas in County Kildare, was similar to the ostentatious country houses of the Elizabethan period. Like Burghley, Woollaton or Hardwick, it was a symbol of wealth, authority and superiority.

On the eve of the Scottish war, Wentworth had much to be proud of in his administration of Ireland. He had increased revenue to the extent that he could finance a substantial armed force; he had countered every opponent and had invariably won; he had revitalised the administration, purged it of its parasitical agents and made it the arm of efficient royal government; he had reformed the Church of Ireland and begun to re-establish its wealth. His economic ventures, though far from novel and occasionally disastrous, showed an awareness of the need for economic growth and development.

Yet at every turn he had so alienated influential individuals and social groups that there was no one in Ireland willing to support him when a crisis arose. As soon as events in England demanded his presence there, his opponents closed in round those left in charge. His task might have been easier if Ireland had been an independent entity, but it was not. The link with England provided hope for Wentworth's opponents, limits on his power and the cause of his eventual downfall. Having failed to cultivate support in Ireland, Wentworth was equally unable to build up a party in England, and, although Charles nearly always backed his judgement, Wentworth's opponents found ready listeners at Court, notably in Lord Treasurer Portland and the circle round the Queen. Charles himself was at fault in failing to give his Deputy any magnanimous gesture of support by way of an earldom, and by showing total trust only when it was too late and extrication was in order. The ill-defined relationship between the Irish and English governments encouraged appeals to the English Privy Council, despite Wentworth's desire for absolute control over Irish affairs: Poyning's Law, by which all legislation and the meeting of the Irish Parliament had to be sanctioned in England, could be used by his opponents as well as by the Deputy.

If Wentworth did create, albeit only by accident, something approaching absolutism, then such control over Ireland was destroyed by the failure of Charles's government to exert a similar control over England. Ireland was different from England, and, while Ireland might be susceptible to a simplistic notion of royal control and a challenge to vested interests, England and Scotland were not. Without the Scottish rebellion, Wentworth's career in Ireland might have been successful; after all, when the Irish rebellion did take place

in 1641 it was merely a revival of the Gaelic Irish nationalism of 1601,
resentful at the Ulster plantation. Furthermore, Wentworth's treatment of the Irish seems positively humane compared to the policies of
Cromwell and William III.

IV

The Scottish war was a turning-point in Wentworth's career. It
aroused acute discontent in Ireland, especially among the Ulster
planters, whose links with nearby Scotland were cemented by ties of
religion and family. They recognised similarities between the Covenanters' cause and their own; both were reacting against the attempt
to impose an English centralised government and Church on an
unwilling people. Even an English Puritan landowner in Ireland such
as Sir John Clotworthy went 'to salute the kirk at Edinboro' ', and
Wentworth stationed 3000 troops in Ulster to prevent a settler rising.
The war also caused the collapse of Charles's government in England
by exerting impossibly high financial demands; and in demanding
Wentworth's presence in England it allowed his enemies in Ireland
the chance to undermine his government. At the same time Wentworth became the chief object of attack of opponents of the Personal
Rule in England.

In August 1639 Charles sent for Wentworth in terms which already
suggested a degree of desperation: 'Come when you will. Ye shall be
welcome to your assured friend.'[13] At the outbreak of the rebellion
Wentworth had seen an opportunity to subject Scotland to the same
controls he had exerted over Ireland, and he still thought outright
victory a possibility. His role was simple: as Charles's only remaining
competent minister with a degree of support in the country, he took on
the load of political decision-making and military control, even
though he had scarcely any experience in the field himself. He was
welcomed at Court as the one figure who might resolve the crisis.
However, he was thrown into pursuing a policy which was not his
own, and the major tactical decisions had already been made.
Strong-willed and resourceful as he was, Wentworth was far from
impregnable; never robust in health, he was plagued by dysentry,
pleurisy and attacks of stone and often forced to direct policy from his
sick-bed.

His absence from England and his political insensitivity led him into a number of miscalculations. First, he assumed that English anti-Scottish sentiment was stronger than sympathy with the demands of the Covenanters, when in fact many Englishmen saw the latter as the logical reaction to Charles I's centralisation and overriding of local interests. Secondly, Wentworth overestimated the amount of money available in England and the ease with which an Irish army could be raised to be used against the Scots. Thirdly, he assumed that, following the example of a loyal and generous Irish Parliament which met in March 1640, the English Parliament would follow suit, inspired by the crisis. Fourthly, he believed that everyone would share his view that, if Parliament refused to help the King in an obvious crisis, then the King was entitled to work without the co-operation of Parliament or even against it to preserve the security of his kingdom. Finally, he did not realise the degree of opposition which the Personal Rule had aroused amongst the landed classes by its attack on their religion, wealth, status and lands. To Wentworth the Scottish war was simply a rebellion against authority, and the confidence with which he proposed the summoning of the Short Parliament exemplifies his views. The failure of this parliament and the increasing problems in collecting both Ship Money and Coat and Conduct Money to pay for an English army ought to have encouraged a cautious and conciliatory approach.

Bolstered by the long-coveted earldom and lord lieutenancy bestowed in January 1640, he relentlessly pursued the policy of victory over the Scots, blind to the weaknesses of the English force led by the ailing Northumberland, who failed to agree with his Scottish royalist counterpart, Hamilton, on any question of strategy. Morale was low and money short. Strafford moreover was no general and his presence with the English troops at the front inspired rather more fear than confidence, despite his dramatic gesture of placing a gallows outside each regimental base to restore order and discipline. By backing Strafford at this stage, Charles was forcing himself into a corner; when, after the abortive negotiations at Ripon, he began a desperate search for alternative solutions and advice, he was seen to be deserting his chief adviser and opening the floodgates of opposition to Strafford. Even at this stage, Strafford still had hopes of an Irish army providing the breakthrough, and this was to be a key factor in his trial. Yet, as early as June 1640, Old and New English opposition had combined to undermine the position of Strafford's deputy, Wandesford.

V

The failure to defeat the Scots is not difficult to explain. What is perhaps more puzzling is why Strafford should become the focus for such a violent attack from the opponents of the Personal Rule in the early months of the Long Parliament, given his extended absence from England. The main charge in his impeachment and attainder was that he was planning to use an Irish army against his English opponents as well as against the Scots. The evidence on either side was – and is – inconclusive, but it is clear that his opponents genuinely feared not what he *had* achieved, but what he might do in future in England. Attacks on evil counsellors were not just carefully veiled attacks on the King; they expressed a real fear of individuals with ability and political power. Just as Pym and his party were later to show a total mistrust of Charles I, so in 1640 they felt threatened by Strafford. Pym accorded Strafford perhaps more respect than he deserved, but it is clear that he believed that Strafford could crush the opposition to Charles and the Personal Rule by military force, and make royal government work. He therefore had to be removed. Strafford's actions in Ireland enabled Pym to cast him in a central role in the Popish conspiracy at Court and provided good propaganda material for a political leader intent on marshalling support and achieving immediate objectives; in the last resort, the factual accuracy of the charges against Strafford were irrelevant if his removal would clear the way for Pym's desired reforms, and there was no chance of Charles taking the opposition leaders into his council while Strafford remained a senior adviser. Strafford was something of a scapegoat; but he was, equally, the director of royal policy in 1640, responsible for the failure of the Scottish campaign and a successful agent of the Personal Rule, albeit outside England.

The propaganda value of the remonstrance sent to the Long Parliament by Irish MPs added fuel to the threatening image of Strafford by emphasising his responsibilities for such things as the decay of trade owing to increased impositions; the denial of the Graces; monopolies; the mishandling of the plantation of London-derry (for which London was heavily fined); the use of High Commission, *quo warranto* proceedings; the lack of parliamentary freedom; court fees; the decay of the gentry, the poverty of merchants and the wealth of customs farmers. All of these were issues with which English MPs could sympathise. Sir John Clotworthy, the Irish

planter who was a relation of Pym by marriage and a client of the
leading opposition peer, Warwick, provided one of the personal links
between the Irish and Long Parliaments; so eager was Warwick to
secure his election that he ended up as MP for two constituencies.
Cork and Ranelagh both had sons sitting in the Long Parliament, and
thirteen Irish MPs were sent to represent Irish grievances. Whilst the
hostility of the Irish Parliament in Strafford's absence shows that his
success at controlling its members was limited, his opponents in
England chose to overlook this and instead exploited fears of his
absolutist inclinations at home. Above all they argued that Strafford
lay at the heart of the Catholic conspiracy which Pym believed to be
dominating Charles's government. While the accusations against
Strafford reflected a wide range of fears and interests, the prospect of
invasion by a Roman Catholic army was foremost in Pym's mind and
demanded the removal of its creator. By skilful propaganda, rabble-
rousing oratory and Charles's inept behaviour, Pym was able to carry
the more moderate of his colleagues in pursuing his attack.

From late in 1640 Strafford's impeachment seemed inevitable and
so he was prepared to accept some of the criticism in order to protect
the King. He had no idea that his own life might be at stake; both he
and Charles were convinced that the worst he had to fear was removal
from office and a fine. At this stage Pym also probably hoped for his
removal rather than his execution, wanting to avoid anything which
might rupture the frail links between the Commons and the Lords.
Nevertheless he was equally resolved to rid the country of the
foremost agent of the Catholic plot at Court – and this sentiment
proved the stronger. The atmosphere of London and Westminster in
November 1640 was such that anything other than a show trial was
out of the question.

When he appeared before the Lords on 30 January 1641 after two
and a half months in the Tower, Strafford faced charges of high
treason under twenty-nine general and twenty-eight specific head-
ings: among the detailed accusations were attacks on his land policy
in Ireland, on his use of martial law against Mountnorris, on the
arbitrary powers of the Irish Church and on his exploitation of the
tobacco monopoly; he was accused of calling the Irish 'a conquered
nation', urging the King to declare war and turning the people
against Parliament – all of them pointed criticisms, yet none of them
treasonable. As Strafford himself pointed out, when accused of
profiting from office, 'I never knew the making of a good bargain

turned on a man as treason.'[14] At his trial he conducted himself with style, wit, accuracy, honesty and dignity. As one observer noted, 'He was opinionated of his own innocence and innocence usually makes men bold and daring.'[15] The trial did not get under way until March, and Strafford's opponents quickly became desperate as they realised that he was likely to clear himself of all charges. While there was still the prospect of various opposition peers and MPs being taken into Charles's Council, the condemnation of Strafford without execution would suffice as a symbol for a change of course, but it was still difficult to fix on him a precise accusation of treason. Concern increased as his impressive conduct won support, reflected by Sir John Temple: 'Truly, his lordship carries himself very gallantly, showing much courage and greatness of mind in his affliction, yet with so much modesty, meekness and humility as none can tax him of arrogancy, contempt of his accusation or any the least neglect to his accusers.'[16] The Commons failed to unite on the idea of accumulative treason, by which treason was committed not by a single act but by the combination of a number of non-treasonous acts, a concept described by one MP as 'arbitrary treason'. Finally, they had to rely on the insecure memory of the deaf Sir Harry Vane, who recollected Strafford's statement that he had intended to use the Irish army 'to reduce this kingdom' – article 23 of the impeachment; further delving produced some vague evidence that 'this' referred to England and not to Scotland, as Strafford maintained. Quite simply, MPs knew in their own minds that Strafford was guilty; they wanted his removal, yet could not find the necessary legal means to effect it. Mob violence and religious tension exacerbated the sense of panic when the impeachment eventually collapsed on 10 April 1641 over a procedural problem caused by the 1352 Treason Statute. Under this the evidence of *two* witnesses was needed to secure conviction; no one could be found to substantiate Vane's evidence.

On 16 April the Commons passed the resolution quoted at the beginning of this chapter as the first stage in the process of attainder, by which a simple vote would be taken on Strafford's guilt. Even at this stage there were doubts about Vane's evidence and the nature of Strafford's intentions, but the decision to go ahead was more an emotional and political than a legal one. Many MPs assumed that their extremism would be moderated by the negative vote of the Lords, and so, on 21 April, with only 263 MPs present, the bill was passed by 204 votes to 59. The Lords sat on it for two weeks, but popular pressure and the revelation of the Army Plot at the beginning of May, skilfully exploited by Pym to keep up the level of political intensity, pushed them into passing it on 7 May by 26 votes to 19. A large number of peers chose to be absent. Attainder was an extreme measure, prompted in part by the pressure of the London mob after the Army Plot had been made public. The latter had confirmed the worst fears of Strafford's intentions and showed Charles's capacity for tactless gestures. In a petition presented to the Lords, Londoners expressed 'fear and jealousies of the sudden execution of some dangerous design upon the City and the kingdom and the making way for the escape of the Earl of Strafford, the grand incendiary' and called for 'the speedy execution of justice upon the Earl of Strafford for prevention of the mischiefs that may happen to their lordships and the petitioners, their wives and children who cannot otherwise hope this night to be in safety',[17] reflecting the sentiment, if not the actual words, of the parliamentary leaders. This was not an atmosphere to encourage calm, reasoned debate. The summary execution of the Earl highlighted Charles's political impotence and the ineffectiveness of his moves to save his minister. Strafford's fall was total; his family got little of his wealth and it retreated into provincial obscurity, while the King failed to get the political bargain he had hoped for from his opponents. The execution solved nothing.

VI

In immediate terms, the sacrifice of Strafford seemed pointless and served only to lessen Charles's reputation in the hands of opposition propagandists, who could now add callousness and cowardice to their list of accusations. His failure to save his minister merely emboldened his opponents; the death of the Earl of Bedford removed the one figure who might have bridged the political chasm. It is tempting to see Strafford as a martyr to some great royalist cause, yet he was in many ways a narrow-minded, pretentious, ambitious civil servant, caught up in issues and emotions beyond his comprehension or control, without the sense of humility to realise the limits to his own competence – all failings which precipitated his final confrontations. This may seem a harsh judgement, and the comments on his success in Ireland should not be forgotten. None the less, Strafford's accusers were wrong in suggesting that he had introduced absolutism into

Ireland in an effective way; if there was a degree of absolutism there, then even at its best it was superficial and cosmetic, and collapsed shortly after Strafford's departure. The alienation of a large section of the political nation in England, Ireland and Scotland could be justified only by the success of political objectives, and Strafford patently failed to achieve such success.

His whole career must throw into doubt whether any overall solution was available to those tackling the problems of administrative and financial efficiency, and his death was in part an assertion by the landed and merchant classes, as represented in Parliament, of their reaction to the government's policy of change in the traditional forms of religion, finance, social standing and administrative practice. Yet, if seventeenth-century England had developed differently, historians might well have seen Strafford as an English Richelieu, the precursor of absolutist greatness. It is part of Strafford's tragedy that he failed to perceive both in English and Irish society those factors which determined a different political outcome from that of French history.

5. John Pym

JONATHAN WATTS

WHEN, in January 1642, Charles I attempted to arrest five members of the House of Commons, he was acting according to the conspiracy theory of political opposition: a fundamentally loyal Parliament had been seduced into confrontation with the King by a number of forceful, ambitious and dangerous individuals; remove these individuals and opposition would evaporate. Charles may have been criticised since for failing to see the broad basis of opposition in Parliament, yet his opponents saw the problems of the Personal Rule in the same light – the work of misguided individuals corrupting potentially sound institutions – and they had already attacked, and in one case destroyed, its agents. How important, though, were the parliamentary leaders to the apparent success of the Long Parliament in its first two years? How far was Charles's view of conspiracy a valid one?

John Pym must occupy a central place in any discussion of the Long Parliament and Civil War up to his death in December 1643. His presence is felt in every debate, committee and piece of legislation, yet his precise role is difficult to define. Was he, for example, the leader and political innovator Charles obviously considered him to be, or was he merely the man of the moment, an eloquent and organised spokesman for the majority of the political nation who opposed the Personal Rule? Far from being the revolutionary he is sometimes painted, was he in fact a restraining influence when radical demands jeopardised Commons unity or accommodation with the King? What precisely was he aiming at and what were his motives? Could any Stuart politician be as unconcerned about personal profit as Pym seems to have been? It is hoped here to answer some of these questions, despite the scanty historical evidence for some crucial stages of his life.

Pym's career falls into four sections. The 1620s illustrate his political origins and the development of his ideas, his knowledge of government and his parliamentary expertise; the connection with other politicians who formed the core of the opposition in the Long Parliament also dates from this period. During the Personal Rule, lack of evidence obscures much of Pym's career. It is possible, however, to see how the up-and-coming politician of the 1620s was affected by the changed political circumstances of the 1630s and how the opposition group, which seemed so prepared for the breakdown of government in 1639, organised itself and built contacts with the political, commercial and Puritan interests of London. Next, there is the period of Pym the parliamentary leader in the build-up to Civil War, where his aims, methods and achievements need examination and explanation. Finally, there is Pym the war-leader, under pressure to provide money, men, munitions and morale for a Parliament at war with the King.

It would be presumptuous to suggest that this chapter is any more than a brief survey of the published material on Pym. Until Conrad Russell completes his biography of Pym, there can be no adequate account, and various aspects of Pym's life remain obscure to a writer working from secondary sources. Nevertheless, such is Pym's importance to the politics of mid-seventeenth-century England that some assessment of his career needs to be made on the basis of existing knowledge, however inadequate in some places it may be.

I

The Pym of 1621 or 1624 looked an unlikely candidate for political greatness. As an MP he was without friends in the Commons, had little to contribute to committees or debates, and possessed a background, opinions and style which set him apart from the English landed classes.

John Pym was born in 1584 near Bridgwater in Somerset, and matriculated from Broadgates Hall in Oxford in 1599. In 1602 he was a student at the Middle Temple, the conventional finishing-school for the late-Elizabethan gentleman, though he never practised at the bar. His mother's second marriage was into the Rous family of Cornwall, whose influential connections and strong Puritanism were to remain important to his death, epitomised in Francis Rous, his contemporary at Oxford and consistent political colleague. In a period when MPs were nearly all men of local standing, Pym was an exception; attempts to establish himself as a country gentleman in Somerset and his wife's county of Hampshire both failed, and he was a political figure with no county community to support him. His one claim to status was his appointment in 1607 as Receiver of Crown Lands for Wiltshire, Hampshire and Gloucestershire (the royal official to whom rents were paid *en route* to the Exchequer); yet, unlike Cranfield, for instance, who used such a post to provide speculative, short-term capital, Pym was totally disinterested, concerned only to protect the King's revenue from those who were using it to their own advantage, and this in a period when profit was the main incentive for holding office.

Elected MP for Calne in 1621, probably on the strength of his receivership, he achieved some minor fame in the 1624 parliament when his election for Chippenham was challenged and eventually overthrown in a dispute over the franchise. Perhaps realising the security provided by a patron's support, from 1625 onwards Pym represented Tavistock, in the gift of Francis Russell, from 1627 the Earl of Bedford, a property speculator and landowner whose patronage Pym probably acquired through the Rous West Country connection and who provided the first link with the political grouping which was to dominate his career.

Under James I, Pym was a reluctant speaker in the Commons; yet his few contributions in 1621 show an interest in two aspects of government – religion, especially the Catholic threat, and royal finance – together with an intensity of manner and expression and a desire for detailed and accurate information on which to base his arguments. From 1626 onwards he took the stage more often and played an important role in crucial debates, such as the attack on the Arminian preacher Mainwaring, the attempted impeachment of Buckingham, the campaign which led up to the Petition of Right and the condemnation of the growth of Arminianism in 1628 and 1629. What happened to turn him into a political activist?

In the early 1620s the overall impression of Pym is of humourless and unambitious dullness, with few interests outside his parliamentary and official responsibilities, and few close associates on any level. Yet one issue could rouse him and that was the defence of the English Church in the face of the threat from Catholicism. His heated if uninspired words in the 1621 Parliament on the need to enforce the anti-recusancy laws and the attacks on specific Papists in 1624 failed to move his fellow MPs, who in the years before Arminianism became powerful saw the spirit of an outdated Elizabethan Puritanism in Pym's manner; with Buckingham, an intimate of the radical Protestant divine John Preston, promoting a pan-European, Protestant war, the English Church seemed secure enough in its traditional forms and beliefs, and the Catholic threat from Europe was being countered. Even Pym was only encouraging the enforcement of existing laws and had faith in James I as the protector of Protestantism. However, the accession of Charles I produced in Pym a marked change of tone. In the past, to attack Catholicism was merely to encourage and expand existing policy; now he was faced with the prospect of Arminianism, a fundamental threat to his own brand of English Protestantism, both in its attack on predestination and in its implied toleration, if not support, for Catholicism. Whatever the Arminians may have intended, their opponents clearly saw them as moving England towards Rome. Nicholas Tyacke has suggested that the Calvinist theology of the English Church was established orthodoxy by the 1620s, and families such as the Rouses and the Russells strongly believed in divine election. After about 1625, the Habsburg successes in the Thirty Years War made quite credible the prospect of an aggressive Roman Catholic revival backed up by all the agents of the Counter-reformation so chillingly described in Foxe's best-selling *Acts and Monuments*.

Some doubt has been expressed as to the rigidity of division between English Arminianism and the conventional religion it was allegedly threatening. It is perhaps better to think of a number of co-existent strands to English Protestant thinking in the 1620s, including among them the belief that Catholicism was the doctrine of Antichrist, but also including as an alternative a respect for and a readiness to argue with the Catholic Church and dogma as reformed by the Counter-reformation. Pym and his associates clearly fit in with the first strand and, if religious opinion was broader and Arminianism less divisive than Tyacke suggests, it only serves to heighten Pym's intellectual isolation and his somewhat old-fashioned view of religious polarities. Whichever interpretation of religious feeling is accepted, Pym's own position is utterly clear: any hint of Catholicism was to be treated with the deepest suspicion.

Always on the lookout for potential threats, Pym was one of the first to attack Montague in 1624, and in 1628–9 he considered the

destruction of the English Church an issue of greater importance than
the payment of Tonnage and Poundage, over which the session was
eventually curtailed. He believed that the King was being subjected
to bad advice, and his attacks concentrated on those putting forward
Arminian views – Montague, Mainwaring, Buckingham and the like.
It is important to remember that, when Pym or his contemporaries
attacked ministers or officers for misleading the King, they genuinely
believed that this was the case, and that it was not a device for
indirectly attacking the King. As early as 1621, Pym had been
summarily imprisoned, almost certainly because of his criticism of
two of Buckingham's monopolist clients, Lepton and Goldsmith;
when, later, Buckingham himself became the target, it was because
MPs believed he *was* the cause of failure at home and abroad. Pym
delighted in giving the evils he condemned a human face.

If religion was Pym's first passion, it was matched by concern for
the King's revenue. His attitude was clear: if the King was to govern
effectively and protect the people and their religion, then he must
have resources adequate to the task. In view of the amount written on
parliament's desire to control the royal purse strings in the early
Stuart period, it is surprising to find Pym repeatedly arguing for
larger subsidies than most MPs wanted, and observing that there was
no point in demanding full-scale involvement in Europe unless the
necessary cash was forthcoming. Perhaps his isolation from the
county community made Pym unaware of the effects of taxation on
those who had to pay, but he had the sense to realise that only by
providing income as required by the King would Parliament ensure
future sessions; the more troublesome and less productive Parliament
became for the King, the more likely he was to do without it
altogether. When Pym arrived at Westminster, Cranfield's programme of financial reform was well under way and was, indeed,
beginning to lose some of its original impetus. Pym's views were
similar to those of the reformers, that the King was being defrauded of
his rightful income by incompetence and dishonesty, and that the
country was the chief victim of this. His experience as Receiver gave
him a detailed knowledge of the workings of Crown finance, and his
speeches show an acute understanding of the complexities of royal
accounting. It is no accident that much of the reform he advocated in
1640 was concerned with settling royal finances and that, when there
was the possibility of his gaining office under the Crown, he was

rumoured to be getting the post of Chancellor of the Exchequer. The
financial organisation he bequeathed to the parliamentary side in the
Civil War was one of its greatest assets.

It was his attitude to religion and finance which determined Pym's
views of government and the roles of Crown and Parliament within it.
Far from deliberately provoking confrontation, he sought to use
Parliament only as a means of assuring effective royal government by
providing adequate resources and appropriate legislation. His advocacy of impeachment was not an attempt to exert parliamentary
control over royal ministers, but a means of bringing to account those
who were defrauding the King and making royal government less
effective than it should have been. Under Charles I he found himself
in something of a dilemma, like many MPs who believed in monarchy
but resented some of the monarch's actions. By 1628 he was attracted
to the cause of the 'ancient constitution' and the rights and liberties of
the people – slogans cultivated by those who saw in Charles a threat to
law and property, and who developed the concept of some past, and
largely mythological, political utopia. Pym, though, saw his position
merely as that of a corrective to an innovating royal government;
religion – or, to be more precise, English protestantism – was one and
the same with the rights of the individual, and the Crown was obliged
to uphold them both by maintaining the law.

Just as Charles was being misled into religious change by evil
counsel, so his methods of government were being perverted. Even in
the crisis of 1628–9, Pym was reluctant to antagonise Charles
completely and saw that more could be achieved by keeping open the
door to co-operation. When Selden and Eliot pressed forward with
demands over Tonnage and Poundage, Pym and other MPs were
unwilling to risk the probable results of such confrontation with the
King. One very clear point which emerges from this debate is that
Pym believed in co-operation and compromise, not conflict, as the
first means of gaining political change. When other MPs rushed into
extreme measures, Pym kept his head and looked to the traditional
forms and techniques of government.

If in the early 1620s Pym had been an isolated figure at
Westminster, by 1629 he had acquired some firm political allies. An
analysis of Pym's relationship with his patron, the Earl of Bedford,
shows that a similarity of stance may be the cause as much as the
result of links of patronage: they shared a deep belief in the imminent
destruction of English Protestantism by the forces of Arminianism,

and both showed a solemn and meticulous attitude to life. The rewards a client such as Pym could hope to receive from a patron outside the Court and opposed to Buckingham were very limited. The personal link provided contact between two like-minded figures in the two houses of Parliament. Yet in the 1620s Pym seems to have been closer to the political circle of the Earl of Warwick, and in particular to Warwick's client, Nathaniel Rich, who might well have become the leader of the Long Parliament had he not died in 1637. It is an overstatement to suggest that the initiative and political leadership came from the Lords rather than the Commons, but the opposition movement of the 1630s was focused around a number of leading peers, and these same lords provided a continuity of leadership and experience largely absent from the Commons until the Long Parliament was well under way.

By 1629 Pym had overcome some of the disadvantages which faced him on first becoming an MP. His lack of county standing had been remedied by links of patronage and political and religious ideology; his unimpressive manner concealed a passionate devotion to his religion and a deep understanding of royal finance. Far from acting the revolutionary, he was prepared to conciliate, and believed in traditional forms of government and a traditional role for Parliament. He had no wish for fundamental constitutional change. If he opposed some of Charles's measures, then it was because Charles was changing accepted forms. In this he reflected the views of many MPs and provides further evidence to suggest that relations between King and Parliament before 1629 were not the start of the breakdown which led to the Civil War. Indeed, Pym was considerably more loyal to Charles in the 1620s than many other MPs, again indicating that the strength of opposition in 1640 did not derive from constitutional changes earlier in the century but was the result of the utter alienation of the political classes by the Personal Rule and by the figure of the King himself.

II

If the Personal Rule *was* responsible for the strength of opposition to Charles in 1640, then events in the 1630s must play a central part in forming the views of leading opponents such as Pym. Even though the evidence for this period is very limited, it suggests that he remained as detached from the bulk of the political nation (the landed gentry and aristocracy) as he had been in the 1620s, and that religion rather than political change remained his primary concern.

For some time historians have been interested in three London colonising enterprises of the 1630s – the Providence Island, Massachusetts Bay and Saybrooke companies – and have attempted to see them as part of an underground opposition movement during the Personal Rule. The evidence for this is largely based on the personnel of the companies and their known links with Puritan activists in the City. Pym himself was treasurer of the Providence Island Company, and two of the Feoffees for Impropriations, responsible for appointing Puritan preachers to London parishes, were members of the board. Pym was also involved in the Saybrooke Company, along with Lord Saye, Lord Brooke, Warwick and Nathaniel Rich – all aiming at the establishment of a colony in Connecticut. The Massachusetts Bay Company, much wider in its financial backing, included at least seven of the Feoffees; and the names of Hampden, St John, Knightley, Barrington and Mandeville, all of them political activists, appear in connection with these companies. Yet to see these organisations as a deliberately constituted opposition movement would be to over-dramatise matters and misunderstand the motives for involvement. Most of the political connections had been established by 1629, notably that between Pym and the Warwick circle, and meetings to plan political strategy had taken place before and during the parliamentary sessions of 1628–9. Interest in setting up New World colonies also existed before 1629, and there were two, linked motives for it. A colony provided the opportunity to set up an exemplary Protestant state: in the case of Saybrooke it was to be a blueprint for reformed English society and institutions when the corruptions inflicted by Caroline government had been removed. Providence Island was more simply a refuge for 'vexed and troubled Englishmen' from the attempts to undermine the English Church. A further motive was that a base in the West Indies or North America provided an opportunity for attacking Spain in the Caribbean and so weakening what was believed to be the sustaining power of European Catholicism. In the late 1620s debates on the war had often made reference to a colonial campaign against Spain in the West Indies, though the sceptic is entitled to question whether opponents of Arminianism with an interest in the West Indies used this as an excuse for defending their investment.

One of the reasons why there is more evidence about colonising-ventures in the 1630s may well be that such ventures proliferated. This was a sign not of effective opposition to the government, but of despair. Pym's justification of moderation in 1629 had been that, if confrontation with the King forced him into ruling without Parliament, then all hope of stemming governmental change was lost. The Personal Rule gave added impetus to the desire for emigration: the rule of Antichrist was imminent and the belief that emigration was the only answer for the dedicated opponent suggests that Charles was being successful, though it remains unclear how realistic Pym's own apparent plans for settlement in the New World actually were. At Pym's funeral Oliver St John was to comment that in the 1630s, 'fearing that popery might overgrow this kingdom', he wished to make 'some plantation in foreign parts where the profession of the gospel might have its free course'.[1] Money was the main factor preventing these enterprises from getting off the ground, and a number of those involved were heavily in debt by 1640: an MP's exemption from arrest for debt was one, albeit minor, reason for prolonging the Long Parliament. One contemporary asked, 'could Saye or Pym and their beggarly confederates have found money to levy an army against their liege lord, that had not money to pay their own debts, had not London furnished them'?[2]

The links between the various members of these companies certainly did exist, but on a much more informal and possibly wider basis than that of business associates. The first link was a geographical one: they all lived in London for at least part of the year, and the area around Gray's Inn Lane was something of a centre; there Pym had his lodgings and Providence Island had its headquarters; Warwick House and Brook House were nearby; the anti-Arminian preacher and friend of Pym, Richard Sibbes, performed at Gray's Inn and had connections with the Feoffees. Outside London, Barrington Hall, the home of Sir Thomas Barrington, Preston Capes, the seat of Richard Knightley whose family had a long tradition of religious radicalism, and Lord Saye's Broughton Castle saw meetings of the future opposition leaders, showing the very obvious second link between them: opposition to the Personal Rule and in particular its religious policies. Pym was a close friend of John Goodwin, the minister of the Puritan church of St Stephen's, Coleman Street – along with St Antholin's, the centre of preaching in the City. He also cultivated the support of leading City Puritan politicians, among them Isaac Pennington, who as MP during the Long Parliament helped create the strong links between London and the opposition. The precise relationship between Pym's circle, the Feoffees for Impropriations and leading merchants is unclear, and some of the tensions which arose between the City and Westminster in the early part of the Civil War suggest that co-operation and identity of interest may not have been total, and that the spirit of moderation already shown by Pym was less to the taste of extremer elements in the City. Even in an environment where Pym's views were common, he remained isolated, sharing with City merchants their interest in Puritanism but not their concern for commerce.

A third link between members of the group was family and patronage. A number of those involved in the Providence Island and Saybrooke companies were related by marriage, and Warwick's patronage was of prime importance. However, the figure of Bedford, so crucial in 1640, was largely absent from the commercial concerns. It is possible that the role he played as a bridge between the Court and the Long Parliament implies that he was more acceptable as a spokesman than his aristocratic colleagues who made a more open show of opposition during the 1630s.

In discussing the progress of Pym's career, the 1630s is the most difficult period of all, so scanty is the evidence, and it is here especially that scholarly elucidation is required. When Parliament met in 1640, Pym was part of a highly organised group of political leaders in the Commons and the Lords, clearly used to working together and sharing common beliefs and objectives. While evidence exists from the 1630s indicating close links of business, patronage and family between many of them, Pym never seems to be at the centre of things and his activity seems shadowy at the very least. The precise nature of his relationship with his aristocratic and merchant friends remains unclear, as does the development of the political and organisational skill he showed once Parliament was under way. Why *he* rather than some other figure – for example, Hampden or St John – should emerge as the leader in 1640 is puzzling in the absence of adequate evidence.

As far as Pym is concerned, the 1630s emphasise the characteristics already noted. Religion remained his main concern. If he objected to the absence of parliaments, it was because they would afford an opportunity to correct Charles's misguided policies rather than because of any abstract political theory. His proposed emigration showed the depths of his religious despair at Charles's apparent success in paving the way back to Rome. As the decade progressed, Pym realised the strength an organised opposition group could have. He cultivated the friendship of leading City politicians, merchants and financiers, and strengthened the relationships established in the 1620s with those who were to become, with him, the leaders of the Long Parliament. By establishing a power base in London and linking the various interests there alienated by the Personal Rule, Pym ensured the support of the City after 1640 and provided the ready-made organisation the opposition needed when Parliament was eventually called.

Pym's personal political activity in the 1630s seems limited. He was probably involved in the campaign against Ship Money, but Hampden's failure to illegalise the tax and Charles's success in collecting it were considerable setbacks, and Ship Money failed to become the *cause célèbre* some writers have held it to be. The Scottish rebellion, however, provided the prospect of governmental collapse. While it is unlikely that the rebellion itself had anything to do with the English opponents of the Personal Rule, once it had begun English opposition leaders were in touch with their Scottish counterparts. Their motives were two-fold: first, any trouble from Scotland would put impossible financial demands on Charles and would make more likely the calling of a parliament; secondly, the aspects of the Personal Rule against which the Scots were rebelling were very close to those which the English hated – interference by a centralising government in traditional spheres of influence, unnecessary administrative change, the challenge to accepted authority in the localities and, above all, a threat to traditional forms of religion. Pym may not have been in contact with the Scots, but he approved of their action.

III

When, on Wentworth's recommendation, Parliament met in April 1640, Pym was the foremost speaker in the Commons. He opposed demands for supply to meet the Scottish rebellion and voiced religious and political grievances in long speeches, advocating co-operation with the Lords in discovering and rooting out evil within the government. The session was quickly dissolved, but events soon overtook the King and the defeat of the English force at Newburn in

August made the calling of another parliament inevitable. In the meantime Pym was meeting with his political allies to plan future strategy, and the Petition of Twelve Peers stated their position clearly; of the signatories, at least seven already had links with Pym's circle and were to play a full part in the campaign of opposition to Charles. Pym's study was searched to find evidence of complicity with the Scots.

There seemed to be no doubt that Pym would be leader of the Commons when it reassembled in November 1640, and he had prepared himself for the role. As the one figure with concrete proposals and an immediate plan for action, he could focus the nebulous grievances of the ordinary backbencher. This, along with his impressive political connections with known and influential opponents of the Personal Rule and his detailed knowledge of the political scene, recommended him as a leader to MPs who knew they wanted action but were uncertain as to what form it should take. From then until his death, Pym was the leader of the Commons and a vital factor in determining the direction and intensity of opposition, the move towards war, and the eventual success of the parliamentary forces in the First Civil War. To understand his role, certain questions have to be answered. What were Pym's motives? What were his policies? How did he intend achieving them? What challenges were there to his position, ideas and methods? What effect did the outbreak of war have on his leadership?

Pym was obsessed with one totally dominating idea: that there was a Catholic conspiracy to destroy the Protestant Church in England. All his actions after 1640 can be attributed in the end to this overriding emotion, and the fact that the basis of his activity was essentially irrational and emotional explains much of its intensity. His marked reaction to Arminianism in the 1620s had already shown his fears for the safety of the English Church, and, once convinced of the existence of the Papist conspiracy, he found his suspicions confirmed everywhere he looked. The strong hold of the Arminian bishops over the Church, the new links with Rome, a pro-Spanish foreign policy, the increased importance of churchmen within the state and, above all the Catholic clique around Henrietta Maria, all pointed to the truth of Pym's belief; and fresh evidence presented itself to him month after month. While Charles himself was not directly implicated by Pym, he was accused of taking the advice of Papists, the 'malignant party', and the removal of such counsellors was a primary aim. Pym's precise charge was that, by allowing the growth of Popery, Charles was dividing the nation; remove the grievance, restore unity, and strength and prosperity would ensue, while England could also take her rightful place in the defence of European Protestantism. In the 1620s the divisive nature of Charles's religious policy was seen by Pym, who criticised those who sought to promote divisions by the use of the factious term 'Puritan' with its overtones of disreputable sedition. Useful though the term 'Puritan' is to historians, Pym clearly found it insulting and a symptom of a deliberate policy to denigrate those who opposed Arminian innovations and defended the traditional forms of the English Church. The evil counsellors were, in Pym's words, 'destructive to religion and laws by altering them both', and the connection between law, religion and politics was deeply imbedded in Pym's mind. As to their policies, 'these ill counsels', Pym argued, 'proceeded from an inclination to popery and have a dependence in popery and all of them tend to it. The religion of the papists is a religion incompatible with any other religion, destructive to all others and doth not endure anything that oppresses it.' Moreover, the culmination of the plot was imminent – the two Army plots and the Irish rebellion were only the most dramatic manifestations of a conspiracy involving a Catholic underground in the provinces, various peers, prominent courtiers, the Queen and her entourage, and various foreign powers. The speed, zeal and intensity of parliamentary activity in the months before the Civil War can only be understood if the presumed immediacy of the Catholic threat is realised. There was, of course, no Catholic plot, but this is irrelevant when considering the strength of Pym's views and their acceptance by a wide range of the population. Just as in the twentieth century the irrational fear of Communism can inflame tensions and encourge the suspension of political disbelief, so in the seventeenth century the fear of Catholicism was a potent force.

At the start of the Long Parliament, Pym believed that Charles could be persuaded to change his policies, and he provided the King with a clear programme of reform. First came the removal of the evil counsellors, the instrument of the Catholic threat, and their replacement by advisers in whom Pym and other MPs could have confidence. When the Nineteen Propositions were passed in June 1642, this demand had become a bid for parliamentary control over ministerial appointments; but, at least until the death of Bedford in May 1641, there was the real possibility that Pym and Charles's more moderate critics might be taken on as royal counsellors. Bedford's plan involved his own appointment as Lord Treasurer with Pym as Chancellor of the Exchequer. Their prime function was to settle the King's finances. Parliament would pay off his debts, revise the subsidy assessments and take steps to reform the financial administration – a scheme that has the hallmark of Pym the accountant. In return the meeting of parliaments would be guaranteed, lands of delinquents would be confiscated, along with those of the deans and chapters of cathedrals, and wardship would also be abolished. Bedford's death, along with the insistence of the Commons on the execution of Strafford, and the King's and many MPs' mistrust of such a compromise and reluctance to agree to it, prevented the plan coming into effect. Secondly, all practical steps were to be taken to remove the Papist threat by disarming Catholics, incapacitating them for office, purging the Church of Arminians and initiating witch-hunts against provincial Catholics. Thirdly, as though to recommend this course of action to the King, Pym insisted on the reorganisation of royal finance and its placing on a sounder footing than hitherto, a clear sign that he was no enemy to monarchy as such and that he linked Catholic counsel with financial mismanagement and the consequent inability of Charles to play some part in promoting the Protestant cause outside England. While Pym supported moves to destroy the machinery of the Personal Rule and to introduce Puritan reforms of the Church by legislation, neither policy was among his priorities.

Quite how Pym chose to implement his programme is not as obvious as might at first appear, given the relative strengths of King and Parliament. Unlike most backbenchers, Pym was not interested in legislation, and many of the bills which were passed acted as a sop to MPs who wanted positive signs of achievement and saw parliaments as a means of creating new laws. He had consistently favoured the granting of supply before redress of grievances, seeing the illogicality of demanding good government from an impoverished King; yet most MPs refused to adopt a realistic attitude to government finance, if only for fear of reaction among their taxpaying constituents, who demanded value for money. Pym's notion of Parliament was in many ways like that of James I: he saw it as a point of contact between government and governed and, in Pym's case, between political leader and provincial rank and file. If Pym could prove to Charles that he had the backing of the political nation as represented in Parliament, then the King would be obliged to accept change, for the sake of practical survival if not as a matter of honour. Parliament was also a means by which Pym could exploit local feeling to increase national tension and put further pressure on the King. Legislation only had a minor part to play in such a policy and was just a symptom of change. Two crucial signs would be Charles's willingness to act over ministers and the Church.

In practical terms it was not difficult to convince the King of the need for change, so great was the animosity toward the Personal Rule. Yet no settlement was forthcoming, owing to disunity within the ranks of Parliament as well as the intransigence and untrustworthiness of the King. Most of Pym's political skill was devoted not to dealing with his opponents, but to marshalling his supporters in Parliament. A study of his activities between November 1640 and January 1642 provides a model for political management. Pym was intent on maintaining an intensity of feeling in Parliament to see his programme through, and every revelation of Papist misdemeanour was exploited, with no distinction between truth and rumour. Urgency and crisis justified the curtailment of debates. Much of the work of Parliament was siphoned off to specialist committees under the direct control of Pym and his immediate colleagues. Membership of such bodies was confined to those nominated by the political leadership, which enabled Pym to circumvent possible hostility. He could bully the house into agreement, stun it by dramatic revelations and continually impress it by the speed, efficiency and breadth of his own work.

Pym was prepared to give in on minor issues at dispute and allow MPs their head, provided the results did not conflict with his own aims. He had to cope with the ignorance and half-digested ideas of provincial backbenchers and their permanent refusal to vote money even for causes sanctioned by Parliament itself. Popular disturbances were increasingly seen as the result of Parliament's attack on royal government, and the fear of a breakdown in law and order tempted waverers away from the leadership. Pym was equally frustrated by practical problems such as the plague, a long, hot summer, annoyance at the length of a parliamentary session which kept landed gentlemen away from their estates, and the consequent absenteeism which often threatened to make the House inquorate, a tendency which was exacerbated as the strength of the royalists grew at the end of 1641. Nonetheless, at each point when control of the Commons seemed to be slipping, news of some fresh Catholic intrigue served to rekindle the sense of crisis in which Pym flourished. The Lords proved even more difficult to manage, despite the presence of skilled supporters, and the King's efforts to build up a royalist party there came close to success. Disputes between the two houses were common, but Pym's tact, management, propaganda and oratory nearly always prevented the deadlock from becoming too destructive. All of these features of Pym's parliamentary activity can be seen in the period leading up to the outbreak of war, and the following cursory glance at events is meant only to illustrate some specific aspects of Pym's role.

The attack on Strafford and other agents of the Personal Rule was a logical consequence of the conspiracy myth, and Pym repeatedly returned to the persecution of delinquents. The removal of Strafford, evil genius of the conspiracy, would provide room for new ministers from the ranks of the parliamentary opposition, who in return would settle royal finances. Eager to prevent a split with the more moderate House of Lords, Pym fought against the demands for Strafford's execution, but was more strongly swayed by an unwillingness to alienate popular feeling and threw in his lot with those wanting blood; while he may have made attempts to hold the middle ground, up to 1642 at least, he always sided with extremists in the end. Popular sentiment, especially in London, was a force he could use, despite its potential for antagonising those who saw Pym's policies as an encouragement to anarchy. Further, Pym realised that in Parliament the Commons and not the Lords held the key to success, although the role of the Lords should not be underestimated. As Strafford's trial drew to its close, Pym issued the Protestation, the first of many propaganda documents, whose oath provided a quick guide to where support lay; Pym was keen to divide the country into those who were for and those who were against his policies. The revelation of the Army Plot helped push Pym to a more extreme position and helped him carry support with him in, for example, the hounding of Strafford. The essence of the supposed plot was that the King would lead his army in the North to London, attack his opponents in Parliament and liberate Strafford from the Tower; in the meantime a force from France would invade. In this mixture of fact, rumour and imagination Pym saw the first true evidence of the Catholic conspiracy in action:

I am persuaded that there was some great design in hand by the

papists to subvert and overthrow this kingdom . . . and though the
king be of tender conscience, yet we ought to be careful that he have
good counsellors about him and to let him understand that he is
bound to maintain the laws and that we take care for the
maintaining of the word of God.[3]

This was Pym's political creed in a nutshell. His taste for the dramatic
was shown in the way he examined all the details of the plot before
revealing it in all its horror to the Commons in June, to revive the
tension temporarily relieved by Strafford's death. Work on the plot
was undertaken by a specialist committee and, as in many matters,
the Commons got to hear the substance only after it had been worked
over by the leadership.

Meanwhile, the problem of money became serious. In the North
there were two impatient armies, both demanding payment. Sympathetic as Pym was to the aims of the Scots, English anti-Scottish
feeling was growing and the situation in the North was volatile.
Parliament could not be convinced of the need for reasonable
measures to raise money, and even some of Pym's closest colleagues
backed this view. Settlement with the King had been Pym's aim
during these few months, and he had failed to produce his side of the
bargain. Strafford had been executed, no financial scheme was
forthcoming – though Parliament did eventually pay off the armies –
and the extremists went unchecked. The death of Bedford in May
removed one figure acceptable to both Court and Parliament, while
the King, always remote from the political nation, developed an
increasing mistrust of the Commons leadership. The scheme for
bridge appointments therefore came to nothing.

With the prospect of Charles's visit to Scotland planned for August
1641, the political and religious pressures of that summer were
considerable. Trust of the King was evaporating, and rumours of a
second Army Plot, to be consolidated in Scotland, made a settlement
even more urgent, though even Pym could be optimistic enough to
suggest that Parliament could 'lay a foundation for such a greatness of
the kingdom as never any of his majesty's ancestors enjoyed'.[4] Is this
the talk of a revolutionary? The Ten Propositions made up a set of
emergency proposals issued in June 1641, and they show Pym's chief
concerns. After a clause on the disbanding of the armies, the
document is almost entirely concerned with the attack on Catholicism
and Parliament's role in it. Even the clause on 'the security and peace

of the kingdom' demanding preparations for defence resulted from the belief that a Catholic invasion was imminent, a view which explains the concern for increased parliamentary control over the militia and the ports. Infiltration of the officer class was one of the frequent points made about the Catholic conspiracy. The overall implication of the Ten Propositions, though, was that Pym was demanding recognition of an important role for Parliament in the executive work of government.

At the same time, the Root and Branch Petition for the abolition of episcopacy was given parliamentary time, to satisfy its London supporters and give vent to the anti-Arminianism of many provincial MPs. While Pym was probably inclined to a more moderate scheme of reform, he could not afford to reject so useful a source of propaganda to back up his campaign. Ever since the days of Elizabethan Puritanism, bishops had been accused of obstructing the true reform of the Church and 'in their wealth, pride and tyranny' were now held responsible for the evils of Church and state, an accusation which the career of Laud helped justify and which connections with the Army Plot helped elaborate. The Petition was therefore simply an expression of anti-Arminianism; yet, because Charles chose to make a stand on the issue of bishops, it was bound to become a central issue, irrespective of any inherent importance the subject may have had. The proposals as revised by Parliament provided a moderate scheme of reform, accommodating MPs' concern to exert greater lay control over the Church. Opposition was there but, as Lord Falkland observed, 'They who hated the bishops hated them worse than the devil, and they who loved them did not love them so well as their dinner.'[5] One of Pym's favourite procedural tricks was to leave voting until late in the day, when only zealots remained in the house.

Despite zeal, a programme of reform, the pressure of time, the revelation of Papist intrigue and the breaking of the financial deadlock by a reform of the subsidy, settlement still eluded Pym. Indeed, apart from a few statutes abolishing some of the most obvious agents of the Personal Rule, there was little which had been achieved to provide Pym with the political security he required. Nothing of Pym's programme had been put into effect, yet the measures which had been passed, such as the Triennial Act, were enough to convince many MPs that something of a settlement had been reached, and they were becoming frustrated at Pym's demands for further pressure and his failure to come to a formal settlement.

With the King in Scotland and the Commons in recess during September, Pym, in charge of the Recess Committee, was in his element deciding on business, putting decisions into operation and continuing the witch hunt against Catholics. Rumours of the 'Incident' in Scotland were exploited to their full propaganda value and increased demands for control of military resources when Parliament reassembled in October. It was also suggested that Parliament should have a negative voice in the appointment of ministers, showing increasing lack of faith in Charles's intentions. But it was the Irish rebellion in October which confirmed Pym's view that England was about to be reduced to Popery. Convinced that the rebellion was promoted by English Catholics, he was now prepared to countenance political extremes, and for the first time expressed serious doubt as to whether settlement with the King could be reached.

Trust was at the centre of the dispute. Under no circumstances would Pym allow Charles an army to put down the Irish which could then be turned against Parliament. The Grand Remonstrance, published at the height of feeling over the rebellion, was not a revolutionary document in itself, but many were shocked at the provocative and popular tone of this appeal to the nation. Widespread mob violence in the provinces and the behaviour of the London populace, urged on by straitened economic circumstances, led to a general belief in the imminent breakdown of law and order. The progress of Root and Branch and its encouragement to sectarianism was seen to be adding to the sense of anarchy. In this atmosphere, and with the support of skilled politicians such as Hyde, Falkland and Culpepper, a strong royalist reaction against Pym's leadership developed, and for the first time Parliament, which had always worked by consensus, took on a pattern of faction. Soon after the crisis there were demands for the registration of protest votes against the parliamentary leadership. At the same time the gap between the Commons and the Lords widened. Pym's grasp seemed to be weakening.

The events leading up to Charles's attempt to arrest the five members in January 1642 are well known. The Common Council elections in the City returned an administration sympathetic to Pym, while Colonel Lunsford's appointment to the Tower alienated any remaining royalist support in the City. Given Pym's reliance on the theory of the Catholic conspiracy and the erosion of his support, Charles's attempted coup was a disastrous blunder and undid much of the work which Pym's own extremism was doing to generate royalist support. It is to Pym's credit that he kept his following, and royalist MPs increasingly absented themselves from the Commons as confrontation between King and Commons leadership continued, neither side able to trust the other. Pym's aims remained constant: he was putting pressure on Charles to provide an acceptable form of monarchical government. If to do this it was necessary to provide a military threat, 'assertive moves taken in a defensive spirit', then Pym was prepared to risk war, and the Militia Ordinance was the result. As with many of Pym's schemes, little about it was new. The Ordinance had a good constitutional pedigree of use in emergencies, and the form of this one had much in common with the traditional methods of raising the militia.

Between January and June 1642, Pym's extraordinary powers of hard work, day-to-day management, investigative skills, political judgement, and ability to play one group off against another kept him on top. In Parliament he was able to moderate extremist claims, while in the Nineteen Propositions he put forward an ultimatum to Charles containing proposals more radical than anything envisaged hitherto: ministers were to be appointed only with the consent of Parliament; all public business was to be debated in Parliament; and, in effect, parliamentary sovereignty was to be recognised. He could allow those who wanted a settlement a free hand while preparing an effective military force; what could he lose? Money still presented a major problem and his links with the City were useful in providing a basis for the recruitment of an army; negotiations with the Scots provided the promise of further support. Increasingly the local enforcement of parliamentary decisions was becoming important and the block of local-government inefficiency was difficult to overcome. In MPs Parliament had a ready-made system for bringing the provinces into line with a central authority, though Pym's lack of sensitivity to local feeling made relations difficult.

In such a brief survey of so complex and confusing a period, much has to be omitted, but fuller accounts only serve to emphasise the central role of Pym. Undoubtedly, he was saying what MPs wanted to hear and he was helped by a King who was tactless in the extreme, prone to impetuous gestures, and incapable of arousing trust. Yet the survival of the opposition movement between 1640 and 1642 owes a great deal to Pym's ingenuity, hard work and obsessive belief in the Catholic threat.

IV

The outbreak of Civil War did not alter Pym's overall aims and methods. The ideas outlined in the Ten Propositions still formed the basis of his policy. All that had changed was that the King had shown himself to be untrustworthy and had now chosen, according to Pym, to wage war on his people in defence of his Papist government. Pym's justification for entering the Solemn League and Covenant with the Scots in the face of hostility from his own side summarises well his attitude to the whole war:

> If a man have a disease in his body and a medicine in his hand to cure it, but before he can take it one comes to him sword in hand to kill him, shall he not cast away his medicine and betake himself to his sword; or shall he take the medicine and suffer himself to be killed.[6]

Settlement with the King was still his aim; as the threat of warfare had failed to produce a spirit of compromise, so a challenge on the battlefield, if not outright defeat, would force Charles into accepting Pym's demands and produce a monarchical government acceptable to the parliamentary leadership. Pym's problem was simple: he had few soldiers, little money, no strategy, no administration, and supporters of dubious reliability. In the face of this, Charles had the country's residual royalism behind him, reinforced by the fear of anarchy and the desire to avoid a protracted war, a clear military strategy – to regain London – and the prospect of military aid from abroad. A number of ex-parliamentary royalists were working out a convincing theory of constitutional royalism acceptable to many former critics. Above all, although the latter months of 1642 were dominated by half-hearted military encounters, a propaganda war and a desperate search for a non-military settlement, 1643 brought royalist success on such an astounding scale that there was real fear that all the gains won by the Long Parliament would be lost in a total royalist victory.

To Pym's advantage were his own expertise as a parliamentary manager and political organiser; the Commons provided the structure for linking the provinces with the centre; the City provided finance and manpower, and prevented their use by the King; and the zeal and obsession which motivated Pym were shared by many parliamentarians. On the other hand, the problems of maintaining a united front were considerable. As already suggested, backbenchers were loath to put their money where their mouths were; resentment grew over Pym's bullying tactics; keeping the localities in step with the central administration proved impossible; and maintaining morale in the army was difficult, and not helped by the half-hearted attitude of Essex after the royalist victories of 1643. Extremist pressure, especially from London, was kept up to encourage Pym to work for all-out victory before settlement was considered. Once the parliamentary side looked as though it would lose, much of its support would disintegrate. In the face of these challenges Pym established a war machine which enabled Parliament to hold on during the crucial campaigns of 1643 and 1644; his financial and administrative reforms provided the basis for the military breakthrough which brought Parliament victory in 1645. It is the purpose of this final section to consider the system he set up from organisational, financial, military and political points of view.

As in the period before the war, Pym's relationship with Parliament itself was uneasy. Aware that the strength of his position lay in a show of support in the Commons and the Lords, he chose to work chiefly through his parliamentary committees, which were easily packed with his own supporters. By far the most important of these was the Committee of Public Safety, a group of about twenty lords and MPs who managed the war-effort, appealing to the Commons only when necessary. Their brief was wide: to determine military strategy in the long and in the short term, to exercise control over the localities, to supervise finance, to distribute supplies to the forces, and to develop links with foreign powers. Given that Parliament had never been an executive body, the Committee of Public Safety has quite accurately been described as the privy council of King Pym, reacting to the day-to-day changes in military and political fortune. The cliquish nature of the Committee invited criticism, notably from the radical opponents of Essex in 1643, who wanted a more forceful pursuit of war and suggested an independent London force under William

Waller, and the Committee began to lose the confidence of the Commons itself. None the less, it enabled Pym to exclude radicals from general policy decisions, and his expulsion of Henry Marten from the House showed that he would not tolerate continued, destructive criticism. Private meetings between Pym and London politicians ensured the continued support of the City, and it was Pym's capacity for compromise which prevented the opening of a rift over Essex, by his decision to accept the need for a more intense military campaign.

For some time it has been accepted that Pym was the leader of a 'middle group' in Parliament, opposed to the peace party, who wanted a settlement with the King at almost any price, and the war party, who wanted all-out victory before negotiations. However, views were not as clear-cut as this suggests and many MPs followed Pym's pragmatic line of pursuing whichever policy seemed appropriate at a given time. As before 1642, in any crisis he always allied himself with the war party but saw the decision forced on him by Charles's intransigence. None the less, he sought to moderate extremist claims in the hope of preventing faction rifts and reconciling especially those who feared the results of social and religious radicalism.

However good the central administration might be, its effectiveness was dependent on the efficiency of its agents in the localities. Here Pym was far less successful, and the network of local parliamentary committees provided a ramshackle and confused administrative system. The primary function of these committees was the enforcement of parliamentary ordinances, particularly those concerned with recruitment and finance. Their strength and efficiency depended on the local parliamentary leadership, which usually came from families of accepted local standing. As in much of his policy, Pym built on existing foundations and provided an alternative government which closely followed traditional forms. In areas of royalist strength, local committees had little effect. Elsewhere, it was difficult to control them from the centre: for example, money collected locally rarely got to the parliamentary treasurer at the Guildhall and was often used for paying the troops in the vicinity. Though seemingly confused, this system had its advantages. In some respects the Civil War was not a national war at all, but one fought out in each county, and a strong and independent local administration aided the survival of provincial parliamentarianism. Within each county, committees were often accused of harsh and arbitrary measures, suggesting at least a degree of effectiveness.

Pym realised early on the key role of finance in promoting success, and he spent much time in cajoling the Commons into passing the necessary financial legislation. His old skill in exploiting each fresh crisis, be it defeat or plot, in the end produced a series of ordinances which ensured an income to sustain the parliamentary army. The Act of £400,000 in March 1642 was the first step forward: a modified form of Ship Money, it provided the finance to set up a basic army. It was superseded in 1643 by the weekly – later monthly – assessments, which, like Ship Money, brought more people within the tax threshold and managed to tax the real wealth of the country. The sequestration of royalist lands proved a popular expedient with those who could use political justificaiton for settling old scores with royalist rivals in the localities. The seizing of recusants' estates was a continuation of Pym's policy of attacking papist delinquents and helped simplify the struggle into one of personalities rather than ideologies. The inadequacy of these sources pushed Pym into demanding compulsory loans from his supporters and it was with some reason that people complained of a parliamentary financial burden greater and more ruthless than that of the Personal Rule. Pym justified all by the existence of an emergency and carried most MPs with him. If money collected in the provinces did not always reach London, it was generally used for the war effort and not for private gain. Finally, Pym introduced the excise, a purchase tax, widely applied and capable of unlimited expansion; it was collected effectively at the local level and provided Parliament with a continuing source of financial support, increasing in importance as the war progressed.

Pym realised that military success was not just a matter of finance: the recruiting, training and equipping of troops was equally important. His volunteer army, with its local loyalties and frequent refusals to serve beyond county borders, was inadequate for breaking the military deadlock or countering the royalist successes of 1643. Various measures were intended to remedy this. Impressment was introduced and an augmented Eastern Association army was put under the direction of the Earl of Manchester to provide a crack fighting-force. Even so, it was difficult to resist the pressure from London to raise its own force and challenge Essex's unenthusiastic leadership, and it was in an attempt to block radical faction, as well as produce a show of strength, that Pym entered into negotiations with the Scots. Few Englishmen wanted Presbyterianism, but Pym saw it as a necessary price to pay for preventing the extinction of the parliamentary cause: political, not religious, issues were at stake. The signing of the Solemn League and Covenant was to be Pym's last major achievement. Even though the Scots turned out to be less useful than anticipated, they enabled Parliament to hold out against the royalist revival and set the stage for the move to victory in 1645.

Despite all the evidence for Pym's activity organising the parliamentary war effort, his precise methods of working are not clear. How far, for example, was he dependent on others to draw up legislation and produce innovatory schemes? What were his activities outside Westminster and the City? How much of the political debate and planning took place in private? As suggested earlier in this chapter, the present state of research does not allow for any but the most speculative answers to such questions. In the same way as it is difficult to pinpoint the exact nature of Pym's character, so it is impossible to define precisely his methods of work.

On the other hand *what* he was trying to achieve does seem clear. Settlement with the King was his aim, but only on terms which would satisfy Pym. As Charles showed himself to be less and less trustworthy, so Pym demanded more stringent controls and limitations on the King as the price for an end to the Civil War. By 1643 the defence of Protestantism and the defence of Parliament had been united in Pym's mind. A victory for the King would threaten them both.

V

At his funeral in Westminster Abbey on 15 December 1643, ten of Pym's colleagues acted as his pall-bearers. Already, splits within the parliamentary side were observable, but Pym had been able to hold them together and his funeral symbolised the respect in which he was held by all those who espoused the parliamentary cause. There was a feeling that his death heralded a new phase: 'The enemy rejoiceth as if our cause were not good, or as if we should lose it for want of hands and heads to carry it on. No, no beloved! this cause must prosper . . . this cause must prevail'.[7] There were to be disputes over the progress and tactics of the war up to 1645 and beyond; yet the foundations which Pym had laid were the key to Parliament's eventual victory. Would things have turned out differently if Pym had lived longer and not killed himself by overwork? The answer is, probably not. For Pym, the only thing preventing a settlement with the King was the King himself; and, while Charles continued to act in a devious and untrustworthy way, Pym was prepared to use all means available to oppose him. Therefore, without a change of heart on Charles's part, it is difficult to see that Pym could have done anything except pursue all-out war. His aspirations may have been those of a middle group, but the policies of the war party provided the only practical course he could follow.

Pym *was* an unlikely leader. He is an isolated figure in the world of seventeenth-century politics, remote from the county community, often alone in Parliament, honest and scrupulous, a man with no apparent interests outside his all-consuming passion for religion and state finance; his failure to train a successor suggests a modesty about his own role. His effect on the course of politics was dramatic, yet without the groundswell of popular opposition to Charles I and his government, even Pym's hopes would have come to nothing. To that extent his success was that of voicing and focusing the views of a wide range of disillusioned English men and women.

6. Sir Henry Vane the Younger

TIMOTHY EUSTACE

For most students of the seventeenth century Sir Henry Vane is a rather obscure figure who drifts in and out of the story of the 1640s. Yet few civilians played a more vital role in securing victory for Parliament in the Civil War and for England in the Anglo-Dutch War of 1652–4. The fact that such an outstandingly able administrator, and such a committed religious Independent, should in 1653 quarrel so bitterly with Oliver Cromwell that he was excluded from all government activity until 1659 tells us something about Cromwell but rather more about the religious fervour which dominated Vane's life and which so influenced developments in England during this period. Those seekers after truth, those who presumed themselves to be the Elect of God, gave an impetus to the rebellion of the 1640s which as much as almost anything else ensured its success on the battlefield and then helped it to take the totally unexpected path to regicide and republicanism. Vane's life illustrates the character of these remarkable fanatics, for whom religious truth was always the paramount issue, one which gave them the unshakeable belief in the rightness of their cause that led to the events of January 1649. Although Vane was not one of the regicides, it is not surprising or illogical that Charles II should have so vindictively insisted on his execution in 1662.

Thus an examination of Sir Henry Vane's life should help us to reach a better understanding of the religious psychology which can seem so alien to our age and yet which is so crucial to an understanding of the events of the middle two decades of the seventeenth century.

I

Henry Vane was born in 1613. His father, Sir Henry Vane senior, was a loyal courtier and official under both James I and Charles I, frequently sent on trips abroad and in 1640 appointed Secretary of State. A substantial landowner in Durham and Lincolnshire, Vane senior was anxious to set his son on a similar path to worldly success. In 1631 the eighteen-year-old Henry was sent with a diplomatic mission to Vienna, after having spent a year in France and the Netherlands developing a skill in languages rare amongst English gentlemen of that time. In 1639 he was appointed Joint Treasurer of the Navy, gaining a substantial income from Ship Money receipts but also proving his worth by curbing wasteful expenditure. In 1640 he was knighted and married a wealthy bride. His future seemed assured.

However, he had already selected a different path. In 1618, while at Westminster School under the guidance of the Puritan Lambert Osbaldeston, he believed he received his 'awakening dispensation' – his personal absorption of God's grace. This marked a fundamental turning-point in his life, persuading him to become a Separatist by rejecting the Church of England. He was prevented from matriculating at Oxford University because he refused to swear the oaths of allegiance and supremacy; his bride in 1640 was Frances Wray, the daughter of a Puritan and herself a 'seeker' after truth. It was quite clear, even in 1632, that the young Vane was reluctant to become a member of Charles's Court. An avowedly pacifist outlook alienated him from the aristocratic Court. Discussions with Bishop Laud, arranged by his father, merely resulted in angry disagreement over Vane's opposition to kneeling at Communion. It was his religious nonconformity which persuaded him to join the Puritan settlements in America – an idea encouraged by Laud, who believed that personal experience of the intolerant Puritan settlements would soon cure the young man of his radical enthusiasm. So it was with royal permission for a three-year visit to America that Vane sailed in 1635 as an agent of John Pym and John Hampden to protect the interests of the Saybrooke Company in the Connecticut River Valley, a colony patronised by a group of men interested in establishing godly communities free from persecution but soon to achieve greater fame by their political opposition to Charles.

In fact Vane got no further than Boston, Massachusetts, then barely six years old, primitive and uncomfortable, the largest town in this raw colony, restless, energetic and rapidly expanding. The colonists, not all of whom could be described as 'Saints', yet whose government was dominated by those who had emigrated to escape growing persecution by the Church of England as Arminianism developed, faced a threat to their autonomy through a dispute over the validity of their charter, and Vane, with a father at Court and a royal letter in his pocket, was seen as a valuable ally at this time of crisis. Within five months of landing he was made a freeman of the colony, and two months later, in May 1636, was elected Governor, despite his youth, insistence on growing his hair to a non-Puritan length, and especially his inexperience of both government and American affairs.

The responsibility of power brought Vane his first real crisis of conscience when he felt compelled to arrange for a military expedition which resulted in the effective destruction of the Pequot Indians, who had been provoked into making vicious raids on settlements; his pacifism was reluctantly subordinated to his duty to the settlers. But of greater significance was his involvement in the great debate at this time centred on Mrs Anne Hutchinson.

This formidable lady arrived in 1634 and soon gathered a congregation about her. She preached of the duty of each individual to follow the prompting of his own 'inner voice', and was one of the first women to become a leading figure in religious affairs. Vane was immediately attracted to her ideas, which seemed to reinforce those he had developed himself. Their demand for complete freedom of worship resulted in Vane quarrelling with most of the leading citizens of Massachusetts, and hence being replaced as Governor in 1637. He returned to England just before a purge of his associates was carried out in Boston, which included the banishment of Mrs Hutchinson, who moved to the tolerant community at Rhode Island and later died in an Indian massacre.

The important aspects for our survey concern the beliefs which Vane developed at this time, to which he remained true for the remainder of his life. They were predominantly Antinomian – that is, rejecting the validity of any written moral law; each individual member of the Elect (those in receipt of God's grace) must follow the dictates of his own conscience, formed directly and individually by God. The rejection of all external authority, the purely individual response inherent in these ideas, caused them to be viewed with horror by most Englishmen – and indeed such beliefs could and did lead to outbreaks of notorious amorality.

But for the more serious believers, such as Vane, a firm belief in God's word and in their responsibility as agents preparing for the Second Coming of Christ ensured the strictest standards of behaviour and a determination and confidence in the rightness of their cause which gave strength and perseverance. Vane was a faithful husband and careful father, plain living and privately honest, certainly less corrupt than most of his contemporaries in office, and above all permanently devoted to fostering God's work as he saw it.

But his beliefs also required him to reject all structures in the Church. Bishops, presbyteries, all who claimed authority over men's consciences, were in defiance of God's Word. Vane worshipped at home when the Spirit moved him (and not necesarily on Sundays). He was to become the leader of a small group of family and friends completely under his influence, for whom one can feel some sympathy; Baxter described his religious writings as 'so cloudily formed and expressed, that few could understand them'[1] and anyone struggling to read *A Retired Man's Meditations*, written in 1655, is likely to agree. The true union of man and God required at least a second 'awakening' or inward receipt of Christ, necessary for permanent salvation – even Quakers and other Puritan sectarians were seen as knowing only the First Coming of Christ into their souls. Only those experiencing this second awakening were the 'true adherers' to the cause – the Saints required to prepare England for the imminent Second Coming of Christ.

Such ideas were not so uncommon in the ferment to be created by the freedom of religious debate after 1640. They illustrate one of the driving forces in the Rebellion, and illustrate both the attractive dedication of those involved and the tendencies which provoked increasing horror amongst those who saw the fabric and stability of society threatened by such emphasis on the free and individual soul, a universal liberty of conscience. 'Why should the labours of any be suppressed, if sober, though never so different? We now profess to seek God, we desire to see light.'[2]

II

Despite this, in 1640 Vane was still a royal official, elected MP for Hull and then knighted, all through his father's influence at Court.

Yet the young Vane was to be instrumental in securing one of Charles's bitterest defeats, the attainder of the Earl of Strafford. It is uncertain whether it was by accident or design that in 1641 he found his father's note on the Privy Council meeting in March 1640 at which Strafford had declared that Charles had 'an army in Ireland you may employ here to reduce this kingdom'; certainly he went through considerable soul-searching, and a probably related bout of fever, before he showed the papers to John Pym, whose skilful use of them, by implying that Strafford was referring to England and not Scotland, ensured a substantial vote in the Commons against Strafford. The episode brought Vane into the limelight: by late 1641 he was described by Hyde as one of the 'stout seconders' of the parliamentary leadership, and in December was sacked from office by Charles (as was his father). He was appointed to many important commmittees, in particular organising naval supplies, pledging £20,000 of his own credit to that end, and was instrumental early in 1642 in securing the support of the Navy for Parliament, so vital to its prospects in the coming war; he was regarded as sufficiently popular in London (perhaps because of his religious radicalism) to be sent frequently to the City to negotiate loans, as in March 1641, when he helped secure £100,000. In September 1642 he was appointed to the Committee of Safety, formed in July as Parliament's executive, presumably as a useful ally of Pym.

Parliament, however, was not a completely united body. Already in the winter of 1642 a peace party under Denzil Holles was emerging, with support from sections of the London mob demanding an end to the war. One of Pym's primary tasks was to create at least a semblance of unity and to prevent the outbreak of debilitating factionalism. Vane did not assist. As early as December 1640 he had spoken in support of the London petition demanding the abolition of episcopacy; it was the ensuing Root and Branch bill which led to his first major speech in June 1641, in which he declared bishops to be the source of civil strife as preachers of 'the lawfulness of arbitrary power'. In August he moved for the impeachment of the bishops, and in November refused to speak in support of the Grand Remonstrance because it urged religious conformity. Now openly more radical than Pym, at least in his religious views, he opposed peace negotiations in December 1642 as likely to reduce the determination to win, and was emerging as a bitter opponent of the cautious war strategy of the Earl of Essex.

Yet he was still chosen by Pym as the leading negotiator to secure the Scottish alliance in 1643. Possibly Pym, certainly the Scots, were more aware of his enthusiasm for victory than his objective of religious liberty. His energy and enthusiasm brought him popularity, and he had already proved himself as a skilled negotiator. Within ten days he had drawn up the Solemn League and Covenant, including the clause that the Church should be reformed 'according to the example of the best reformed churches' but also 'according to the word of God'. The Scots, made aware of the urgency of the situation by the recent surrender of Bristol to the royalists, found it difficult to dispute the validity of such a phrase, while confident that their Presbyterian Church was indeed 'according to the word of God'. Vane privately disagreed.

At this stage he undoubtedly believed in the necessity for the Scots alliance, and was energetic and successful in securing the funds necessary for paying their expenses. But within a year he had become their bitter and outspoken opponent, so helping to develop a third group within Parliament, determined on total victory free from dependence on the half-hearted and self-interested Scots – the war party, led by Vane and Sir Arthur Haslerig. This group, more ruthless than the one guided by Pym, was later, partly owing to Vane's pre-eminence, to be known as the Independents (misleadingly, since several Presbyterians, such as Zouch Tate, were part of the group). The royalists were quick to spot this emerging split. In 1644 Lord Lovelace approached Vane offering a religious settlement which would preserve episcopacy but guarantee 'liberty of conscience'. Further attempts were made in 1646 and even 1648 to seduce him with promises of toleration, but with no success. Vane was far too suspicious of episcopacy and increasingly of the trustworthiness of the promises of the King, although some Presbyterians were to accuse him of holding treasonous secret talks.

Instead, throughout 1644 Vane was hectically involved in securing outright victory. He attended the Committee of Both Kingdoms on most days, and was instrumental in securing for it effective control over peace negotiations, having ensured a membership which gave a working majority to the war party; thus the risk of a compromise peace settlement was avoided. His actions often showed scant regard for the supremacy of the legislature, since he frequently sent orders or made arrangements *before* Parliament had taken any such decision. Urgency matters in wartime; but such behaviour tends to devalue his claims that Parliament 'ought to be sacred to the ears of all true Englishmen'. In October 1659 he was again to sacrifice belief in the primacy of Parliament to the expediency of the moment. Confirmation of Vane's emergence as a leader of the war party came with his seconding of Zouch Tate's 'Self-Denying Ordinance', shortly followed by the creation of the New Model Army. (It might be noted that Vane, as an official sacked by Charles and reinstated by order of Parliament, was thereby exempt from the terms of the Ordinance.) The New Model Army, with many Presbyterian officers and largely recruited from the armies of Essex and Manchester, was not at first a radical force.[3] Indeed, Vane's political base was still small – a group of Independents in the Commons and not so many more in the country. Most Presbyterians were very suspicious of his intentions, while emerging political radicals such as the Levellers were aware that Vane, a substantial property-owner, was socially conservative. From June 1645, when he lost his majority on the Committee of Both Kingdoms as the receding fear of defeat reduced support for the vigorous war party, he absented himself from its meetings, reluctant to be associated with decisions of which he disapproved, and so providing a hint of his doubts about democratic principles.

So a shift towards religious radicalism within the New Model Army, apparent by 1647, makes the developing relationship between Vane and Oliver Cromwell significant.[4] The two men contrasted greatly in character but shared comparable objectives, in particular a demand for religious toleration. Vane needed more support, and Cromwell needed skilled allies in the Commons. Full alliance was not yet established, but over the next five years the two men were often to find themselves working at least along parallel tracks.

'The Independents perhaps owed their victory in the Civil War more to Vane than to any other single man except Cromwell.'[5] His contribution at least in part included the loyalty and efficiency of the Navy, the creation of the Scottish alliance and the New Model Army, the raising of substantial loans from London, much of the detailed, grinding but vital work of the Committee of Both Kingdoms, and the debating and organisational skills necessary to prevent MPs from losing heart and accepting peace on inadequate terms. His energy and clear-sightedness were indeed essential and invaluable.

III

The surrender of Charles in 1646 did not make life any easier for
Vane. Parliament had secured military victory, but Charles refused
to accept the logic of this situation and was aided in his procrastinat-
ing negotiations by the divisions now clearly emerging amongst his
opponents. The Scots rapidly lost interest in English affairs,
demanded their back pay and retired to Scotland. The moderate
majority in the Commons, led by Holles and Philip Stapleton –
normally if not entirely accurately referred to as the Presbyterians –
held prolonged talks with the King on the basis of his acceptance of
Presbyterianism and parliamentary control of the armed forces for a
certain number of years. They also published an ordinance to
suppress blasphemy, imposing rigorous punishments such as life
imprisonment for an incorrect view of infant baptism. Realising the
unpopularity of the continued existence of the Army, owing to its
arrogant indiscipline and the high taxes it necessitated, they proposed
to disband many regiments, remove others to Ireland, allow no
officers above the rank of colonel except for General Fairfax, and
require all officers to take the Covenant.

All of this was repugnant to Vane, to Cromwell and the Independents, the other major grouping in Parliament, who had few clear-cut
policies beyond toleration and the preservation of the Army. For the
first half of 1647 Vane seems to have been mostly absent from
Parliament, reminding us of his absence from the Committee of Both
Kingdoms in 1646 when again he could not secure a majority. He
decided to form closer links with the Army as the only means to
preserve Independency; and physical threats against him by the
London mob in June 1647, clear evidence of the widespread desire for
a quick settlement and of hostility towards those demanding harsh
terms from the King, may have encouraged this further. It was almost
certainly Vane who warned Cromwell in May of the rumoured plan
to remove the King to Scotland, so enabling Cornet Joyce to seize
Charles before this could occur and take him to the Army's
rendezvous at Newmarket.

Yet Vane's attitude towards the growing quarrel between Parliament and Army was still uncertain and confused. Lilburne was to see
him as linked with Cromwell in a 'design . . . to keep the poor people
everlastingly . . . in bondage and slaverie'.[6] But Vane, one of the
parliamentary commissioners sent to negotiate with the Army in July

1647, was also one of those who signed a letter dissenting from its decision to march on London and was openly opposed to any plan to force a dissolution of Parliament. Only the invasion of Parliament by the London mob on 26 July, culminating in the holding-down of Speaker Lenthall, persuaded Vane along with sixty-four other MPs to join the Army on Hounslow Heath. The alliance of the Presbyterian Commons with the City of London, both anxious for the return of the King and normality and the disbandment of the Army, alarmed Vane anew and pushed him at last into definite co-operation with the Army. It was Vane who presented the Heads of Proposals to Parliament on 6 August (won over completely by the proposal for separation of religion and state and the abolition of tithes) and who accepted the intimidation which led to the withdrawal of many Presbyterians from the House and so gave the Independents a majority within the Commons. Nevertheless, Vane was not prepared to join Sir Henry Marten and Colonel Rainsborough in their demand for the abolition of the monarchy, lacking their political radicalism. He seems to have hoped that Charles would reject the Newcastle Propositions, as he did, and so be prepared to discuss the more pragmatic Heads of Proposals, giving special emphasis to the role of the Privy Council as well as to the co-existence of Anglican and Puritan churches. As always, Vane showed little interest in the details of the political settlement and no real commitment to radical political change. The freedom of each man to commune with God in his own way was for him the overriding question.

The flight of Charles to the Isle of Wight, and the consequent outbreak of the Second Civil War, interrupted all such discussions. Presbyterians and Independents drew together to resist the surge of royalism in the country and the Scottish invasion; Parliament and Army co-operated again, under the executive leadership of the Derby House Committee, of which Vane became a leading member. He agreed with the Vote of No Addresses (to the King) in January 1648, while in May he supported the Commons' vote not to alter 'the fundamental government of the Kingdom by Kings, Lords and Commons'. Yet, when in August, the fighting over, Parliament repealed the Vote of No Addresses, Vane argued that Charles should not and could not be trusted. Despite this support for the Army's now clearly stated point of view, he was chosen as a member of the commission sent to Newport to negotiate with Charles. His part in this episode is unclear. Many (including Hyde and Holles) believed that he intended to prolong the talks while the Army strengthened its position by crushing the Scots; certainly, once the Army had arrived near London, Vane declared in the Commons on 2 December that further talks were of no value, and that government must be settled without the King's agreement. He lost the vote, and four days later Pride's Purge took place.

Vane's behaviour during the next two months confirms his ambivalent attitude towards republicanism. He played no part in Pride's Purge, remained absent throughout the succeeding debates, took no part in the King's trial (although he did observe it), and on the day of Charles's execution calmly called at the Navy Office to sign documents. He could not accept the validity of the trial and execution, but neither could he quarrel with the Army, the only hope for securing true liberty of conscience. He refused to sign the parliamentary oath of approbation of the trial and execution, yet continued to hold office, and by February was playing a leading role in the proceedings of the Rump Parliament.

IV

The Rump Parliament forms a unique period in English history – four years of government by a one-chamber Parliament. It would be misleading to assume from this that it was of a very radical nature. In social balance it differed little if at all from the full Long Parliament, consisting predominantly of landowners (such as Vane himself). Many of those sitting after Pride's Purge were not republicans, and from February 1649 the Rump was anxious to persuade moderate MPs to return to its ranks to give it greater credibility. A significant group of lawyers, such as Bulstrode Whitelock, prevented any major reform of the law; the disturbing growth of radical religious sects, so much more extreme than most Puritan groups in the early 1640s, cooled the ardour of many for complete toleration; and the routine of necessary administration gave little time for major programmes of change. Failures to reform were owing more to lack of inclination than to lack of skill or hard work.

Rather more than 200 MPs were eligible to sit in the Rump; rarely did more than sixty do so; and perhaps only thirty to forty were full-time politicians at Westminster.[7] Their leaders were divided: Marten and Scot were republicans, Vane was not; Marten was

1. Lionel Cranfield, Earl of Middlesex, by Daniel Mytens.

2. George Villiers, Duke of Buckingham, sketch by Rubens.

3. William Laud, Archbishop of Canterbury, copy of Van Dyck.

4.   Thomas Wentworth, Earl of Strafford, with Sir Philip Mainwaring, by Van Dyck.

5. John Pym, by Samuel Cooper.

6. Sir Henry Vane the Younger.

7. Edward Hyde, Earl of Clarendon, after Hanneman.

8.   Anthony Ashley Cooper, Earl of Shaftesbury, after J. Greenhill.

9. Thomas Osborne, Earl of Danby, Studio of Lely.

10.   Robert Spencer, Earl of Sunderland, the English School.

thought to be too immoral to be influential in religious discussion, while Vane was unclear and surprisingly inactive in this area. Even where the radicals dominated committees, little that was radical emerged: some small legal reforms, a revised Blasphemy Act, some efforts to spread the gospel. Greater reliance was placed on local administration than on central legislation to deal with social problems. Only the Navigation Act, the war with the Dutch and the proposed Union with Scotland emerged as major achievements.

There was no undisputed leader of the Rump – perhaps another reason for its relative lack of achievement; Scot, Marten, Haslerig and Vane were all influential, but none predominated. However, no one worked harder than Vane. A member of the Council of State, he also sat on committees for the compounding of royalist estates, for law reform, for Irish and Scottish affairs, for electoral reform, for treaties and alliances, for trade and plantations, and for foreign affairs, and was most active on the Naval Sub-committee. He frequently started work at 7 a.m., attended committee meetings virtually every day, travelled to Scotland to arrange the Union and to Chatham to organise the Navy, and still managed to be a regular attender at parliamentary debates. As early as August 1649 he complained that his health and family duties were suffering, but he did not relax.

One of his major achievements was the plan for the Union with Scotland, begun in November 1651 by a committee led by Vane and St John. This committee overrode royalist and Presbyterian opposition in Scotland, sequestered the land of those involved in the invasions of England in 1648 and 1651, arranging for it to be leased at low rents to the poor, and guaranteed general toleration. Vane was probably responsible for most of the drafting of the plan which he placed before Parliament in March 1652, although it did not come into effect until Cromwell enforced it in 1654. Efficient management and religious toleration were undoubtedly Vane's personal contributions.

He also took a leading role early in 1651 in instigating negotiations, led by St John, to bring about the union of England and the United Provinces. The failure of these talks, clear by June, led Vane to withdraw from the discussions, leaving the initiative to St John and Marten. He disapproved of the ensuing war and supported Cromwell's efforts from March 1653 to secure peace. Yet no civilian played a greater part in ensuring victory, as will be seen below.

The destruction of the Rump resulted from Cromwell's dissatisfaction with its proposals for replacing itself. In May 1649 Vane was nominated chairman of a committee to consider electoral reform and future parliaments. Not until January 1650 did it report, and debates on its proposals occurred only intermittently, with a burst of activity after the battle of Worcester (owing to Cromwell's pressure) and again in March 1653. There were too many complex factors: the franchise, redistribution of seats, the size of Parliament, and, especially, whether the next election should be a 'recruiting' or 'fresh' election. On the first three points Vane favoured a £200 real property franchise (thus in fact reducing the number of electors), a redistribution to increase the number of county seats at the expense of the boroughs (hence reducing aristocratic patronage), and a total of 400 seats. On all these points there was eventual agreement, and the proposals were incorporated almost *en bloc* into Lambert's Instrument of Government. The decision which discredited the Rump was its insistence on having 'recruiting elections' – that is, the existing incumbents to hold their seats without facing re-election and to check the validity of the election of new MPs, so claiming the right substantially to decide the balance of the new parliament. For Vane this was essential. Only by this means could the godly party hold on to power, ensure toleration, prevent the return of monarchy and give itself time to gain credibility. One of the greatest proofs of Cromwell's strange and uncertain political understanding was his opposition to this and his impetuous destruction of the Rump when it suddenly decided to enact this scheme on 20 April 1653 despite personal assurances by Vane and others the previous evening. Only Vane's scheme, however unpopular, could have given some constitutional veneer to the military rule necessary to enforce Cromwell's own aims; essentially a programme for a great spurt of by-elections, it would have preserved a greater degree of constitutionality than any one of Cromwell's later efforts to arrange for amenable parliaments.

But by then Vane and Cromwell had quarrelled, largely because of Cromwell's retreat from the idea of total religious freedom to one incorporating some limits and standards (namely, the Triers and Ejectors), and because of Cromwell's growing impatience with the bumbling Rump while Vane clung to the continuance of the Rump with its semblance of constitutionality. 'The Lord deliver me from Sir Henry Vane', Cromwell replied when Vane, on the dissolution of the Rump, called out that 'it is against morality and common honesty'.

Vane's work with the Navy deserves special emphasis as undoubtedly his finest achievement. Appointed Joint Treasurer by Charles in

1639, he soon developed an interest in and understanding of the needs of the Navy. In 1642 he was appointed Sole Treasurer by Parliament; in 1645 he helped remodel the Navy after the Self-denying Ordinance. Although in 1650 he sold his office of Treasurer, the predominant loyalty of the Navy and lack of complaint from sailors throughout the 1640s confirm his achievement. 'He has discharged with as much clearness and freedom from corruption as ever Treasurer did',[8] wrote Giles Greene, a colleague in the Navy department but a political Presbyterian.

The Rump appointed a sub-committee of the Council of State to run the Navy, and Vane dominated this. In March 1650, when five new ships were needed, Vane arranged parliamentary approval in one day, transferring funds from the Army to the Navy; in April he encouraged recruiting by securing an act to grant one tenth of the proceeds from captured ships to the sailors; in September he arranged for more funds designed for Cromwell's army in Scotland to go to the fleet sent to capture Barbados. Then, in December 1652, immediately after Blake's defeat by Tromp off Dungeness, Vane arranged the setting-up of a new more efficient committee to administer the Navy. He visited the fleet, discussed its needs with Blake and other officers, and visited Chatham dockyard to ensure the speedy supplying and fitting-out of a fleet to intercept the Dutch fleet returning from the Caribbean. At the same time he persuaded Parliament to raise taxes for the armed forces from £90,000 to £120,000 a month, arranged for higher wages and regular payment to secure voluntary enlistment, and provided increased help for the sick and wounded. Within four months he had reorganised the Navy and laid the foundation for Blake's victories and England's triumph.

V

Vane was invited to attend the Nominated Assembly in 1653 but sarcastically refused, rejecting Cromwell's patronage. He might favour government by the godly elect, but not the strange assortment of fanatics and men of substance selected by the Army Council. He did, however, try (unsuccessfully) to win election to the First Protectorate Parliament, and then in 1656 published *A Healing Question*, a discussion of the problems of England's government. This acknowledged the need for firm secular government until the Second

Coming of Christ, but only if it guaranteed liberty of conscience and security of property. However, the franchise should belong only to 'the whole party of honest men adhering to this cause', in effect the Fifth Monarchists, amongst whom Vane could be counted. Another section demanded a Council of State distinct from and subordinate to the legislature – a notable contrast with his own use of power as a Councillor during the Rump's rule.

In 1656 he was also active in opposing the major generals and associated with a potential Fifth Monarchist rising, resulting in a summons to appear before the Council. This he ignored, and so was imprisoned from September to December. A wide gulf now separated Vane and Cromwell, who had worked so closely together a decade earlier. They still shared some of the same objectives: a godly, tolerant society, efficient government protecting the rights of property-owners, some moderate social and legal reforms, and power overseas; but they now differed on the scope of toleration to be permitted and especially on the means to attain these ends. Vane had come to reject his earlier flirtation with the Army commanders; he preserved a sufficient attachment to the idea of Parliament (whatever its specific format) to ensure an increasing hostility to the reality of military rule.

For five years, therefore, Vane was effectively out of politics, concentrating on developing his religious ideas, on writing and on preaching to an intimate and exclusive band of uncritical family and friends.

1659 saw Vane return vigorously to the centre of politics. This is not the place for a detailed examination of the hectic, often confusing events of that year. There were three main periods. The Protectorate survived until April, during which time Vane, elected MP despite attempts by the government to prevent this, worked closely with Haslerig to obstruct the regime. Filibustering tactics achieved nothing positive but slowed down essential provision of supplies, so weakening the government. Vane and Haslerig concentrated on denying the constitutionality of the Protectorate, Vane shrewdly pointing out that only the validity of the Rump made Charles's execution a legal act; but they failed to prevent the Act of Recognition confirming Richard Cromwell's authority.

Vane therefore supported the Army's removal of Richard Cromwell and recall of the Rump. From May until October he served with Haslerig on the Committee of Safety and then the Council of State, still supervising naval affairs but now with a greater interest in foreign affairs, in particular the negotiations for an alliance with the Dutch for joint mediation in the Baltic to restrain the increasing power and demands of Charles X of Sweden. But Haslerig, a truer parliamentarian, quarrelled with Vane over the former's ideas for a wider franchise, his belief in majority rule and his tactless rejection of Army demands, especially the confirmation of its high command. Vane favoured a narrower franchise, a government shaped to protect the rights of the minorities (the extreme sects), and a more tactful relationship with the Army, essential to preserve those rights.

So, disillusioned by the attitude of the majority of MPs, Vane provided public support when Lambert expelled the Rump, blaming Parliament for provoking the quarrel; he served on the Committee of Safety, and unsuccessfully attempted to win the support of the Navy. Again he found himself out-manoeuvred. The recall of the Rump at the end of December following riots, petitions and the intervention of General Monk resulted on 9 January in an order for Vane to leave London, enforced on 13 February probably through the influence of that formidable Presbyterian Mrs Monk. Vane now found himself vitriolically attacked in pamphlets as a Fifth Monarchist, Papist, Jesuit and hypocrite, and, rather inelegantly, for having been 'shit out of the Rump'.

He made no effort to hide or escape once Charles II returned to England. On 1 July he was arrested and held in the Tower. Despite some efforts by the Commons, the House of Lords insisted on his exclusion from the Act of Indemnity, although the Commons did secure a plea to the King to remit execution. Not until June 1662 was he brought to trial, for treason against not Charles I but Charles II, by appointing Army officers in May 1659 (to keep Charles out of the country) and reviewing his regiment of volunteers in December. These petty charges were based on the invalidity of all parliaments since 1649, so preventing Vane from making any effective defence. Even at his execution on 14 June, undignified but successful methods were used to prevent him making a speech to the public, although there was widespread respect for his dignity and bearing on the scaffold. 'Certainly he is too dangerous a man to let live if we can honestly put him out of the way':[9] Charles's comment, and his order that Vane be executed on Tower Hill, recall the attainder and execution of Strafford twenty-one years earlier, the event which marked Vane's emergence as a leading politician and radical rebel.

VI

Sir Henry Vane's career can seem confusing because he was so often self-contradictory. Talk about the 'sovereignty of Parliaments' comes at a time when, as a member of the Council of State, he was issuing instructions two or three days before such measures were approved by Parliament. He talked of the essential independence of Parliament, but accepted Army intervention in 1647 and 1659, whilst rejecting it in 1653. He opposed the King's execution, yet within a month was on the Council of State alongside the regicides. He was sometimes lenient, at other times vengeful; he would argue for the voice of the people to decide, yet reject majority decisions. Generally acknowledged by fair-minded critics as uncorrupt, he took only £200 per annum in fees between 1642 and 1645, yet after the Self-denying Ordinance took £16,000 by the end of 1647, for reasons still unexplained, and received substantial compensation when he gave up the post of Treasurer of the Navy in 1650.

Uncertainty and contradiction in his political beliefs and behaviour stem, as in Cromwell, from two ideas generally seen as incompatible in the seventeenth century: liberty of conscience, and a belief in the necessity of protecting property and preserving its owner's influence. He never showed any interest in programmes for economic reform or social upheaval. Lilburne was not being unfair when he described them as 'silken Independents'. Vane, even more than Cromwell, failed to align these two ideas.

But his passionate faith and trust in God, and in God working through him, though often leading to political confusion and contradiction, were characteristic of so many in those years of free expression and experimentation. Words written to his wife shortly before his trial illustrate this mentality: 'They that press so earnestly to carry on my trial, do little know what presence of God may be afforded me in it and issue out of it.'[10]

If, like all the revolutionaries of the period, he failed to win widespread support or to secure any lasting achievement, his total commitment to his own beliefs and his energy and skill in administration deserve respect, and provide some understanding of the forces which give credit to those turbulent years.

7. Edward Hyde, Earl of Clarendon

TIMOTHY EUSTACE

FEW politicians have played so significant a role for so long as did Edward Hyde, first Earl of Clarendon. More than any other man he shaped the emergence of 'constitutional royalism' from 1641; for nearly ten years he acted as chief adviser and tutor to the young Charles II in exile and greatly assisted in ensuring his triumphant restoration; finally he served as leading minister during the years in which monarchical government was re-established. To these achievements must be added his monumental and stylish *History of the Great Rebellion* and *Life of Himself*, fascinating and revealing if not absolutely accurate works. It was his tragedy that he achieved the pinnacle of his career when political circumstances had changed beyond his comprehension, and when he was a generation too old to fit easily into the relaxed mores of the Restoration Court. His long political career shows a consistency of belief and behaviour rare in any age, an admirable virtue which probably contributed significantly to his ultimate failure by 1667.

Throughout his life he showed an interest in history. He criticised Hobbes's *Leviathan* because it showed little historical knowledge. His own legal training helped him to study England's political past as a means to discovering solutions to contemporary political problems. As will be shown, he began writing his own *History of the Great Rebellion* as the best way to educate Charles I into becoming a wiser King. Amongst its most notable features is the fair-mindedness of his comments on most of his political opponents; indeed, his character judgements are invaluable sources for all students of the period. His actions and policies as Lord Chancellor were influenced substantially by his reading of England's recent history. It is a salutary warning to historians that this led him to misjudge the situation so badly. All this makes it the more surprising that almost 150 years should elapse

157

between the publishing of T. H. Lister's three-volume biography of 1838 and R. W. Harris's study of 1983.

Where recent writings have impinged on his career (such as those concerning the restoration of the Church of England) there has been wide disagreement. B. H. G. Wormald in 1951 challenged many assumptions about Hyde's translation from parliamentary leader to royalist adviser, and thus illuminated many aspects of his character as well as clarifying some aspects of the growth of royalist support in the early 1640s. It is to be hoped that at least some proportion of the enthusiastic research devoted by historians to the period leading up to the Civil War will soon be extended to the period after 1660 – much of Charles II's reign contains a mass of unanswered questions. In the meantime this chapter attempts to explain why the intelligent, humane and perceptive politician whose ideas seem so wise and sensible in the 1640s should fail so lamentably in the 1660s.

I

Edward Hyde was born into a moderately prosperous but not influential Wiltshire family in 1609. Educated at Oxford University (for which he retained a lifelong affection) and at the Middle Temple, he was, as he confessed, a rather casual student. His father's death in 1634, when he became head of the family, and his second marriage (to Frances Aylesbury, daughter of a Master of Requests), induced him to become a more determined and successful lawyer. He was appointed Keeper of the Writs and Rolls of the Common Pleas, and won the approval of William Laud for his competence. Indeed, he became a colleague of the Archbishop by assisting in the raising of money for the repair and rebuilding of St Paul's Cathedral. His own comments on Laud balance recognition of his abilities and his efforts to make the churches more seemly places with criticism of his excessive prejudice and hot temper. Yet the impression one gains of Hyde's life up to 1640 is that of a cultured lover of good conversation and interesting ideas rather than an ambitious and hard-working lawyer, and the most significant aspect of his life during the 1630s was his membership of the Great Tew Circle.

Centred on Lord Falkland's house near Oxford, this grouping of young gentlemen and scholars (including Sidney Godolphin, Ben Jonson, Edmund Waller, Gilbert Sheldon, John Hales and William Chillingworth) was a centre of intellectual probing and civilising behaviour. As Hyde wrote in his *Life*, 'if he had anything good in him, in his humour, or in his manners, he owed it to the example, and the information he had received in, and from that company'.[1] Discussing religion and philosophy, much influenced by the writings of Erasmus, the members of the Circle emphasised the value of the use of reason, and condemned controversy and overreliance on the writings of previous ages, especially the early Fathers of the Church, to whom both Catholic and Arminians were at that time appealing. Only the simplest beliefs were seen as necessary for salvation, and these were self-evident in the Scriptures; details of structure and doctrine were seen as 'inessentials'. Wormald has summarised their ideas as 'unity in diversity through charity'. Problems would only develop when those with vested interests ('professional ecclesiastics') squabbled over inessentials, such as the validity of *jure divino* episcopacy. (Did bishops receive their spiritual authority through a direct line of 'laying-on of hands' going back to St Peter and Christ, or where they merely a convenient form of ecclesiastical authority?) From this approach Hyde developed his analysis of the difference between religion (those few unchangeable, incontrovertible truths) and 'Religion of State' (the changeable superstructure of hierarchies and details of liturgy and practice). The latter should be decided by the Prince to ensure good order and overall unity, but exact uniformity in details need not be required. It was an essentially pragmatic approach, in great contrast to the often frenetic religious ferment of the mid-seventeenth century. This rational, intellectual, calm approach to ideas and ideology was, as Hyde admitted, to have considerable influence on him. As a statesman he was to follow the same path; and passion and commitment to inessentials, irrational responses to rumours and inability to forget wrongs done in the past were tendencies he found difficult to comprehend.

Even while indulging in such convivial company and theorising, Hyde as a practising lawyer had become greatly concerned by what he saw as the excessive activities of the royal courts during the Personal Rule. The summoning of Parliament in 1640 seemed the opportunity to remove these violations of the law. He launched an immediate attack on the Earl Marshal's Court and emerged at once, despite his lack of parliamentary experience, as a leading critic of the Personal Rule. Having failed to persuade Laud to prevent the dissolution of the Short Parliament (realising that it was a potentially constructive body) he threw himself even more energetically into the early reforms of the Long Parliament. He joined in the attack on the prerogative councils of the North and the Marches and on certain judges (such as those involved in Hampden's Case). Active on the committee dealing with all these topics, often serving as chairman, he was a clear and unequivocal critic of the King's misuse of his authority; of the Council of the North he said that 'this "discretion" [of punishment] hath been the quicksand which hath swallowed up their property, their liberty'.[2] He was equally vehement in the impeachment of Strafford and the accusations against Finch, so emerging as a powerful critic of Court policies and personnel. Religious arguments provoked him rather less. He was not concerned with 'inessential'; he recognised the errors of Laud, but this did not lead him to challenge the principle of episcopacy, nor the King's right to govern the Church. Unlike his friend Lord Falkland, who was at first prepared to support the exclusion of bishops from the House of Lords, Hyde was a consistent defender of the structure and traditions of the Church. In an attempt to curb his comments he was appointed chairman of the committee on the bill to abolish episcopacy in the summer of 1641. It was an interesting ploy, but doubly ineffective. Not only was he not silenced, but he was summoned by the King, gratified to observe his staunch attitude, who requested him to delay the bill until Charles's visit to Scotland, which Hyde agreed to do and successfully achieved. Thus by June Hyde was in contact with Charles, and apparently co-operating with him in the handling of Parliament.

It is however far too simple to assume that it was religious conservatism which drew him to the royalist side. Indeed it has been convincingly argued by Wormald that Hyde did not become a royalist until well into 1642, and even then he was not seeking a 'royalist victory'. For Hyde, 'royalist' and 'parliamentarian' were at this stage meaningless and dangerous terms. The King had been certainly ill advised, possibly wrongly intentioned, and Parliament had fulfilled its duty by pointing out and removing areas of misgovernment; but the King was 'head and sovereign of the whole', merely assisted by his Estates and not being just one of those Estates, as Falkland argued. Parliament should no more aim to dictate to the King or usurp an executive role than the King should attempt to destroy the power of Parliament. This belief in a balanced structure of government was to be severely battered by ensuing events, but remained Hyde's target well into the war period and essentially for the whole of his life.

There were two more vital stands to his thinking. In the growing hysteria of the winter of 1641 he saw the threat of political disintegration – of disorder possibly leading to tyranny by either side; and he placed both the blame and the possible cure for this in the hands of certain individuals. Throughout his political career he believed that problems could be overcome by individual settlement (note his behaviour from 1659 onwards). At first dubious about the Earl of Bedford's plan to introduce parliamentary leaders (such as Pym and St John) onto the Privy Council, he came later to believe that Charles erred in waiting for proof of service before offering office to his critics. The King should have taken the initiative (even at York in 1640) in order to secure for his service those who were critical of his past government but were not determined to demand radical changes (the earls of Bedford and Essex, even Pym in 1641). The key to the growing crisis was mistrust, and the King must take the initiative to overcome this barrier.

These concerns led to a substantial change of emphasis in Hyde's actions in the second session of Parliament (from October 1641). He approved of the narrative section of the Grand Remonstrance as 'true and modestly expressed', but the proposed further changes, especially for parliamentary approval of the King's ministers, he regarded as preventing rather than securing a settlement, since Charles could not possibly agree; and he succeeded in delaying publication of the document, which was 'not lawful', until 15 December by threatening to publish his own counter-protest. Greatly concerned at the widening gap between the Court and most MPs, he accepted the invitation to co-operate with Sir John Culpepper (the leading opponent of Pym at this stage) and Lord Falkland, meeting them almost every night to discuss ways of protecting the King's authority from being overwhelmed. It was Hyde who wrote the skilful reply to the Remonstrance, in which the key points were his emphasis on how readily Charles had accepted the reforms of early 1641 (hence admitting his errors), and that his good intentions were confirmed by changes in the Privy Council (to include Culpepper and Falkland, former critics), which had given its full approval, and so guarantee, to the reply. Further, Charles promised to accept any legislation necessary to secure the reforms already made, and to accept a law for the relief of 'tender consciences' on things 'inessential' in religion. Such a programme of moderate changes resulting from a balanced interchange of views by King and Parliament was how Hyde believed normality must be restored. He had himself rejected the office of

Solicitor General since it would entail the sacking of Oliver St John, so even further alienating the parliamentary leadership from the Crown.

This compromise approach was effectively destroyed by succeeding events – rumours of Army plots, the bishops' protest of 30 December, above all the attempted arrest of five MPs – of which Hyde had no foreknowledge and which horrified him. Initially, it is true, these errors compelled Charles to attempt Hyde's line of compromise, ironically first by signing the Bishops' Exclusion Bill (14 February), which Hyde still opposed as an unwarranted interference in the composition of the Upper House; and so the more moderate Lords were encouraged to rally to his support. Many hoped that a balancing of the strength of both parties would lead to a settlement. The key issue was control of the militia. Hyde drafted several of the King's statements during the prolonged discussions, offering royal acceptance of parliamentarily appointed officers if a definite time limit was agreed, and if there should be statutory backing for any extra powers they might need. It was Pym's rejection of these offers which helped persuade Hyde that compromise in the present situation was impossible.

Thus we observe a further change of tack. Charles, largely through his own errors, which served to justify Pym's growing demands, was too weak to negotiate a solution to the conflict. He must therefore appeal to the public (Hyde seemed to be learning from Pym) to build up sufficient support to compel Pym to moderate Parliament's demands and in particular to reduce his own reputation for untrustworthiness. Having failed to persuade Charles to stay near London rather than obey the Queen's insistence that he travel to the north, Hyde urged him 'to shelter himself wholly under the law, to grant anything that by the law he was compelled to grant, and to deny what by the law was in his own power, and which he found inconvenient to assent to'.[3] Moral not material authority was what was necessary. Meanwhile Hyde would reverse the situation by illuminating the excesses of Pym – his use of the mob (so justifying Charles's absence from London), the harsh treatment of the Kentish petitioners who in March 1642 requested a rapid settlement with the King, and other actions 'invading the public liberty', illustrating that 'they are not unwilling to be tyrants'. It was a shrewd and partially successful plan, aimed not at raising a party to fight for Charles but at sufficiently undermining Pym's credibility and strength to force him to realistic negotiations. Hyde continued to sit at Westminster, although less regularly as he faced possible arrest owing to suspicion of his activities. This arose despite efforts to keep his contacts with Charles and authorship of his declarations secret (Charles himself once locking them in a room to ensure private discussion, and promising to destroy all correspondence). Only in May, on Charles's instructions, did Hyde finally leave London for York, to join the royal party there.

Was he at last a royalist? At the time, and throughout the war, he was assailed by the ultra-royalists, such as his former friend Lord Digby, for his 'spirit of accommodation', and the military courtiers despised and resented him. His letter to Charles suggesting that 'Your Majesty well knows that your greatest strength is in the hearts and affections of those persons who have been the severest assertors of the public liberties'[4] implies his interest in the support of the middle ground rather than the avowed royalists. He was anxious for Charles to secure the Earl of Northumberland as Lord High Admiral at the Oxford talks in January 1643 and similarly to welcome the earls of Holland, Bedford and Clare when they briefly detached themselves from Westminster that summer.

On both occasions Charles followed his wife's unforgiving advice and refused to greet the earls. Indeed, it is hard to find much influence brought by Hyde on the royalist councils during the war, especially after 1643. He was in the inner council of six at Oxford, where he resided at All Souls' College from October 1642 to March 1645. He assisted in raising money, especially from Oxford itself, and was appointed Chancellor of the Exchequer in March 1643, one month after being brought onto the Privy Council and knighted. All this was administration rather than advice. He did play a leading part in the Oxford and Uxbridge negotiations (1643 and 1645); both of course were unsuccessful, owing primarily to Parliament's insistence on a Presbyterian settlement, despite Hyde's offer at Uxbridge of substantial modifications to the Church of England and reforms such as the prohibition of pluralism. Yet only the summoning of the Oxford parliament can be seen as primarily his achievement. Over 170 MPs and eighty-two peers seem to have attended this 'parliament' in 1644, designed to expose the sectional nature of the Westminster parliament and as a protest at the Scottish 'invasion'. The parliament voted taxes of £100,000 and an excise, but achieved little of real significance. It is noteworthy that Hyde saw it effectively as a convention, to be joined when possible to the Westminster 'convention'. He was at least successful in dissuading Charles from ordering the dissolution of the Westminster parliament, a most tactless and pointless intention.

Gradually the rigidity of Parliament drove Hyde to realise the need for outright victory just when the prospects for such a victory were ebbing away. He became bitter towards the 'faction of malignant, schismatical and ambitious persons'. His final year in England before his exile was an unhappy period spent as a member of the Prince of Wales's Council in the west. Unable to control the bickering of Goring and Grenville and the resentment of all soldiers at civilian interference, he could do little to prevent parliamentary advances. His only success was to prevent the removal of Prince Charles direct to France, which would have been a gift to parliamentary propagandists. Instead in March 1646 he accompanied the prince to the Scilly Isles, a month later fleeing to Jersey to escape the parliamentary navy.

II

From 1646 until 1660 Hyde was in exile, suffering great poverty, often separated from his wife and family (of whom he was genuinely fond), frequently ill and with no certainty of a return to England. Yet he remained amazingly cheerful and active. In Jersey he commenced his *History of the Great Rebellion* – at first as a lesson to Charles of his errors in the past and guidance to wiser behaviour in the future; later as a justification of the actions of the martyred King. He also began his *Reflexions on the Psalms* and studied French literature and classical studies, working up to ten hours a day.

All this was despite a series of disastrous setbacks for his hopes. Prince Charles ignored his advice and followed his mother's orders to sail to France in July 1648. The Queen appeared to contemplate handing over the Channel Islands in payment for French aid, and Hyde even planned to call in parliamentary aid to prevent this betrayal of English interests, which fortunately did not become necessary. But he could not prevent the King's alliance with the Scots in 1648, any more than his drafting of letters from Prince Charles to General Fairfax and to several European monarchs prevented the King's execution. He was summoned in 1648 to join the Prince in France, was robbed by pirates on his way, but had little political influence once he arrived, facing as he did the hostility of Henrietta

Maria, Digby, Jermyn and Prince Rupert. His hope in 1649 of a return to England via Ireland was destroyed by Cromwell, following which the young Charles was to ignore his advice and sign the Covenant to win Scottish aid, to his ensuing humiliation. Hyde probably agreed to go on an embassy to seek Spanish aid in 1649 more to escape the embarrassments of the Scottish trip than in the hope of gaining effective help. Indeed, although he joined in further negotiations with Spain in 1655–6, he essentially believed that 'a foreign aid . . . will never reconcile those hearts and affections to the King and his Posterity, without which he hath no hope of reigning'.[5] He experienced little more than humiliation in Madrid, and was expelled in 1651.

In November 1651 he was again summoned to join Charles, and this time was able to establish himself as the most trusted advisor to the young King (now free of his mother's domination), the leading member of a guiding committee of four, although not until 1658 did he receive the rather empty title of Lord Chancellor. He still faced the hostility of the Queen Mother and her circle, but they failed to shake Charles's trust in him. An accusation of decrying Charles's behaviour and lack of commitment to business behind his back was countered when Charles himself pointed out that Hyde had spoken even more freely to his face!

There were more serious problems. The poverty of the little Court was highly embarrassing (Hyde had to borrow from friends to pay the postage on official documents); links with the French Huguenots (essentially Presbyterians) had to be avoided; royalists at home had at some stages to be roused from despair, at others discouraged from over-rash ventures. Hyde realised that both Penruddock's and Booth's risings were premature, but could not prevent all such actions. A plan to appoint a new master of the Court of Wards had to be resisted as politically disastrous. The miniature Court was forced out of France in 1654, and failed to secure effective Spanish aid in 1655.

Despite all this Hyde remained confident that success would be achieved, and that the King's enemies would be divided and fall; his study of the Psalms confirmed his belief in the working of Divine Providence. The essential point was for the royalists to avoid errors: God would restore England to its true constitutional path in good time.

III

If there is one achievement almost universally ascribed to Hyde, it is the success of the peaceful and untrammelled restoration in 1660. Hyde was to write of 'such an extraordinary influence of divine providence, that there appears no footsteps of human power in the deliverance',[6] and it is tempting to agree with him. Certainly the royalists played little part in creating the divisions within the Army; certainly the Rump brought final discredit on itself in the early weeks of 1660; certainly Monk showed no inclination to seize the power probably within his grasp. It is also true that the Convention of 1660 had a much larger proportion of royalists (supporters of a virtually unconditional restoration) than is often realised, forming probably the largest grouping until many of the younger MPs drifted off to their estates in the summer.[7] In many ways the crown fell into Charles's hands without him needing to stir.

Yet that is not the whole story. The prime essential for Charles was to avoid any tactless actions which could damage his prospects. Hyde had more success with son than with father. It is true that in 1659 Charles ignored his pleas and dashed to Fontarabia to try to gain the assistance of France or Spain now that they were at last ending their war. This chimera failed, and Hyde was able to exclude all foreign participation in the events of 1660, thus avoiding English resentment and keeping Charles free of foreign obligations. Equally, Hyde was prepared to negotiate with anyone – Fleetwood, Lambert, Monk among potential leaders, but also a whole range of less significant individuals – and was kept frantically busy coping with a mass of correspondence, differentiating between men of value, and those less useful or trustworthy, winning over by dint of private promises (of pardon, title, or office) men such as Admiral Montagu and Anthony Ashley Cooper. By using individual communication rather than public declarations Hyde gave himself a much freer hand. Furthermore, as early as 1656 he had written to Ormonde, 'When they are obstinate to insist on an unreasonable proposition that you find it necessary to consent to, let it be with this clause, "If a free Parliament shall think fit to ask the same of his majesty".'[8] Thus early did the crucial clauses of the Declaration of Breda emerge.

By 1658 Hyde had been persuaded that Monk was the best hope for securing the King's return, and indirect contact was made through his brother Nicholas. In fact Monk was one of the last people openly to admit his intention of a restoration, and real negotiations only began in March 1660. At first Monk suggested terms (demanding in particular only five exceptions to a general indemnity, and safe possession for holders of confiscated royalist lands) which Hyde regarded as unacceptable and, thanks largely to the strong position the royalists were in owing to his mass of correspondence, was able to modify to those expressed in the Declaration of Breda of 4 April.

Thus the various pitfalls – English resentment at foreign interference, Presbyterian terms such as the 1648 Isle of Wight Treaty, a military counter-reaction – were avoided. Charles kept a low profile; private treaties were made with many influential men; the tide of royalist reaction in England was gently fostered (young royalists were encouraged to win seats in the Convention); and an apparently moderate and undemanding King graciously agreed to return on terms to be decided by his people in Parliament. In all this Hyde had played a crucial and successful part.

Thus he returned from fourteen years poverty-stricken exile to observe the surge of emotional rejoicing – though perhaps a little surprised to hear reports of the celebrations at Ripon in which girls in white dresses were crowned 'in honour of their "Virgin–King" '.

IV

There is no space here for a discussion of the powers of the monarchy in 1660. It is more appropriate to examine Hyde's own views on the correct structure of English government, and then to examine how successfully he put these into operation.

It was natural for Hyde, as an historian, to search for lessons on how to avoid the mistakes of the past. He had been a parliamentary leader in early 1641 and assumed that those hectic months had seen the correct guidelines laid down. Hence the prerogative courts were illegal, and the Court of Wards and last vestiges of the feudal system encouraging interference in men's property best left unrevived. The King must realise that prolonged periods without Parliament could lead to a dangerous gulf in understanding and knowledge between Crown and nation. Yet government must be by king, not king and Parliament; that is, the king must have full power to appoint ministers, decide government policies, protect England's interests by controlling all foreign relations, govern the Church, and have the final prerogative power (control of the armed forces, and dispensing power) necessary for efficient and fair government. Thus the Crown had lost its excessive powers, but preserved its initiative in government. Parliament should be freely elected (and left free of Court influence during its sittings), its functions the traditional ones of granting the necessary funds (especially now that Crown Lands were negligible) and presenting advice and grievances. It must ignore its executive experience during the Civil War and Interregnum; attempts, for instance, to supervise government expenditure were constitutionally unacceptable.

If these ideas seemed to pave the way towards a revival of the Personal Rule, by preserving much of the royal prerogative and limiting the functions of Parliament, the prevention of such a course lay in Hyde's belief in the central role of the Privy Council. 'The body of it is the most sacred, and hath the greatest authority in the government next the person of the king himself.'[9] In this paramount organ of government the king should meet regularly his ministers of state, selected from men of outstanding social or political significance. There he would listen to the advice of the most influential of his subjects, not professional bureaucrats or foppish favourites. It was a body which should bind together all the departments of state and supervise a coherent administration of policy. Neither Elizabeth, who had dominated her Council, nor the early Stuarts, who had allowed favourites to predominate, or excluded significant interests, had followed such a course. Nor was it forward-looking, since Hyde saw no close connection between Parliament and such a Council, which would not be selected by Parliament, nor necessarily represent its factions. It was essentially a medieval idea, socially prestigious but taking little account of the growing complexity of government and the need for specific expertise. Indeed, he disliked the tendency of the Council to set up sub-committes (such as that on trade and foreign plantations). The growing size of the Council (soon verging on forty members), and the admixture of royalists and former Presbyterians, did persuade him to set up a 'secret' committee for foreign affairs in June 1660, which in reality decided a whole range of policy decisions. But it was essentially a smaller version of his ideal Council, consisting as it did only of men holding high office.

V

[Although Edward Hyde was not created Earl of Clarendon until April 1661, it will be convenient to refer to him by this title from now on.]

There has been much controversy about Clarendon's attitude towards the religious settlement of the Restoration period. Bosher has argued that he was throughout a staunch Anglican, Abernathy that he consistently worked for comprehension, Green that he started as an Anglican but ameliorated this position to keep Charles's favour, Witcombe that he began by favouring comprehension but shifted to intolerant Anglicanism to keep the favour of Parliament.[10]

Certainly there is much conflicting evidence: letters written at the same time to men of differing religious attitudes often express substantially different ideas. He could write of the 'seditious designs' of the Presbyterians (1661) and that 'I am not much in love with your Presbyterians' (1659), and yet strive to protect Presbyterian ministers hounded by Anglican JPs, and give full support to the Act for Settling Ministers passed in September 1660 protecting the Presbyterian ministers established during the Interregnum by confirming their livings. It is important to remember what has been noted earlier – his idea of 'Religion of State'. The structure of a Church was changeable, and therefore we can expect a pragmatic approach; it was to be decided by the prince, so we can expect an emphasis on prerogative freedom of action. Certainly all historians are agreed that he followed a pragmatic, even devious, course until 1663, and it seems likely that he was not totally committed to any precise settlement, adjusting his ideas as circumstances altered.

Certain extraneous factors must also be noted. The Presbyterians played their cards badly. Predominantly out-manoeuvred in the Convention, overwhelmed in the Cavalier Parliament, they were divided and disorganised, overconfident and overdemanding (especially so in the case of Baxter). Foolishly hostile to toleration for any other group (Independents or Catholics), they lost potential allies and made comprehension difficult to justify. Also, even by the summer of 1660 a great Anglican reaction could be observed in the country. The Prayer Book was soon widely in use, JPs were quickly in action persecuting non-Anglican ministers (probably 695 were forced out of their parishes during 1660[11]), and petitions came from counties such as Northamptonshire and Somerset for the complete restoration of the Church of England. The elections to the Cavalier Parliament confirmed this trend, and from that moment any concessions to non-Anglicans would have to be forced through in the face of vigorous opposition from Parliament and most of the gentry. The Anglican clergy had done valuable work winning the support of the gentry during the Interregnum, then and later the work of Gilbert Sheldon being most influential.

Clarendon himself did much to support the Anglican Church. He was an old friend of Sheldon, had powerfully resisted a Presbyterian settlement in the 1640s and 1650s, and made little effort to interfere while the bishops and deans extracted large sums of money from the new leases as they regained control of Church lands. Charles's coronation was according to the full Anglican rites, and the bishops took precedence over the lay peers. He described the Prayer Book as the 'best we have seen', far superior to the Protestant services he had seen abroad with their 'great and scandalous Indecency'. He never doubted that monarchy and Anglicanism were necessarily co-existent, and that episcopacy was essential for good order.

Yet the predominant impression one receives is that, certainly until the end of 1662, Clarendon sought a settlement based on comprehension, although he differentiated between acceptable moderates such as Baxter, Calamy and Reynolds and radicals such as Zachary Crofton and various 'seditious preachers'. The offer of bishoprics to the former was not just the 'taking off of the leading men' – if more than Reynolds had accepted, there would have been a substantial impact on the episcopal bench. The Worcester House Declaration of October 1661 (after meetings between leading Anglicans and Presbyterians at Clarendon's home) offered very real concessions, and many of its suggestions (for presbyters in each diocese, and suffragan bishops) were long-term reforms rather than mere delaying gestures. Clarendon persuaded the Lords to block the Commons' efforts to reverse the Act for Settling Ministers; and he delayed the business of Convocation in 1661 to enable the Savoy House Conference to reach a settlement first, and was distressed and disappointed when Baxter's unyielding stance prevented it from reaching agreement. With the passing of the Act of Uniformity in 1662, Clarendon proposed a proviso whereby the King might retain in a living any minister he thought suitable – a move rejected by the Commons. He then suggested a three-month suspension of the Act (blocked by the judges) and a plan in August for individual dispensations for some Presbyterian ministers. Sheldon's success in preventing this plan led to a bitter quarrel between the two old friends. Less publicly Clarendon had often intervened to ameliorate the actions of persecuting JPs in the counties, and attempted to secure financial support for those ministers driven from their livings.

The culmination of this problem arrives with Charles's Declaration of Indulgence of December 1662, the uncertainty about Clarendon's attitude being harder to elucidate owing to his prolonged absence from Court (October 1662 to March 1663) through illness. The detailed draft of the document was drawn up by Henry Bennet, who had suggested such a plan in the summer. Although Charles, Bennet and other Councillors visited his bedside to discuss it, and his ally Secretary Nicholas raised no objection when it was discussed in full Council, Clarendon wrote to Ormonde (in code) to express his disapproval of the scheme. It seems likely that he believed the Declaration was too general and loosely worded, and his concern about Charles's intention to assist the Catholics may account for his doubts. He was at least totally consistent in his opposition at all times to any toleration for Catholics.

The explanation may well be that he favoured the use of the King's dispensing power when there was specific justification, but was dubious of the use of the suspending power against the clearly stated will of the political nation. As he wrote in Charles's speech accepting the Act of Uniformity, 'the execution of these sharp laws depends on the wisdom of the most discerning, generous and merciful prince'.[12] Having failed to achieve comprehension, the most that could be achieved was individual relief for moderate nonconformists. After failing to give support to Bennet's attempt to give the Declaration statutory backing in March, he was used no more as Charles's spokesman on religious affairs and took virtually no part in the debates on the Conventicle and Five Mile acts. It all seems more like a disillusioned retreat from his hopes for comprehension up to 1662 than a specific change of course, even if he did try for political reasons in his later years to appear as the staunch defender of Anglicanism, thereby giving his name to the Clarendon Code.

VI

Despite intrigues by opponents in the Convention and at Court, Clarendon was from the very start Charles's leading minister. He realised the necessity of giving several Presbyterians important positions, but key offices went to his supporters the Earl of Southampton (the Treasury) and Edward Nicholas (Secretary of State), and he could also rely on the help of the Earl of Ormonde until he left for Ireland in 1662. Clarendon dominated the Committee for Foreign Affairs and the naturally indolent Charles was content to leave the details of supervision of the administration to him, although Clarendon rejected Ormande's suggestion that he should become a 'first minister', since the English 'would not bear a favourite, nor any one man who should, out of his ambition, engross to himself the disposal of the public affairs'.[13] It was partly for this reason that he was so infuriated by his daughter Anne's clandestine marriage in 1660 to the Duke of York – the outbursts of resentment and envy were often vitriolic. He was also reluctant to receive titles (rejecting the Garter), and, although he accepted a gift of £20,000 as a recompense for his sufferings in exile, and thirty acres in London and Westminster, he rejected the offer of 10,000 acres in the Fens, since it would then be harder to restrain the King's extravagance to others. He faced perennial niggling hostility at Court, especially from Lady Castlemaine, the Duke of Buckingham, the Earl of Bristol and Sir Henry Bennet. The appointment of Bennet as Secretary of State in October 1662 in place of Clarendon's associate Sir Edward Nicholas was a serious blow to the Chancellor's position at Court; many saw this as the beginning of the replacement of the 'old guard' by the new generation of young royalists, such as Bennet, Bristol and Sir Charles Berkeley. The attempt by Bristol to bring about his impeachment in 1663 (for selling of offices, advising the sale of Dunkirk and other mostly imagined crimes) was in fact premature, ill-founded and effectively destroyed by Charles's support for his Chancellor. Bennet and Buckingham, however, were already starting more effective campaigns for his removal, as will shortly be observed.

Unfortunately Clarendon's supremacy did not ensure efficient government. His insistence that 'men of quality' rather than men of business should hold high office, and his insistence on supervising all aspects himself and discouraging initiative in junior officials resulted in a hidebound administration. In particular his support for Southampton prevented essential reforms in the Treasury and he sneered angrily at Sir George Downing and 'fellows of his condition' who saw the need for substantial improvements. He took some small measures to speed up the work of the Court of Chancery, but his period of office was a regrettable hiatus between the Protectorate and later periods of reform.

Even more serious was his handling of Parliament. This was clumsy and uncertain, promising Parliament much initiative (in the Declaration of Breda) then resisting many of its recommendations; denying the Court's right to interfere in parliamentary affairs, yet showing resentment when Parliament made specific demands. He formed an unofficial committee to create a link between the Court and Parliament but it was too casual and unclear in purpose to have much effect. When Charles insisted on adding Bennet and William Coventry to this committee, Clarendon replied that 'meetings and cabals in Parliament had always been odious in Parliament', but he had to accept with distaste the new scheme of bargainings and wheedlings, promises and presents, to win votes. Only in 1664, when he arranged for the backbencher Sir Robert Paston to suggest a grant of £2.5 million for the coming Dutch war did his restrained approach really work. His own personal interventions in the Lords could be more effective, as when in 1661 he dissuaded the House from passing the first Bill of Uniformity and demanding thirteen more exemptions from the Act of Indemnity. By 1664 he was losing control of the House of Commons, vainly trying to keep foreign policy out of its debates and unsuccessfully resisting its demands, in 1665, to appropriate supply and, in 1666, to set up commissioners to examine the war accounts. Such demands he saw as 'a new encroachment which had no bottom'.

Legislation in this period therefore did not always reflect his own policies. He failed to secure an effective royal veto on the nomination of mayors in the Corporation Act; he failed to prevent the passing of the Irish Cattle Bills (to protect the rents of English landlords by blocking imports of cheap Irish cattle) in 1663 and 1666. It was only with the greatest difficulty that he was able to curb the vindictive desire of many to exclude large numbers from the Act of Indemnity (in the event only ten were executed). Those measures beneficial to royal power – the Militia Act, the extended Treason Act, even the relaxed Triennial Act of 1664 – were the result of the enthusiasm of MPs rather than any orchestrated government programme.

On the contentious issue of the land settlement, Clarendon accepted the impracticality, as well as unfairness, of expecting a restoration of the situation before the war, as many royalists wanted. Crown lands must be regained at once, Church lands when possible (he envisaged this taking some time); others must fend for themselves. No statute could cover all the various complications and individual experiences, and with much land in the hands of ex-soldiers (whose loyalty he still regarded with concern) and merchants (whose loans were urgently needed) widespread confiscations or forced sales were not to be envisaged. His calm thinking made him understand that royalists had no option but to be loyal, and the mass of those who had prospered during the Interregnum should not be provoked. Unfortunately 'indemnity for the king's enemies and oblivion for his friends' succeeded in winning the loyal adherence of neither group, although it is not easy to imagine a feasible alternative.

Clarendon has been much condemned for the inadequacies of the Restoration financial settlement. In reality the figures *agreed* by the Cavalier Parliament, to provide an income of £1.2 million to match estimated expenditure, have been shown to be realistic proposals,[14] and Parliament did show its willingness (for instance, by the Hearth Tax) to make up the shortfall obvious by 1663, and to make substantial grants for the Dutch war. There was certainly financial discomfort at first (since in 1660 income was less than £800,000), but by 1664 the situation looked much healthier. Only the war itself, together with the Plague and the Fire of London, and indeed the failures of the government itself, caused the years 1664–70 to be ones of dire financial difficulty. It is almost certainly true that Clarendon, aware of Charles's tendency to extravagance, preferred to keep the Crown's finances tight rather than comfortable. It was a not unreasonable approach from one who remembered the 1630s, and there can be no certainty that Parliament would readily have voted unjustifiably larger sums.

Burnet claimed of Clarendon that 'he had not a right notion of foreign matters'. This is rather too harsh. He was regarded as a skilled negotiator, and did have a specific policy: to avoid war if England's interests could be otherwise protected. He would have preferred a Protestant royal marriage, but was soon converted to the advantages of the Portuguese offer: 'we have very ill luck if, in the East and West Indies, they [the merchants] do not make incredible benefit by the concessions'.[15] Similarly, he probably did not suggest the sale of

Dunkirk, pointing out to Parliament in May 1662 the losses likely 'if it were in enemy hands', but once persuaded of the financial necessity (it was costing over £100,000 a year merely to garrison, let alone maintain) he was the principal negotiator and raised the French offer from 2 million to 5 million livres, by originally demanding 12 million! He was also responsible for negotiating the Dutch treaty of 1662 which attempted to settle commercial differences. Predominantly Clarendon favoured a French rather than Spanish alignment, and both the Portuguese marriage and the sale of Dunkirk can be seen as aiming to consolidate this. By 1667, however, he had become concerned about the developing French threat to the Netherlands; but he did not feel politically strong enough to challenge Charles's continuing pro-French policy.

The developing conflict between English and Dutch trading companies he regarded with great concern. The African conquests of 1664 were made 'without any shadow of justice', although he regarded New Amsterdam as legitimate English property. Above all he was aware of the nation's unpreparedness for war. When war came he was proved all too correct. The English at least held their own for the first two years, but the only justification for the war was outright and overwhelming success. The disaster of the Medway in 1667 resulted as much from the effects of the Fire of London as from ministers' misjudgement of Dutch intentions – there simply was no money to borrow for the future. But no government can escape the blame for such a fiasco, particularly with such clear evidence of gross inefficiency in the naval dockyards. Clarendon's failing was neither to equip the nation for war nor to prevent its outbreak. This resulted not from misunderstanding the European situation, but from political failings at home.

VII

The downfall of Clarendon must be seen in two distinct stages. His removal from office was near-inevitable, and not unreasonable. The failures of the war, weak Crown finances, inefficient government and the hostile attitude of Parliament were all ultimately his responsibility, since he attempted to supervise virtually every aspect of government. Charles was tired of his prickly, proud and often abrupt Chancellor. Remarks such as 'Indeed you are to blame that you have not given your warrant', and the often arbitrary fixing of times and places for meetings were unlikely to preserve Charles's affection, and there had been angry quarrels over Clarendon's hostility to Lady Castlemaine. But it was not just personal spite. Parliament was no longer prepared to tolerate his continuance in power, and a hiatus between Crown and Parliament was inevitable if he were not removed. Sir William Coventry was insistent that he must go in order to permit necessary reforms in the administration. On 26 August 1667 Charles requested his resignation. Clarendon refused, hinting that he could still manage Parliament. Four days later Charles sent Sir William Morrice to demand the return of the Great Seal. Clarendon was devastated, while Lady Castlemaine and most courtiers quite literally danced with delight.

However, impeachment was not inevitable. Many in Parliament, infuriated in particular by his suggestion that summer of a dissolution and by the continued maintenance and billeting of troops after the ending of the war, wished to take further action, but they were not in a majority and without Court encouragement and indeed pressure there was no chance of success. Coventry was satisfied, and refused to join in the impeachment. Bennet gave reluctant support, fearful of his own impeachment. The pressure came from the Duke of Buckingham, with a group of ambitious politicians – Thomas Osborne, Edward Seymour, Sir Richard Temple. Already planning the distribution of offices, they realised that the father-in-law of the heir to the throne must be politically destroyed to prevent any possible comeback, whatever Charles might promise. By 5 October Buckingham, playing on Charles's vanity and perhaps inclination to cruelty, had convinced the King, who seems to have believed Buckingham's claim to have potential control over the Commons, that Clarendon must be impeached.

Seymour introduced the attack, but the Seventeen Articles presented to the Commons did not amount to treason, merely predominantly unsubstantiated claims about the acceptance of bribes or giving of evil advice. The first Article was rejected by 172 votes to 103. Only Article 16, of betraying war secrets to the French, was accepted after an unproven accusation made by Lord Vaughan. Thus no specific charges could be presented to the Lords, who, rigorous as always in their demands for legal proof, rejected them, and a bitter struggle between the Houses ensued. Clarendon would have been safe if Charles had not shown his intention to take the affair

out of Parliament's hands and hand it over to a Commission of
Twenty-four Peers, appointed by himself to ensure condemnation of
the man who had governed England for him for seven years.
Clarendon saw the threat, and on 27 November fled to France, after
first securing a promise that his estates would be left untouched.
Three weeks later Parliament passed a bill of perpetual banishment.

For nearly seven more years he survived his second period of exile.
Again his energy was undiminished. He completed his *History* and
wrote his *Life*, studied Italian, and composed a mass of other writings.
Life at first was as difficult as in the 1650s – he was almost murdered
by a group of unpaid English sailors in 1668, and only the signing of
the Triple Alliance, dividing Louis from Charles, reduced Louis's
hostility to his residence in France. He died in 1674 in Rouen. Charles
had refused him permission to return home for his final days,
although his family was allowed to bury him, without memorial, in
Westminster Abbey.

VIII

The truth is, his behaviour and humour was grown so insupport-
able to myself and all the world else, that I could no longer endure
it, and it was impossible to live with it, and do those things with the
parliament that must be done, or the government will be lost.[16]

Unappealing as Charles's treatment may be, his explanation of the
necessity to remove Clarendon cannot be disputed – except in his
assumption that his government would be better handled in future.
Clarendon by 1667 was enormously unpopular with courtiers,
Cavaliers, Presbyterians, Catholics and the mob, who had placed a
gibbet outside his new house in the Strand, unluckily completed in
1667 just when Londoners were suffering so much from recent
disasters, from which Clarendon seemed so obviously exempt.

He was almost certainly not corrupt. He rejected the offer of a
French bribe during the Dunkirk negotiations, and Charles frequently mocked his scruples. He made much money, and collected
many presents, particularly a fine collection of paintings, of which he
was especially fond, but so did all chancellors and leading ministers.
He was, however, proud, often heated in his treatment of others, and
careless of the need to generate popularity at Court and in the

country, while his arrogant treatment of officials prevented much-needed reforms in the administration. More significantly, his ministry appeared to lack direction. He was too often prepared to give way, over comprehension and the Dutch war in particular, betraying his own beliefs and stated aims. The result was a failure of his intended policies and the hostility of several significant sections of the community. By 1667 he had very few, mostly rather obscure, supporters in Parliament. He had lost touch with the political developments of the Restoration period.

This was his greatest failing. In looking at his career before 1660 one must admire his intelligence, range of interests, moderation, common sense and patience. From 1660 one is disturbed by his willingness to give way on policies in which he believed, and his unwillingness to work at the personal relationships necessary for success as a seventeenth-century minister. He became too complacent, too obstinate in resisting changes that were necessary in the structure of government, too isolated to be able to insist on his own policies consistently. It was tragic that a man so successful in securing the King's return should be so unsuccessful in preserving the affection of the people, which he so clearly understood to lie at the basis of royal power.

8. Anthony Ashley Cooper, Earl of Shaftesbury

TIMOTHY EUSTACE

> In friendship false, implacable in hate,
> Resolved to ruin or to rule the state.
>
> Dryden, *Absalom and Achitophel*

FEW politicians have aroused as much venemous hatred as the first Earl of Shaftesbury. Dryden's piercing character assassination expressed the views of virtually all those who supported Charles II during the Exclusion Crisis. Shaftesbury did have some popularity with the London populace, but few of the Whigs in Parliament felt great affection for him, and their successors of the post-1688 period showed no inclination to restore his reputation after Tory propagandists had demolished it. It is unfortunate that his destruction of most of his papers (in order to prevent Charles's government from using them to secure his conviction) has removed the most useful evidence for understanding his motives; without them his actions all too often give an impression of inconsistency and ruthlessness, both of which characteristics were mercilessly exposed by Dryden. Most historians have found him a somewhat perplexing subject – Professor Clayton Roberts has described him as 'a cross between a John Pym and a second duke of Buckingham'.[1] Professor Haley's invaluable biography of Shaftesbury goes some way towards restoring his reputation, but his character remains somewhat elusive.

Yet Shaftesbury, more than any of his contemporaries, understood how to mould and create a political party, the first such party to emerge in British politics. Its failure during and immediately after the Exclusion Crisis should not blind us to the insight and skill he showed

179

between 1673 and 1681 in developing techniques of political opposition which served as a lesson to succeeding generations. His previous experience of office during both the Interregnum and the first thirteen years of the Restoration period makes his career even more illuminating on the politics of the seventeenth century, and on the responses of a member of a wealthy gentry family to the many political changes in his lifetime. It is worth considering not only his political significance, but also whether the friend and patron of the great political philosopher John Locke could have been as unsympathetic and selfishly ambitious as he is often portrayed to be.

I

Anthony Ashley Cooper was born at Wimborne, in Dorset, in 1621. His father, Sir John Cooper, died in 1631, so the person with the greatest influence on his upbringing was his maternal grandfather, Sir Anthony Ashley, an Elizabethan courtier and official, and a friend of Sir Walter Ralegh. The young Anthony was without doubt brought up to be aware of the glorious Elizabethan past and its contrast with the less impressive Stuart era. A year at Exeter College, Oxford, ensured a Puritan education. Add family links with Sir John Eliot and one can see the background from which many of his later ideas might emerge, especially since Dorset was a Puritan county which showed much disaffection to the Crown in the 1630s.

For some time there was little sign of the emergence of such ideas. He enjoyed the traditional upbringing of a prosperous member of the gentry. A year each at Oxford and Lincoln's Inn prepared him for his expected role in local government; marriage in 1639 to the daughter of Lord Keeper Coventry ensured his election for the borough of Tewkesbury in the Short Parliament, and a useful Court connection. An income of around £3000 allowed him to maintain a standard of living to match that of many nobles, and ownership of large estates in the south-west established him as a young man of considerable local influence. Intelligent, interested in practical affairs and estate management, skilful at influencing people around him, his only apparent disadvantages were his short stature and later ill health, which was to plague much of his adult life.

In October 1640, however, he failed to gain election to the Long Parliament, his connection with the Court now turning to his disadvantage as the country reacted against the dissolution of the Short Parliament. So he was absent from Westminster during the events which led to the Civil War, and there is no record of his attitude to the issues being debated. Much of his family background suggested support for Parliament; his connections with the Coventrys (with whom he now spent most of his time) drew him strongly to the royalist camp. Although he visited Charles at Nottingham and was made Deputy Lieutenant of Dorset, it was only in the summer of 1643 that he returned home after much procrastination and raised a regiment to fight for the King. This hesitation in choosing which side to fight for was of course common to many of the gentry at this time.

Far more unusual was his decision in February 1644 to travel to London and swear loyalty to Parliament and the Covenant. Any explanation of this event must be tentative. He clearly disliked the arrival in Dorset of Prince Maurice, who sacked Dorchester after Sir Anthony had been one of those who persuaded it to surrender, and who ensured his removal from the governorship of Weymouth. This interference by brash soldiers in his county, the influence of Henrietta Maria and the 'hot-heads' on Charles, and the Cessation in Ireland may all have combined to persuade him that the royalists posed a greater threat to the traditional customs and forms of government, national and local, than Parliament. It was a brave move, since Parliament's victory was by no means certain, and most of his estates lay in royalist territory. In the event, his prospects improved rapidly. As an important parliamentary leader in Dorset, he took part in the vicious sacking of Abbotsbury, and in 1647 was made Sheriff of Wiltshire, also regaining his estates. We do not know his views on the developing conflict between Parliament and the Army from 1647. The execution of Charles had no apparent effect on him, and he continued to serve as a JP and commissioner of taxes. But his second marriage, in 1650, to Lady Frances Cecil related him to the Earl of Salisbury, a moderate supporter of Parliament.

Then in 1652 the young Sir Anthony, still only thirty, became quite suddenly a figure of national significance. He was named a member of the commission set up by the Rump Parliament to reform the law, and so came into direct contact with Oliver Cromwell. The next year he was appointed to both the Nominated Assembly, in which he sat on most of the important committees, and the Council of State. He was one of the leading moderates in both Council and Assembly, active in suppressing Lilburne's 'scandalous pamphlets', opposing the abolition of tithes until a viable alternative had been found, and taking a major part in the dissolution of the Assembly in December, disturbed by its inefficiency and the outbursts of its radical minority. He was one of the fifteen men appointed to the new Council of State under the Instrument of Government, where again he was active on committees, especially those dealing with what were now emerging as his main political interests – law, finance, and trade. In 1654 he was elected MP for Dorset in the first Protectorate parliament.

Close links with Cromwell were now developing. The two men had different backgrounds and careers, but both shared a belief in wide toleration, were essentially pragmatic, had a keen interest in major reform of the creaking and unfair legal system of the time, and in the final instance desired to protect the interests of the gentry. Sir Anthony, a man of wealth, local significance and energy was admirably suited to the needs of the administration. He frequently visited Cromwell's house, and soon after the death of Lady Frances Cooper in 1652 there were rumours of a possible marriage between Sir Anthony and Mary Cromwell.

Instead, in 1655 he married Margaret Spencer, sister of the first Earl of Sunderland and niece of the Earl of Southampton – both royalists. This third and most contented marriage was to last his lifetime. It was only possible because he had already quarrelled with Cromwell. He had become concerned about the drift towards military rule confirmed in the establishment of the rule of the major generals, stopped attending the Council, and argued publicly that it was illegal to collect or pay taxes not voted by Parliament. In 1656 he was excluded by Cromwell from sitting in the second Protectorate parliament and was only allowed to sit in 1658 after the creation of the Upper House, which he then proceeded to attack as politically subservient and socially insignificant.

Despite this, in 1655 and again in 1659 he refused offers from Charles of a pardon and reward if he would assist the royalists. He continued to be a supporter of Parliament against any risk of arbitrary government. His speeches emphasised the traditional rights of Parliament and the people, and argued the need for the landowning classes to dominate the political machinery of the country. After Oliver Cromwell's death, he continued to oppose the Protectorate, but its collapse did him little good. In May 1659 he was voted onto the Council of State by the restored Rump, but in July stopped attending it and retired to Wimborne. By then there were strong but unjustified

rumours that he was a royalist. Still supporting republican government, he was one of those who persuaded the agents of General Monk
that he could be sure of widespread support against the other
scheming generals, and actively promoted propaganda for the recall
of a free Parliament.

But he was overtaken by the changing mood of the country, and the
political skill of Edward Hyde. Back on the Council of State again in
January 1660, he was a member of the Suffolk House group (with the
Earl of Manchester, Fairfax, Holles and others), who hoped to ensure
that Charles would sign the articles of the proposed Isle of Wight
Treaty (1648), including the clause that Parliament should have the
right to nominate the King's ministers for a period of twenty years.
But the Declaration of Breda out-manoeuvred them, and Sir
Anthony, one of the parliamentary commissioners, was required to
greet Charles's return on terms which he almost certainly regarded as
too generous. Despite having come to individual terms with Edward
Hyde, he was a late and uncertain convert to the Restoration.

II

Nevertheless, his position in 1660 turned out to be a promising one.
He was not greedy for titles, as were so many; he had proved his
ability on parliamentary committees, had emerged as a leading
moderate politican, opposed to Cromwell, had earned the respect of
Hyde, and was married to the niece of the new Lord Treasurer. So his
elevation to the Privy Council, and in 1661 to the post of Chancellor of
the Exchequer and to the House of Lords as Baron Ashley, was the
result of proven ability and useful contacts. He worked hard to
confirm this. He was a government spokesman in Parliament and sat
on forty-one of the fifty-four Privy Council committees, and his ability,
hard work, efficiency and honesty were soon being remarked upon.
Pepys was to write in 1665, 'My Lord Ashley, I observe, is a most
clear man in matters of accounts, and most ingeniously did discourse
and explain matters.'[2] An insistence on receiving detailed information and clarity in organising and understanding those details were
features that distinguished him from many royal officials.

Yet although Charles visited his house at Wimborne twice in 1665
he was never quite an intimate of the King, and so had limited
political power, especially as he was becoming increasingly opposed

to the Earl of Clarendon. In 1662 his sympathy for dissenters led him to support the first Declaration of Indulgence, after having opposed the Act of Uniformity. He argued that the best way to achieve toleration was to persuade the Anglicans to trust the King; clearly the royal prerogative could be a beneficial instrument. He also opposed Clarendon over the Second Anglo-Dutch War, despite his knowledge of the government's financial weakness, because his connections with many London merchants had persuaded him of its necessity. Nevertheless he played no part in Clarendon's downfall, and opposed his committal to the Tower. He had little time for the manoeuvrings and in-fighting at Court, and disliked the vindictiveness of the attacks on Clarendon. Although his quick wit made him a frequent member of Charles's drinking-parties, he was already uncomfortable in the Court's selfish and cynical atmosphere.

Further promotion, therefore, seemed unlikely. In 1662 he had supported the royal prerogative over the question of toleration, and did so again in 1672, arguing then and later that royal supremacy in ecclesiastical affairs was correct and beneficial. But in 1666 he opposed the House of Lords' vote to allow royal dispensations in the Irish Cattle Bill (intended to limit the import of cheap Irish cattle), a bill which as a Dorset landowner he fervently supported. In 1667, when the Earl of Southampton died, Ashley did not, as expected, succeed him as Lord Treasurer, and only just scraped onto the new Treasury Commission, although he soon became one of its most regular and expert members. His contributions during the period of the Commission were substantial. He cut down on claims made on the Treasury, and encouraged the replacement of the customs farmers by commissioners to collect the revenue direct. He opposed the Stop of the Exchequer as undermining the credit system on which the government depended. Yet his skill and financial expertise did not make him one of the most influential members of the Cabal, and he seems to have had little influence on the King. Significantly, he was only informed of the 'public' clauses of the Treaty of Dover; as a Treasury commissioner, it would be his responsibility to find the money needed for the ensuing war.

Then in 1672 his prospects suddenly improved. He was created Earl of Shaftesbury and in November appointed Lord Chancellor. With only one year's legal training, he was not an obvious candidate to be a successful Chancellor, but he had long been interested in legal affairs and had no doubts of his own capability, expecting to hold the office for several years. In a major speech in 1673 he expressed his belief that 'the ease and safety of the people [are] inseparable from the greatness and security of the crown'.[3] But Charles had appointed him primarily for the role he could play in Parliament. Before the 1673 session of Parliament, he issued writs for thirty-six by-elections to the Commons, a move to increase the size of the Court party and one for which he was to be strongly attacked for usurping the role of the Speaker. His famous speech at the opening session required Parliament to support the war: 'But you judged aright [in 1664] that at any rate *Delenda est Carthago*, that government was to be brought down, and therefore the King may well say to you, this is your war.'[4]

Money was indeed voted (though not enough), but only on condition that the 1672 Declaration of Indulgence was withdrawn. Shaftesbury urged Charles not to give way; toleration was more important than the war. Charles ignored his pleas and a breach began to appear. The Test Act widened it. Shaftesbury supported it ostensibly to get money voted for the war; his previous behaviour suggests that it was more on principle, as his suspicions of James Duke of York's Catholicism were confirmed. Concern about the true nature of the Treaty of Dover and about the possible emergence of a Catholic absolute monarchy in England created a great division between Chancellor and King. Outright hostility with James now developed, and James and Lauderdale urged that he must go. In November Charles agreed, and Shaftesbury was required to resign; in May 1674 he was removed from the Privy Council. Shrewdly, he demanded a royal pardon for all his actions before handing over his seals, a protection as much against Parliament as the King.

III

'It is only laying down my gown, and putting on my sword.'[5] Certainly Shaftesbury had little respect or trust for Charles, and this feeling was reciprocated; and he had become suspicious of James not just because of his religion but also because of his political ideas, which were showing strong tendencies towards absolutism. Thirteen years of considerable service to the Crown had brought high office and prosperity but little real power. However, he had lived with his doubts in 1660 and it is probable that in 1673 his aim was not entrenched opposition but a rapid return to office by persuading

Charles to come to terms with Parliament, and in particular to divorce his wife Catherine in order to remarry and produce a Protestant heir to displace the dangerous James. Such an idea was not too far-fetched. In 1670 Lord Roos had brought in a private bill for a divorce, opposed by the bishops but supported by Shaftesbury in the Lords. Charles had shown a keen interest and attended the debates. Was he interested in such a precedent? Many thought so, and Shaftesbury was for many years to urge this on Charles as the solution to the crisis which was to develop.

Instead Charles turned to Danby and his Anglican, Cavalier policy, and Shaftesbury found himself rejected by the Court and regarded with some suspicion by the Country opposition as an advocate of the Dutch war and the Declarations of Indulgence. His fluctuations during the previous thirty years were held against him, and he had few contacts with the leaders of the Commons, except for a slight acquaintance with William Russell. He was making a considerable gamble, and the prospects did not look promising. He was a sick man, subject to periods of intense pain and hence bad temper. An operation for the removal of a hydatid cyst in 1668 had been successful, but left him equipped with a tube from his side to allow the abscess to drain. (Later, pamphleteers were to make much of this unusual phenomenon, 'a silver tap, through which . . . doth strain . . . both excrements and brain'.)

IV

The period 1674–8 was to be dominated by the policies of Danby. His emphasis on a Protestant foreign policy, on support for the Church of England and on developing links with the gentry, often by bribery and pensions, was an intelligent reaction to the failures of Clarendon and the Cabal, but his work was to be destroyed by three factors: Charles's insistence on continuing his own negotiations with Louis XIV, the growing fear of the implications of James as heir to the throne, and the strong possibility that Danby was more interested in strengthening the monarchy than in desiring that the King should follow parliamentary advice. As a result, by late 1678 his position was crumbling catastrophically. Pensions could persuade men to attend Parliament and to vote for reasonably acceptable policies, but not to support a ministry which they came to regard as treacherous and perhaps tyrannical.

The euphoria of the Cavalier Parliament in 1661 had disappeared. So had many of its original members, 343 by-elections having taken place by 1678. MPs were impressed less by the King's charm than by his immorality, laziness, affection for France, sympathy for Roman Catholics, and failure to select a ministry capable of bringing prestige and success abroad. The First Anglo-Dutch War had been popular enough, but by 1672 fear of the growing power of France and of the Catholic position in England was replacing resentment of the Dutch and suspicion of the dissenters and old republicans. 5 November 1673 was celebrated with more bonfires in London than had been seen for over thirty years. This situation gave Shaftesbury some scope. He had old ties with former parliamentary peers such as Salisbury, Carlisle and Holles, and soon had the co-operation of the Duke of Buckingham, who was anxious to establish himself as the leader of opposition to Danby. He had courage, determination and a useful ability to influence people. In 1674 Shaftesbury strongly supported the bill to prevent princes of the blood from marrying Roman Catholics without parliamentary consent, on pain of exclusion from the throne. This angry protest at James's marriage to Mary of Modena failed, but it enabled Shaftesbury to make his position clear and to attempt to demolish the suspicions which naturally clung to a former minister. He had already warned of 16,000 Catholics near London, ready for desperate measures.[6] A powerful weapon lay to hand, Englishmen's phobia about Catholicism, and Shaftesbury had no compunction about whipping up this hysteria.

The immediate result was surprising. Danby became so active in enforcing the penal laws that James turned against him and made contacts with Danby's opponents, such as the Earl of Bedford and the Marquess of Halifax, and so with Shaftesbury. All were now working to frustrate Danby by securing a dissolution and a new parliament, which Shaftesbury with more justification than James believed would be favourable to his aims. The main conflict came over Danby's Non-resistance Bill,[7] which was defeated, but not before Shaftesbury and his colleagues in the Lords had gained widespread publicity by publishing their Protests (entered in the Journal of the House of Lords), arguing, amongst other points, that exclusion from the House of Lords would be an invasion of their liberties and birthright. This willingness to argue for the special privileges of the Peers was continued in the case of *Shirley vs Fagg*, Shaftesbury denying the right of the Commons to prevent one of their number, Sir John Fagg, from pleading his case before the House of Lords. This antagonisation of the Commons was ostensibly designed to provoke such a deadlock between the Houses that Parliament would have to be dissolved, but it was also consistent on Shaftesbury's part. He had taken a similar line in Skinner's case; and in 1671, even more significantly, he had defended the right of the Lords to amend money bills, a position he maintained even after leaving office.

These hints about the primacy of his aristocratic beliefs were overlaid by his first major propaganda exercise, the publication in 1675 of *A Letter from a Person of Quality to his Friend in the Country*. Possibly written by his friend John Locke, certainly expressing Shaftesbury's ideas, this attacked Danby's Non-resistance Bill as aiming 'to make a distinct Party from the rest of the Nation of the High Episcopal Man, and the old Cavaliers, . . . to allow . . . Monarchy . . . to be *Jure Divino*, . . . to take away the Power and Opportunity of Parliament to alter anything in Church or State'. It was part of a plot going back to the 1640s, and even to Laudianism, and would permit the establishment of military rule. Praise was given to those who had opposed it, notably Shaftesbury, 'a man of great Abilities and Knowledge in Affairs . . . [who] was never known to be either bought or frightened out of his publick Principles'.[8] This strongly worded attack on the whole range of Danby's activities helped to establish Shaftesbury's reputation, but as an opponent of Danby, not the King.

He worked steadily at establishing this position for himself. In 1676 he moved to Thanet House in the City of London, giving himself a valuable base in the heart of the capital, second only to Parliament in its ability to pressurise the government. By then the Green Ribbon Club was emerging as the headquarters of the 'Whigs'. (This title can by now be given to that large section of the Country opposition which was reacting against Danby's methods, the Catholicism of the heir to the throne, and the consequent presumed threat to the independence of Parliament.) The Club's meetings at the King's Head Tavern, under cover of careful secrecy, enabled its members to plan each day's activities when Parliament was in session and to keep in close contact when it was not. It raised money for public spectacles, such as the Pope-burnings on 17 November (the anniversary of Queen Elizabeth's accession and often more widely celebrated than 5

November). Its role in the rapid circulation of propaganda and news was to be invaluable.[9]

The long prorogation of Parliament throughout 1676 meant that Shaftesbury's activities were confined to Thanet House and the Green Ribbon Club. He had many supporters but no real party, as was cruelly exposed when Parliament met again in February 1677. Anxious for a new parliament which would more strongly reject Danby's ministry, Shaftesbury and Buckingham, supported by Salisbury and Wharton, moved that Parliament was automatically dissolved, not having met for over a year (as stated in statutes of Edward III). Opposed in the Lords by Halifax, and in the Commons by leaders of the Country opposition, such as Meres and Sacheverell, who resented this demand coming from men not facing the problems of securing re-election, the four peers found themselves excluded from the Lords and sent to the Tower when they refused to beg for pardon. Three were released by the summer, but Shaftesbury, although unwell, refused to apologise and was confined, admittedly in considerable comfort, for a full year. One notable result of this was his failure to meet William of Orange, who visited England that autumn, preventing him from making contact with a possible alternative to James as heir to the throne. He secured his release in February 1678, his long 'martyrdom' having raised his stock considerably higher than that of the Duke of Buckingham. He now strengthened this support by demanding an immediate declaration of war against France; and, when peace became imminent, in order to maintain his role as a politically active leader, he brought forward John Arnold to describe the activities of priests and Catholics in Monmouthshire, although he failed to secure any extension of the penal laws.

Yet his popularity offered few real hopes for the future. When Parliament was prorogued in July, Shaftesbury retired to Wimborne for the rest of the summer. He was fifty-seven, in ill health, and apparently unlikely to achieve anything constructive in Parliament. He was intensely disliked by Charles and rejected by James, who had renewed his alliance with Danby; his chances of a return to office appeared negligible.

V

When his schemes to make himself a real force in English politics
seemed all but lost, Titus Oates gave them a new lease of life.

(F. S. Ronalds[10])

Let the Treasurer [Danby] cry as loud as he pleases against Popery,
and think to put himself at the head of the Plot, I will cry a note
louder and soon take his place.   (Shaftesbury[11])

There can be no doubt that the Popish Plot gave Shaftesbury the
opportunity he needed. He was in no way connected with its initial
stages, remaining at Wimborne until late October. Indeed it was
Danby who made the most of it, attempting to confirm his anti-
Catholic position; but the Plot ran out of control and Parliament was
able to seize the initiative. The Country party gleefully hounded him,
and the arrival of Montagu and exposure of Danby's letters to Louis,
combined with the hysteria created by the Plot, enabled them to
secure his downfall by March 1679.

Shaftesbury's target was different. He realised early on that
Danby's position had collapsed, and urged a bill merely to banish him
from office and Court – a far quicker process than impeachment. He
argued instead for measures to prevent James from succeeding to the
throne. Absolutely clear was his hostility to, indeed fear of, James:
'Heady, violent and bloody, who easily believes the rashest and worst
councils to be most sincere and hearty.' James's character, religion
and inability to see any point of view but his own, his determination
and energy, his militaristic and absolutist tendencies suggested great
danger to the traditional patterns of government, religion and society
in England. If some of Shaftesbury's methods and language were to
be unattractive, we should not forget how accurate his forebodings
turned out to be.

Titus Oates had not at first implicated James in the Plot. More
intelligent men soon realised that he was the logical beneficiary of
such a conspiracy, and in November Shaftesbury moved in the House
of Lords that he should be barred from the King's councils. No vote
was taken, but the warning was there. In the meantime, Shaftesbury
was very active on the House's committee to investigate the Plot, and,
although little evidence was unearthed, excitement was maintained

throughout the winter. This could without too much difficulty be turned into fear of James succeeding to the throne. As yet Shaftesbury was having little success, and James was exempted from the terms of the new Test Act (excluding Catholics from both Houses of Parliament) which convinced Shaftesbury that the Act was now worthless. However, when Charles at last dissolved the Cavalier Parliament in order to save Danby, Shaftesbury claimed with little justification the credit for forcing this popular move, was widely regarded as the leader of the opposition, and was given a special guard by the citizens of London after rumours of a plot against his life.

Shaftesbury did not trouble to visit Dorset during the elections for the new parliament, feeling confident of success. Once the results were known, he drew up a list of the two 'parties' – 302 for the Whigs, 158 for the Court. In reality the situation was not so simple. The 245 new members were often unknown quantities and tended to be surprisingly independent. The election had been fought on an anti-Danby platform, with lists of his 'pensioners' widely publicised; many who would vote against him showed greater hesitation on the issue of Exclusion, and the Commons resisted Shaftesbury's efforts to dissuade them from an impeachment of Danby as an attack on their power.

The removal and imprisonment of Danby was followed by one of Charles's more startling moves, his acceptance of Sir William Temple's plan for a reformed Privy Council, to consist of fifteen office-holders, and ten lords and five members of the Commons to represent the 'nation'. The appointment of Shaftesbury as its Lord President was intended to prevent him from making more trouble, and to separate him from the rank-and-file Whigs. In this it partially succeeded; Montagu, Sacheverell and many others were bitterly resentful at this 'betrayal' and rejected the new Council's request for money for the Navy. The City of London was also distinctly cool. Shaftesbury had no doubts, and was being consistent both to his own ideas and to seventeenth-century practice: that opposition was regarded most often as a means of forcing oneself into office, in order to be able to influence government policies. He had misjudged the King. Charles had private meetings with the Earl of Sunderland, Temple, even Halifax, but not with Shaftesbury. He did place before the Council his proposals for 'Limitations' if James should succeed to the throne (which would have removed his control over appointments to senior positions in Church and state), but he ignored Shaftesbury's arguments against the proposals, and he did not even consult the Council over the prorogation and dissolution of this parliament.

In the meantime, Shaftesbury arranged for Sir Thomas Player to introduce the first Exclusion Bill on 11 May 1679. This proposal to prevent James from inheriting the throne (no alternative heir was named) passed its second reading by 207 votes to 128, but notable were the number of abstentions, mostly from Shaftesbury's list of supporters, and the speeches against the proposal by many leading Whigs, such as Powle, Capel and Cavendish. The Whig party was not yet an organised force. Its only achievement before Parliament was dissolved was the Habeas Corpus Amendment Act (passed by the House of Lords only because Lord Grey jokingly counted the rather overweight Duke of Newcastle as ten men, the vote being 57 to 52).

Shaftesbury made a public display of anger when Parliament was prorogued in May, and declared that he remained in the Council only 'to be a tribune for the people there'. In fact he was not allowed to play any role in it, and when in October he was sacked for attacking James's move to Edinburgh he lost no power but gained public adulation as a martyr. By skilled propaganda and organisation he now aimed to ensure such overwhelming support for Exclusion in the country that he would be able to pressurise Charles into accepting the inevitability of the policy, and so enable Shaftesbury to gain a majority in the House of Lords, where as yet he could rarely muster more than twenty votes.

This explains the developments over the next two years. Until 1681 Shaftesbury was to believe that Charles could be persuaded. In December 1679 he had a secret night-time meeting with Charles to urge him to divorce the Queen and remarry, whereupon the Whigs would end their hostility. He hoped that the trial of Sir George Wakeman, accused of agreeing to poison the King, would incriminate the Queen and so lead to a divorce. He proposed divorce again in the Lords' debate on Limitations in 1680. Immediately prior to that he had delayed the debate in the House of Lords of the second Exclusion Bill so that Sunderland could have time to persuade Charles to accept it. On no occasion would Charles waver beyond the offer of Limitations, which Shaftesbury realised would be unenforceable once James became king.

Throughout this period, Shaftesbury, with considerable skill, kept up the pressure on Charles. The excitement created by Titus Oates had begun to subside by the summer of 1679. The patrols of the London Trained Bands to maintain order in the capital were halved in size in March, and again in July. (The Trained Bands were securely under the control of the King, who appointed their officers and ensured their loyalty, a notable contrast to the situation in 1641–2.) Shaftesbury, however, was able to turn to his advantage the ludicrous 'Meal Tub Plot' (supposed to incriminate the Whigs in plotting against the government), and to use Thomas Dangerfield, caught planting the false evidence, to give counter evidence against the Papists. In March 1680 Shaftesbury appeared before the Privy Council with news of an Irish plot, and used his unscrupulous agent, Hetherington, to collect a bunch of disreputable witnesses in Ireland, so maintaining public excitement. Until another parliament should meet, there was little more constructive that Shaftesbury could do. The serious illness of Charles in August 1679 had resulted in the return of James to Court, and many politicians returned to his side. Shaftesbury remained strangely quiet at Wimborne, whether through fear or lack of concern is not clear. Although James was sent away once Charles had recovered, only a firm enactment by Parliament seemed likely to prevent the probability of civil war when Charles should die.

Charles did call elections in the late summer of 1679, and these saw a much greater party conflict than any previous election. The Whigs were now well organised. Pamphlets countered the propaganda of the clergy (mostly loyal to the Court); lists of those who had voted against Exclusion were published, the voters being urged to reject them and to place national issues before local ones. Some leading peers, notably Lord Grey and the Duke of Buckingham, toured actively in several counties and had considerable influence. The Whigs gained overwhelming success, many Tories not even risking a contest at the polls. In the elections to the Oxford Parliament of 1681 the Whigs were even better organised. The addresses of instructions to the newly elected MPs, instructing them to refuse a money grant until Exclusion was accepted, to reject any idea of a regency, and to demand annual parliaments and free and independent elections, were clearly based on a model drawn up under Shaftesbury's supervision. He now indeed had a party structure, a means of influencing Parliament and the nation.

This organisation was mainly developed during the period from October 1679 to October 1680 during which Charles repeatedly prorogued the meeting of the second 'Exclusion' Parliament. It was a gamble on his part, arousing great resentment, but it prevented the Whigs from forcing any action and gave the country time to return towards normality. Shaftesbury countered this by a series of Petitions, the first from London with over 50,000 signatures. As with the later Addresses, forms were printed centrally and circulated to the county committees, who organised the setting-up of tables at strategic points and persuaded many thousands to sign. Charles rejected these petitions with contempt (although the Tories imitated them), but they served to keep a party in existence even when no parliament sat and to create a sense of unity and power that prevented too much loss of support for the Whigs. This was vital, as Charles was using this period to purge the lieutenancy and the magistracy of all Whigs. All this time a flood of pamphlets was being published, often scurrilous but remarkably uniform in ideas, emphasising consistently both the unsuitablity of James and the constitutional validity of Exclusion, so keeping these issues firmly before the nation.

It was London that really mattered when Parliament was not in session. There the sequence of trials resulting from the 'revelations' of Oates, Bedloe, Dugdale and others took place, amidst much public excitement. Hostile witnesses and judges were jeered, even attacked. The Green Ribbon Club organised massive demonstrations of support for the Whigs. 150,000 watched the bonfire celebrations of 5 November 1679, and these became progressively more elaborate. On 17 November 1680, to give added excitement to the burning of a 'Pope', live cats were caged in the effigy to be burnt to add realistic sound effects. But, since normally only 400 members of the Trained Bands were on duty, and windows with a good view were on hire for £10, it would be misleading to describe these as dangerous political demonstrations; they were predominantly entertainments and traditional anti-Papist celebrations, watched by crowds which dispersed quietly once the display was over.

Shaftesbury's most dramatic action in London came in June 1680, when, supported by other leading Whigs, he laid charges of recusancy against James and of being a whore against the Duchess of Portsmouth (Charles's mistress). Chief Justice Scroggs prevented the petition from being laid before the London Grand Jury and James was caused little discomfort, but such a deliberate insult had made it clear that the Whigs must succeed or face dire penalties. There was a second, more immediate effect. The Duchess of Portsmouth was sufficiently frightened to make approaches to the Whigs (as had been intended), and her close connection with Sunderland brought him into communication with Shaftesbury. His influence on the King might well be instrumental in persuading Charles to sacrifice his brother's rights.

Petitions, pamphlets, parades, electioneering, intimidation – Shaftesbury organised them all with considerable skill and energy; but only when Parliament met could he achieve anything constructive. The first Exclusion Bill had been foiled by a dissolution. In November 1680, the second bill swept through the Commons in nine days; but in the Lords the oratorical skill of Halifax and, even more effectively, the presence of Charles throughout the debate ensured its defeat. Shaftesbury was now unable to prevent Winnington, Montagu and other Whigs from launching bitter attacks on Halifax and the Tories which he realised would be counter-productive, by alienating moderates from the Whigs. The Commons seemed to be slipping out of his control.

The calling of the next parliament, in Oxford, provoked further petitions from Shaftesbury and the Whigs that they and their witnesses would be unsafe there from royalist anger. Shaftesbury emphasised his complaint by arriving in Oxford escorted by 200 followers. More accurately it would prevent them from using London for support or even a rising; Lord Grey was to say in 1685 that Shaftesbury had proposed such a rising, although there is no other evidence for it. The Oxford Parliament was a fiasco. Charles had the promise of French funds, ignored Shaftesbury's suggestions at a private meeting that he declare Monmouth his heir, and dissolved Parliament after a wasted week.

VI

The dissolution of the Oxford Parliament took Shaftesbury by surprise. It was only in May that he was able to arrange a petition from the Common Council of London requesting a new parliament. The Whigs still hoped for a parliament that autumn, unaware as yet of Charles's French subsidies, but Charles was now on the offensive. He published his Declaration justifying the dissolution, insisted on the trials and executions of the Popish Plot witnesses Fitzharris and College that summer, dismissed Oates from Whitehall, and benefited from the increasing number of Tory pamphleteers. Roger L'Estrange's *Observator* successfully exposed the contradictions in Whig actions and ideas, and in November Dryden's *Absalom and Achitophel* accused Shaftesbury of selfish ambition and ruthless disloyalty.

On 2 July Shaftesbury was arrested and imprisoned in the Tower. Such a move would have been unthinkable four months earlier. Already some of the less committed Whigs were deserting him, and many of the 'professional' witnesses who had assisted the Whigs over the past two years were now willing to act for the Tories. Nevertheless, Charles had acted too soon. The sheriffs who selected the Grand Jury were still staunch Whigs and ensured that it was dominated by Shaftesbury's supporters. When the indictment was heard in November before a crowded Old Bailey, he was accused of trying to compel the King to accept Exclusion and bills to aid dissenters by threat of an armed rising, and of claiming that the King was deserving of deposition and was not worthy to be trusted, being false, unjust and cruel. A succession of witnesses failed to influence a jury which knew that if it accepted the charge Shaftesbury would be tried by a court of peers nominated by Charles. The 'ignoramus' verdict led to great outbursts of celebration, confirmation that Shaftesbury still had a large popular following.

Despite this he could not prevent the upsurge in royal power. Too many of the gentry had been disturbed by the prospect of civil war, were tired of the hysteria, and worried by the constant appeals to the poorer sections of the community. In particular, the Court was able, by very dubious means, to arrange the election of Tory sheriffs in London in May 1682. Shaftesbury was now in danger of being brought before a hostile Grand Jury. On 29 September he went into hiding. At this point there is no certainty about his actions. Those Whigs arrested after the Rye House Plot were to state that he had been planning a rising at this time. It is doubtful if any firm plans were made, but probable that Shaftesbury – sick, in danger, angry and impatient – supported the idea of a rebellion: Charles had frustrated the will of the electorate in three parliaments, accepted the French subsidies, and used tricks to get control of the capital. But there was no prospect of success. Charles controlled Scotland, Ireland, the armed forces and had growing public support. There was no comparison with 1642.

In November Shaftesbury accepted the logic of the situation and fled to the Netherlands. On 21 January 1683, in Amsterdam, he died.

His body was taken to Wimborne, but few dared or even wanted to pay their respects. He died very much alone, an apparent failure unable even to claim a martyr's death.

VII

Shaftesbury's character is still the subject of some uncertainty. Rejected with embarrassment by the Whigs after 1688 as a devious and unsuccessful demagogue, he was vilified without contradiction by the Tories. Dryden's character assassination has been accepted by many as a convenient summary of his career; but Cromwell and Clarendon respected him, and John Locke accepted his patronage and friendship and the two men worked closely for over fifteen years. Was Locke so completely fooled?

We can be more certain about some of his interests. His belief in the necessity for legal reform has been shown; the Habeas Corpus Act provides some memento of this. He worked consistently to provide toleration for the dissenters. Partly this resulted from his own lack of deep religious commitment (he is best described as a deist), but he was to give full-hearted support to the Declarations of Indulgence and in 1680 persuaded the House of Lords to agree to bills to relieve dissenters from some persecution; ironically the dissolution resulting from his insistence on Exclusion destroyed these bills. His hostility to Roman Catholics only became apparent from 1673, but was essentially a political response to his suspicions of James. 'Popery and slavery, like two sisters, go hand-in-hand.' Even though most Englishmen shared this hostility, he can gain little credit from the methods he chose, which resulted in the execution of many innocent Catholics, most notably Archbishop Plunkett of Armagh.

Unlike those of many contemporaries, his anti-Catholic activities resulted from almost entirely domestic issues. He showed little interest in foreign affairs, accepting the two Dutch wars on the advice of others, and only rather incidentally using the French danger as a weapon in 1678. It must be added that there is no evidence that he, unlike his colleagues Buckingham, Holles and even Russell, took bribes from the French.

Where we can find a more positive and personal interest is in colonial affairs. As early as 1646 he purchased a sugar plantation in Barbados. He followed this by investing in Bermuda, in the Hudson's

Bay Company and the Royal Africa Company (in 1672 becoming Sub-governor to the Duke of York). In the 1660s he served on several Council committees supervising trade and the colonies, and in 1672 he became President of the new Council of Trade and Foreign Plantations (soon appointing Locke as Secretary). He took a close interest in all these, showing a flexible attitude to the problems of colonists on such issues as trade with the Spanish colonies. His interest was always with the newer, less-established companies, not with the East India or Levant companies.

Partly this was because his interest was in colonisation, not just trade. This is confirmed by the establishment of South Carolina. He was one of the original proprietors and devoted time and money to the project, encouraging emigration to the struggling colony and sending out frequent plans and instructions. The colony made little progress during his lifetime, but not through lack of effort on his part. Of greatest interest in the context of this essay are the *Fundamental Constitutions of Carolina* drawn up by Shaftesbury, probably with Locke's help, in 1669: eight 'magnates' to own 40 per cent of the land and to form the 'Grand Council'; 12,000-acre indivisible estates; ownership of fifty acres to qualify for the vote, of 500 acres to qualify as a candidate for the Lower House, which was to meet automatically every two years – these suggest a balanced constitution of an aristocratic oligarchy limited by an assembly of property-owners which may be seen as reflecting his ideas about the English constitution.

For Shaftesbury was no radical. At all points he fought for the rights of the local gentry (1644, 1655) and for the House of Lords (1669, 1671, 1675). He praised the abilities and disinterestedness of the nobility, and twice married into their ranks. He incited public hysteria, but never called out the London mobs as Pym had done; everything was kept under the guidance and control of landowners or prosperous merchants.

It is more difficult to fathom his attitude to the monarchy. His desertion in 1644, his doubts in 1660 and his behaviour from 1673 suggest a belief in limited monarchy. Yet he opposed Limitations as impractical, supported and justified the use of the royal prerogative over toleration, and realised the need for a final executive authority in times of danger. He used the Whig party to pressurise the King; but only in 1682, in the desperation of defeat, may he have contemplated the use of force to compel Charles. The King, he believed, should consult and take advice from his leading subjects, not just his favourites, but this was not new or radical in the 1670s. Note should also be taken of his advocacy of divorce and remarriage to solve the Exclusion crisis – he was hostile to James, not to the monarchy. It is possible that he might have hoped to make the Duke of Monmouth a puppet king; but he only fully accepted Monmouth as the alternative to James in 1681 (until then the Whigs had refused to commit themselves), and Shaftesbury, nine years older than Charles and in poor health, was unlikely to outlive him. Others in the party may have wished to reduce the monarchy; there is little evidence that Shaftesbury desired any radical change in its powers. Exclusion for him was personal rather than constitutional.

So we should not exaggerate the radicalism of his aims, as opposed to his methods. He did believe that parliament had a significant and permanent role to play. He favoured the abolition of bribery and overlong parliaments (although these were essentially party points). There is the possibility that he contemplated the reduction of the electorate by raising the qualification to vote, since inflation over the centuries had made a mockery of the forty-shilling freehold requirement, and he saw the need to make the borough franchises more uniform. These were all well-established ideas. The crucial innovatory role played by Shaftesbury, regardless of his defeat over Exclusion, was in the development of the first real political party in England. It had only one clear objective, and was divided over many issues, came from diverse backgrounds, and was often fragmented and difficult to control. Leading Whigs opposed Shaftesbury in the 'automatic dissolution' debate of 1677 (Holles, Sacheverell, Meres), over Limitations (accepted by men such as Powle) and over the first Exclusion Bill (opposed by Cavendish, Capel, Winnington and Jones). Montagu, Winnington, Sacheverell and others frequently disclaimed his leadership and advice, and disliked him. Despite this, a party organisation was formed, which fought two elections with great success, dominating certain areas (London, the Home Counties, the south-west and the north Midlands); developed a sustained publicity campaign; produced uniform and coherent petitions and addresses; and forced Charles to accept the emergence of a Tory party on whose loyalty he was dependent from 1681–5. He had shown the need for, and the means of achieving, the organisation, clarity of purpose, determination and mass appeal of an effective if as yet unsuccessful political party.

VIII

Shaftesbury's failure, which at the time of his death seemed total, was in large part owing to his misjudgement of Charles: a man of 'good parts, excellent breeding and well natured' but weak – 'His Brother, his Minister and His Mistress . . . perfectly govern all matters.'[12] His assumption that Charles would give way under pressure – the foundation of all his actions – was proved wrong. He had no other weapon. Charles had full control of the armed forces, the Church, most of the House of Lords, and with a little care and French help could avoid financial catastrophe. The Restoration monarchy turned out to be surprisingly strong, and the country was in no mood to risk another civil war, merely because of the possibility of a dangerous king in the future. Shaftesbury had found it impossible to undermine Cromwell; he found the same with Charles. Only the peculiar circumstances of 1642 and 1688, both resulting from exceptionally obstinate and foolish monarchs, permitted revolt, which even then required outside intervention to achieve their success.

Shaftesbury's career from 1673 was often unappealing. He was, on occasions, vicious and ruthless, and not entirely honest. He lost many friends. But he preserved the affection of his close intimates, he was prepared to risk the loss of his estates and imprisonment for his beliefs, and was perhaps more consistent than is often allowed. A desire for government with a strong executive but taking account of the interests of property-owners can explain all his apparent changes of direction.

9. Thomas Osborne, Earl of Danby

TIMOTHY EUSTACE and ROD MARTIN

THOMAS Osborne, best known despite his plethora of titles as the Earl of Danby, has a well-established reputation for financial expertise and shrewd political management. Yet by 1679 he was probably the most hated man in England, and his unexpected return to political influence during the early years of William III was barely more successful. It was quite clear by 1674 that Charles II needed a successful and popular first minister. The years of government by the Cabal had led in 1673 to the most humiliating and total rejection of his policies, and royal authority was at a lower ebb than at any time in the century except during the crisis years of 1640–60. Danby's suggested solution to this dire situation looks most sensible: a programme of financial retrenchment at Court, support for Anglicanism in the country and for Protestantism abroad. Few MPs seemed likely to quarrel with any of these policies. The purpose of this chapter must be primarily to explain why this apparently intelligent programme was such a total failure. It will be suggested that Danby was less of a financial wizard than he is often assumed to have been, and that it was not entirely Charles's inconstancy and deviousness that undermined Danby's efforts at political manipulation. There are too many unanswered, and often unasked, questions about the later Stuart period for any really conclusive analysis to be given. However a close examination of Danby's career does suggest that his reputation as a skilled political manipulator and financial expert owes more to self-publicity than to genuine achievement.

I

Thomas Osborne was born in 1632, the year his father was appointed Vice-president of the Council of the North. The sequestration of much of the family's land during the Civil War increased his hostility towards those involved in the rebellion, and marriage in 1653 to Lady Bridget Bertie, one of twelve children of the Earl of Lindsey, confirmed this royalist attitude whilst also ensuring useful connections with many of the aristocracy, in particular the second Duke of Buckingham. This contact brought him the modest reward of appointment as High Sheriff of Yorkshire in 1661, and assistance in securing election as MP for York in 1665. Without much oratorical skill, he relied on conscientious work in parliamentary committees to increase his reputation. He also loyally followed the lead given by the Duke of Buckingham, especially during the impeachment of Clarendon, whom he helped to hound out of the country. His reward in the ensuing government reshuffle was appointment as Joint Treasurer of the Navy; in 1671 he became Sole Treasurer after securing the removal of his colleague Sir Thomas Littleton on grounds of corruption. He could be ruthless in seeking power. Despite the initial hostility of the Duke of York as Lord High Admiral, he rapidly won respect for his industry and skill in administrative work, greatly increasing efficiency by establishing weekly accounts and higher standards of book-keeping. In 1672 he became a member of the Privy Council, as Charles broadened its membership in preparation for war.

By this time Osborne was in something of a quandary, owing to an increasingly ambivalent attitude towards Buckingham. The Duke was his patron; yet Osborne could not assist his patron's support for toleration in 1668 and for the Declaration of Indulgence in 1672, nor did he welcome the Duke's involvement with the Treaty of Dover. His Anglicanism had deep political roots, and he understood better than many at Court the country's growing hostility towards France. Already he realised that the King must have clear parliamentary support, and even in 1669 had drawn up a list of 291 probable supporters in the Commons, predominantly former Clarendonians who wanted the preservation of the existing system of Church government and the promotion of the Cavalier interest (predominantly older royalists from the Interregnum period, staunchly Anglican and suspicious of both former rebels and young courtiers, such as those attached to the Earl of Arlington and the Duke of Buckingham).

Yet his appointment as Lord Treasurer in June 1673, on the resignation of Clifford, was widely regarded as the result of Buckingham's patronage. In reality the support of Clifford and the Duke of York, conscious of his financial ability and his belief in the validity of the royal prerogative, noticeable even during his attacks on Clarendon, probably played a greater part in persuading Charles to make the appointment. It was an unexpected promotion for a relatively junior minister, dashing Arlington's hopes, and there was no certainty that his stay in office would be prolonged or significant.

Other developments opened his path to primacy in government. Both Buckingham and Arlington were attacked ferociously by the Commons for their involvement in the outbreak of the Dutch war. Buckingham's impetuous rush to defend himself before the Commons without Charles's prior consent, hence implying their right to judge the King's ministers, ensured his downfall. Arlington was more skilful in his defence, but was too discredited to remain in power, although as Lord Chamberlain he retained Charles's favour and was still being used for diplomacy in late 1674. He was to remain a problem for the Treasurer.

Danby (as we must now call Osborne – he was created Viscount Latimer in 1673, and Earl of Danby a year later) remained discreetly inactive during this turmoil, although giving Buckingham some support at Court. Instead of hounding his political rivals, he was drawing up a memorandum for an alternative policy to be placed before Charles – the protection of Protestantism at home and abroad, and a careful observance of honesty and economy in financial matters; such a programme, he argued, would enable the government to appeal to Parliament for financial support with some hope of success.

The disintegration of the Cabal was a gradual process, only completed nine months after Danby received the treasurership. But its purpose was destroyed during the 1673 session of Parliament. Charles's policy of securing financial security by an attack on the Dutch trading-monopoly, and by French subsidies and parliamentary support for a popular and successful war, while at the same time granting religious toleration, was hopelessly impractical at that time; and the necessity for such a disparate and self-lacerating ministry to secure the programme confirms this. Yet his earlier reliance on Anglicanism and on one leading minister had been no more successful. It is doubtful if Charles took any conscious decision about the future form of his ministry. It was Danby who beavered his way to the centre, through the crumbling political edifice around him, with a policy of peace, retrenchment and Anglicanism, at least the first two of which had become unavoidable by early 1674.

Danby had come to realise that a pro-French policy, with which he had shown some sympathy in the 1660s, was no longer feasible; by 1673 there was widespread concern about the growing power (commercial as well as military) of France, and public enlightenment about the Catholicism of James and Clifford in 1673 had a dramatic impact. Charles I's reign had been bedevilled by public suspicion about the monarch's foreign and religious policies, and it seemed that his son now faced a similar problem. It required little more than common sense to realise that the Crown's comfort and security could best be guaranteed by an anti-French and anti-Catholic policy. What was more subtle was to argue that the Crown would *increase* its power by following such a policy. Clarendon had realised that Parliament was necessary but had failed to understand how to establish a working relationship with it, and the Cabal had been too much concerned with individual policies and ambitions to achieve any foundation for co-operation between Crown and Parliament, by then financially so essential. Danby was perhaps the first to realise that this co-operation must be established by accepting the need for policies which would have popular backing in Parliament, which could then be stabilised by some ministerial organisation of a group of MPs. This would make possible a secure financial settlement, after which the King could introduce modifications in policy closer to his own inclinations. We cannot be sure if Danby eventually envisaged rule without Parliament; in reality no seventeenth-century king could hope to enforce policies abhorrent to the socially and economically significant classes. Yet there is no doubt that he consistently favoured powerful and effective prerogative government, and did not envisage lasting parliamentary limitations on the King.

His programme was shrewd, an intelligent response to the problems of Charles's reign, but it was dependent on two improbable factors: the whole-hearted commitment of Charles to such a policy, and Danby's ability to overcome the suspicions engendered by thirteen years of wayward and largely unsuccessful government, and indeed to prevent experienced and touchy MPs from seeing through to the purpose of his programme.

II

A debt of over £2.1 million, an annual deficit of around £500,000, and little prospect of parliamentary assistance made Danby's task as Treasurer rather unenviable – perhaps not surprisingly he suffered one of his frequently recurring bouts of ill health in July. Even Charles pointed out that Danby 'had but two friends in England . . . himselfe and his owne meritts'.[1] He did have the support of the Speaker of the Commons, Sir Edward Seymour, and together they ensured that Sir Heneage Finch should succeed Shaftesbury as Lord Keeper – a staunch ally, but a distressingly clumsy government spokesman at opening sessions of Parliament. However the Earl of Ormonde, leader of the Cavalier interest in the Council, disliked Danby, Arlington perpetually intrigued against him, and the Earl of Shaftesbury was a powerful opponent in the Lords. No supplies were voted in the 1674 session to cover the debts caused by the war, although Danby was able to start some financial retrenchment once Charles had been persuaded to end the war in February 1674.

The flood of anti-Catholic pamphlets in 1673 encouraged Danby to develop his political base by ordering the rigorous enforcement of the penal laws, and in December excluding all English Catholics from the Court. Whereas in Middlesex between 1660 and 1672 sixty-two recusants were indicted, in 1674 739 suffered. In late 1674 Danby arranged consultations with the Anglican bishops, from which in February 1675 emerged Privy Council orders to enforce the Conventicle Act, expel Catholic priests from England and prevent the education of Catholic children abroad, and also a threat to seize two-thirds of the Catholics' land. Danby's Anglican policy and alliance were established. It was not wholly successful. Buckingham started to rally dissenting opposition, James waned in his support, and throughout the country JPs were reluctant to take action, even being discouraged by Charles from enforcing the penal laws, so tenuous was Charles's support for his Treasurer.

In the parliamentary session of April–June 1675 Danby had equally mixed fortunes. His main objective was a bill to introduce a test or oath to be sworn by all officials that they would endeavour no 'alteration in the government in church or state as it is by law established' and declare traitorous any armed resistance to the King. Danby's intention was to appeal to Cavalier attitudes against the former rebels, and there was some prospect for this in the Commons.

If successful, it would have blocked all effective criticism of the government, by protecting ministers and policies from parliamentary threats. In the event, it only passed the Lords after a most bitter debate, many peers feeling concern at the threat to their inherited right of attendance, while the Commons, now more aware of the bill's implications, were distracted from discussion by Arlington's attempt to impeach Danby. This vitriolic move by a fiercely resentful fallen minister enabled the government's leading opponent, William Russell, to declare that Danby had 'overthrown and violated the ancient course and constitution of the Exchequer' and received 'great gifts and grants from the Crown'.[2] It was a hopelessly premature attack, since Danby had as yet done little to alarm MPs, and future critics such as Garroway and Colonel Birch were amongst his defenders. The first article was rejected by 181 votes to 105, and in the ensuing debate on the remaining articles Danby was triumphantly vindicated. Even an effort to prevent MPs from holding government offices – the key to Danby's manipulation of MPs – was rejected by 145 votes to 113. Yet this was all that he did achieve. The Commons refused a grant for the Navy, and made impassioned demands for the withdrawal of English troops fighting in Louis's army. Charles was caustic that Danby was better at protecting himself than the King's interests. The prorogation resulting from the deadlock between Lords and Commons over the *Shirley vs Fagg* case[3] gave Danby the opportunity to plan more carefully for the next session, although Charles's acceptance of £100,000 from Louis should Parliament show hostility to France threatened to undermine the whole of Danby's policy unless he could ensure even more substantial supplies from Parliament during the session to commence in October 1675.

Already thirty-four MPs were receiving a total of £10,000 in pensions from the Excise as compensation for changes made in the farming-system. More money could be made available for pensions, and more offices could be granted to MPs as rewards for loyalty to the Court line. This, however, would take time, and many existing office-holders, owing allegiance to former ministers and enjoying life tenure, felt little need to heed Danby's commands. At this stage he could only rely on his own influence in Yorkshire and on that of Seymour over many MPs from the south-west, and send about 100 letters to potentially loyal MPs urging their prompt attendance. The result was disappointing. A vote of £300,000 for building twenty ships was less than Danby wanted, and it was tagged onto a bill appropriating the customs revenue to the use of the Navy, so tying the Treasurer's hands in spending the government's income. He failed totally in his request for almost £1 million to pay for the revenue already spent in anticipation of future income, the voting being 172 to 165. Growing complaints were made about his attempts to influence MPs. Russell and Sacheverell were articulate and influential critics, winning over sufficient MPs to match Danby's group, although it is premature to regard them as an organised party. Danby won a narrow vote in the Lords (50–48) to defeat a call for a dissolution, a move which Charles was seriously contemplating; however the revival of *Shirley vs Fagg* forced Danby to accept a fifteen-month prorogation on 22 November.

III

It was financial expertise which brought Danby to power and forms the core of his reputation; as such, it deserves separate examination.[4] He achieved sufficient success to persuade Charles that he was a minister to be supported, despite differences in policy. Reduction of the armed forces in 1674 saved perhaps £200,000. He was tough, even mildly unscrupulous, in negotiations with the tax-farmers, increasing the Hearth Tax farm by £16,000 in 1674, and the Excise farm by £20,000 in 1674 and a further £10,000 in 1677, at which point he arranged for any excess profits to be paid to the government (£105,000 over the next three years). From Parliament he secured £300,000 in 1675, and a further £600,000 in 1677 (both for the Navy), as well as agreement for a loan of £200,000 secured on the Excise. Then in 1678 came the grant of a Poll Tax (approximately £300,000 in practice, although more had been promised), and in June £619,000 (£200,000 to pay off the loan of 1677, £200,000 to disband the Army, £200,000 for the Navy, the rest for Princess Mary's dowry). To this must be added the extension of the 1671 additional excise on wine and vinegar, renewed in 1677 for three years. It is impossible to produce a precise total (for instance, agreements with the tax-farmers were on the basis of substantial advances, enabling the government to borrow at an earlier date than would otherwise have been possible), but a generalised figure of almost £3 million gives some idea of the help he provided for Charles between 1674 and 1678.

On the other hand, he had several failures. Parliament refused to pay off the anticipations of revenue in 1675, refused to grant an extra £600,000 in 1677, and in 1678 rejected the request for a permanent extra grant of £300,000 a year. Such rejections were neither unprecedented nor wholly unexpected. A more serious criticism is his failure to reduce expenditure significantly. This hovered at around £1,350,000 or so, approximately £250,000 being Charles's 'personal' or Court expenditure. In 1675 Danby set up a Privy Council committee to draw up a plan for retrenchment, and after some heated debate at court an expenditure figure of £1,112,000 was agreed upon. Danby never came near achieving this figure, and a similar plan in 1677 had no greater success. The Treasury had inadequate control over other spending departments, and Danby's political position was never sufficiently secure for him to be able to enforce compliance; he had for instance to permit grants of £55,000 between 1676 and 1678 to the Duchess of Portsmouth to prevent her using her private influence in the bedroom to undermine his position at Court, and more went to the Duchess of Cleveland and Nell Gwynne. Chandaman has pointed out 'the simple Caroline law that the extravagance of the king tended to increase in proportion to his resources'.[5] Corruption and speculation were still rife at Court and in the civil service, and there was little that one minister could do to root it out without more support than Charles was willing to provide. Parliament in the early seventeenth century had been anxious for royal finances to be self-sufficient; now it was determined to grant occasional assistance, but no permanent solution. As Sir Thomas Meres said, "Tis money that makes a Parliament considerable and nothing else."[6]

Other criticisms can be made. Danby was not only (like Cranfield) rather unoriginal – no new taxes, no new forms of credit, only the 1676 commercial treaty with France to give a boost to the carrying trade (although it probably increased England's trade deficit with France). More serious, he was in many ways looking backwards rather than forwards. He favoured tax-farming, although the advantages of direct collection of the customs were already visible. He preferred appointing officials for life (for political loyalty) in place of the growing habit of granting office *durante bene placito*. The increased efficiency of the Treasury was based on a consolidation of the reforms brought about by Downing and his fellow Treasury Commissioners from 1667. Only his insistence that the excise farmers pay over their running cash to the Treasury, to assist in securing loans, can be seen as an innovation.

Even his last two years as Treasurer, when he seemed to win such substantial grants from Parliament, were financially damaging. By promising war against France, he secured between 1677 and 1679 £1,385,000 from Parliament. But expenditure on military preparations amounted to £2,165,000 – a deficit of £780,000. He inherited in 1673 a debt of £1.2 million; he left behind him a debt of £2.4 million, an army of 30,000 to be paid off, a furious Parliament, and a French king unlikely to grant Charles any more subsidies for some time to come.

His foreign policy of course was not motivated purely by financial considerations. Also it must be admitted that few of his problems as Treasurer were susceptible to easy solution, and there is no doubt of his conscientious and meticulous work. He was able in 1677 to establish his credentials before Parliament as a reforming Treasurer. Yet it should also be pointed out that his successors, the Treasury Commission guided by Lawrence Hyde, reduced government expenditure to £1,130,000, while maintaining income at £1,353,000 in 1679–80; personal expenditure was reduced from £250,000 to £100,000. Much of this resulted from Charles's shock over the Exclusion crisis; but Danby's ministry does tend to appear a rather barren patch between the innovations of Downing and the achievements of Hyde.

IV

The long prorogation from November 1675 to February 1677 was used by Danby as a time to strengthen his political position. The most urgent problems lay within the Court. Charles still inclined towards France, and after some wrangling gained his subsidy, shortly followed by a secret agreement with Louis by which neither could make a treaty without consulting the other. Danby could only hope that its negative character might soon be countered by a more positive policy once he could secure parliamentary subsidies. Meanwhile James was fluctuating in his support, increasingly believing that a new parliament would be more likely to grant toleration to Catholics – a naïve chimera unscrupulously encouraged by Shaftesbury. Arlington, Ormonde and Secretary Williamson also urged a dissolution, since Danby had apparently failed to gain control over the Cavalier Parliament. Danby managed to resist this pressure, partly as a result of a survey by Sheldon of the archbishopric of Canterbury showing, probably misleadingly, that over 95 per cent of the population were Anglicans – toleration was both unlikely and unnecessary. However, more positive action was needed. In early 1676 Danby secured the removal from the Privy Council of lords Halifax and Holles for opposing his plans, followed by the dismissal of the Chancellor of the Exchequer, Duncombe. He would brook no rivals, just as he showed a jealous suspicion of all able subordinates, preferring to surround himself with dull bureaucrats or reliable relatives, such as his nephew Charles Bertie, given charge of the expenditure of secret-service funds.

Danby showed equal touchiness towards criticism from outside the Court. He unsuccessfully attempted to drive Shaftesbury out of London, Charles refusing to give sufficient support in this. He attempted to close down the coffee houses in London, as centres of politically disaffected discussion. In the ensuing uproar he was compelled to modify this to an attempt to ban scandalous papers from these premises. He also carried out a substantial purge of JPs, a move which as much weakened his influence by making other office-holders feel threatened as it strengthened his authority in the country. Charles attempted some mediation at Court, but there was enough suspicion and resentment there (not least because of Danby's attempts to curb perquisites and pensions) to make it clear that Danby's career depended more than ever on his successful management of Parliament. Sir Robert Wiseman had already drawn up lists of probable supporters (105 in late 1675). Further investigations added to this list, partly resulting from Charles Bertie's use of 'bribes'. Over £17,000 was paid out to sixty-seven MPs, as Danby's own papers admit; probably a total of £250,000 was expended this way in 1676–8. By 1677 Danby was confident of the votes of well over 200 MPs – enough to give confidence of victory on almost every issue. The preparations for the 1677 session were meticulous: arrangements for proxies for loyal peers who might be absent; estimates that the Court would win sixteen out of twenty-three pending by-elections (Danby's brother and two elder sons were to be successful); letters sent to loyal MPs to ensure prompt attendance; grants of office to waverers; dinners to win over those susceptible to flattery.

Much opposition was aroused by Danby's techniques. Yet some such policy was essential. Parliament met so frequently that its expertise was growing rapidly; it now expressed itself on every aspect of government policy and in 1673 it had shattered Charles's policies and ministry. A minister must ensure the approximately 200 votes necessary for survival. Traditional groupings would help. Danby had seven close relatives in the Commons, and seven others were lords lieutenant, able to exercise some influence in elections. Seymour and the Earl of Bath had 'client' MPs who could be persuaded to give support, although other Court patrons were less reliable. Personal influence could be used, as when Danby won over Sir John Reresby by dining him well. Government office could be used as a bribe, and Danby did develop this (just as prime ministers today have over 100 positions in government to grant to supporters); but it was less easy to remove disloyal existing officers – Colonel Birch, Auditor of the Excise, held onto his office despite criticising the Treasurer, as did Sir Robert Howard, Auditor of the Exchequer, granted office for life by Clifford. Bribery appears less creditable, yet many 'bribes' were often little more than compensation for the prolonged sessions, an expensive burden now that MPs could no longer claim fees from their constituents. There is little evidence of bribes affecting the way MPs voted; rather it affected the regularity of their attendance. It should not be forgotten that by 1677, with bribes available from Danby, France, Spain and the Dutch, the problem for MPs was, essentially, how to avoid accepting a bribe. Even Ogg's statement that Danby 'rejoiced more in the votes of ninety-nine silent legislators than in the conversion of one notable opponent'[7] recognises that bribery was merely to oil the mechanism, not to reverse its direction. Although Shaftesbury was to justify his more sophisticated methods of party organisation by declaiming against Danby's 'plot' against the country, it ought to be admitted that assistance for the government from Parliament was essential. Criticism of Danby's methods should perhaps centre more on their effectiveness than on their morality.

Certainly their effectiveness seemed to be confirmed by the parliamentary session of February–May 1677. Foreknowledge of Shaftesbury's plan to force a dissolution enabled Danby to counter what was made to appear as an attack on Parliament,[8] and James reforged his support for Danby after this threat to the royal prerogative. In the Commons he won majorities of 51 to defeat the call for a dissolution, and to prevent the appropriation of customs revenue to the Navy, and of 33 to continue the additional excise despite the great hostility it aroused as potentially freeing the Exchequer from further dependence on Parliament. The grant of £600,000 for the

Navy was a substantial achievement in peacetime. Yet he had never gained more than 193 votes on any issue, despite hopes before the session of up to 250. His chief spokesman in the Commons, Williamson, was bumbling, and the absence of able subordinates was becoming dangerously obvious. His bill to limit a Catholic successor to the throne by arranging for bishops to control ecclesiastical affairs was regarded both as inadequate, and likely to over-elevate the role of bishops – Anglicanism appeared less strong in the Commons than he had assumed. Once the discussions turned to foreign affairs, the alarm caused by recent French successes led to five addresses for the recall of English troops in France, with which Danby sympathised but which infuriated Charles.

Foreign affairs also dominated the ensuing period of adjournment. Danby had earlier been urging Charles to take more rigorous action against France in order to secure substantial supplies, since if Parliament should fail to assist, 'the people would helpe you destroy that Parliament which should refuse itt'.[9] Such a policy could also win commercial concessions from Holland and Spain, and even provide the potentially valuable support of an army. Charles's refusal to heed this advice had wrecked the parliamentary session. Instead he listened to the optimistic suggestion of the ambassador in Paris, Ralph Montagu, that England's neutrality was so valuable to France that a greatly increased French subsidy was possible. Danby had tried to suppress these letters, but Montagu wrote directly to Charles. Danby at this point (July–August) seems to have feared for his survival at Court, his relative failure with Parliament being compounded by the release of Buckingham from the Tower. Buckingham was soon to meet Charles at Nell Gwynne's rooms, where he poked fun at Danby and more seriously hinted at alternative policies. Reluctantly (his letters to Montagu confirm his hostility to France) Danby joined in the negotiations, making excessive demands in the hope of destroying them, but eventually agreeing to the subsidy of £100,000, inadequate for Charles's needs and ultimately disastrous for Danby.

That autumn, however, it did not seem such a setback, for arrangements were now in progress for a visit by William of Orange to arrange his marriage to Princess Mary. Until August 1677 Danby had expressed doubts about such a marriage, fearing James's annoyance, but now it offered great advantages. It would undermine Charles's agreements with Louis, should lead to a Dutch alliance and so win parliamentary support, and, more selfishly, could help guarantee Danby's position by securing the friendship of the heir apparent (assuming, as most did, that James would predecease his brother). Charles was apparently won over by promises of the domestic political advantages (as he openly admitted to Louis), and James by the prospect of military glory at the head of an English army. Danby found himself in October at the centre of public celebrations, and the intimate of William, the Protestant hero. The agreement on a treaty with the Dutch in December seemed to mark the summit of his work. When Parliament met in January 1678 the Commons promised £1 million as supplies for war.

Yet all this was too fragile and too late. William's anxiety for a speedy marriage resulted from growing political weakness at home, the States General being anxious to end the expensive war. Parliament promised much, but in practice voted only a Poll Tax, which brought in little more than £300,000, while rather more enthusiastically banning the import of French wines, likely to cost the government £290,000 in lost customs duties. The Commons insisted on an immediate war before voting any more supplies; Charles refused to act until absolutely certain of financial support, justifying this with reminders of the second Anglo-Dutch War but in reality determined to prevent any open conflict with France. Danby was linked to a vulnerable political figure in Holland, an evasive King at home and a suspicious Parliament, many MPs demanding war while accepting French bribes, more concerned to destroy Danby's schemes than provide funds for war. Lord Russell, Sir Thomas Lee and others used their expertise to delay any essential decisions, determined as they were to bring about a dissolution. Outside Parliament, Marvell's pamphlet *An Account of the Growth of Popery and Arbitrary Government* served to raise alarm at the prospect that an army raised to fight France might be used instead in England.

It is unlikely that even whole-hearted support by Charles would have guaranteed success. An English declaration of war at this stage would have been too late, and intervention probably on too small a scale, to prevent a truce being signed in May 1678. Danby was able to secure money to pay off the Army, and to cover other past expenses, but he failed in the request for a permanent vote of an extra £300,000 a year. On 19 June the peace talks broke down, and Danby delayed disbanding the Army; on 15 July Parliament was prorogued; on 31 July peace was finally signed, while still the Army remained intact.

True, the money to disband it had been spent on maintaining it since May, but where was the money to come from to continue paying it? Danby had flouted and infuriated the Commons, had driven Louis to despair of English intentions and hence cancel any subsidy, and had failed to obtain sufficient funds to meet the increased expenses of government.

James had frequently suggested the need for ruthless action by the government as it faced recurring political problems: the arrest of leading opposition spokesmen, the dissolution of Parliament, and enforcement of the King's will by military force. Although it cannot be fully proved, it seems probable that Danby was now seriously contemplating the maintenance of an army to give strength to the government; even in 1676 he had envisaged enforcing recusancy fines in order to increase the militia and establish a local paid bureaucracy. Yet such a plan contradicted his programme of winning the acquiescence of the political nation. The nation was now tense, hostile and suspicious, and government finances were rapidly running further into debt and deficit. Remarkably Danby remained optimistic, despite having no immediate plans as to how the army might raise the money to pay its wages, confident that even if Parliament did have to meet again to provide supplies he could secure 218 votes, although he had never achieved more than 170 in the previous session. His prospects for the next session, beginning in October, were in reality not good. Revived fears of Popery and absolutism, of which Marvell had accused him, appeared more genuine that summer, however ludicrous the former and unjustified the latter might be. Yet few could foresee his imminent downfall: his leading opponent, the Earl of Shaftesbury, was at this time retiring in some despair to the country.

V

Two characters were in their different ways to bring about Danby's fall from office. Titus Oates's elaborate inventions at first seemed like a gift, conveniently timed to give the Treasurer the opportunity of proving his staunch Protestantism by a vigorous investigation and at the same time justifying the need for substantial armed forces to protect the King at this moment of danger. As leading minister Danby could not risk ignoring the Plot, however unlikely it seemed. Five months earlier he had written of his desire for 'some small insurrection' as a way of 'getting into some condition of armes and money by the consent of the people'.[10] He arranged a number of arrests, and urged a parliamentary investigation. But the affair got out of hand. The murder of Sir Edmund Berry Godfrey, the failure to discover any convincing plotters, and Shaftesbury's skill in turning the Plot into a weapon with which to attack James led to bitter criticism of Danby, not the hoped-for praise.

Ralph Montagu's ambition to rise from the post of ambassador to Paris to that of Secretary of State now began to play its part. Danby could not accept a staunch exponent of French subsidies in such an influential position, and had arranged his removal from Paris. Montagu came to realise that only Danby's downfall would open his path to promotion. This exponent of a French alliance, absolutism and subsidies won a parliamentary seat and forged links with Whigs such as Russell and Littleton. Given his opportunity by Danby's only partially successful attempt to seize his papers, he rose in the House on 19 December to denounce this action, explaining that the object of the search was certain letters written by Danby, especially that of 25 March referring to the need for a large French subsidy. In the ensuing uproar, the House voted 179–116 to draw up articles of impeachment, ignoring Danby's efforts to discredit Montagu by producing his letter urging subsidies, and also information about French bribes to Russell and other Whigs. The articles declared that he had 'encroached to himself regal power' by conducting foreign affairs without consulting King or Council; accused him of keeping an army and attempting to introduce arbitrary government 'to the great danger and unnecessary charge of his Majesty and the whole kingdom'; of negotiating secret French subsidies to hinder the meeting of Parliament; of arranging large gifts for himself; of spending £231,000 of the King's money on pensions and secret services; and of being 'popishly affected'.

All charges except the fifth (not criminal) were unjustified, unless he was intending to fulfil the second. A courageous speech to the Lords defeated an attempt to order his immediate committal to the Tower, and both Charles and James seemed firm in his support. Danby was supremely confident, removed Solicitor General Winnington and Sir Stephen Fox from office for voting for his impeachment, and replaced the ineffective Williamson by the Earl of Sunderland as Secretary of State. Yet as so often there was a lethal weakness in his position. Charles would give him support, and write 'I agree' on letters between Danby and the French Court, but he could not risk a public impeachment hearing. There was too great a risk of revelation of his own intrigues with Louis, even the terms of the Secret Treaty of Dover. In January 1679 he acted quickly to secure an agreement with moderate Whigs, led by Lord Holles, by which he would dissolve Parliament, call a general election, disband the Army and dismiss Danby, in return for which the moderates promised to vote a reasonable supply and to allow Danby to escape prosecution.

Charles seemed to be attempting a 'parliamentary programme', but his own needs had again blinded him to the reality of the situation. The election was fought essentially on one issue: the attempts by Danby to corrupt Parliament and establish arbitrary government. The first general election for eighteen years witnessed a revulsion against Court intrigues, influence and incompetence, a determination to elect men to speak unrestrainedly for the 'country interests'. Not a single Danby relative or connection was elected, barely thirty of the former 'pensioners' and office-holders were returned, despite a pamphlet campaign by Danby and a renewed attempt at retrenchment at Court. Nor was it simply a disastrous humiliation for Danby: Holles was in no position to be able to guide the House; even Shaftesbury was unable to distract MPs from a vendetta against Danby into an attempt to focus attention on the policy of Exclusion. Charles needed to act quickly. Even before Parliament met he persuaded Danby to accept a pardon (Danby still denying its necessity) and one week after Parliament met he insisted on his Treasurer's resignation, compensating him with a life pension of £5000. Danby was displeased, Parliament was infuriated. Both Houses saw the pardon as an attempt to destroy the power of impeachment, their only effective weapon against the power of royal ministers. Heated debates followed. Charles forced Danby into hiding on 23 March; on 26 March the Lords voted a bill of banishment; on 14 April they agreed after some resistance to the Commons' demands for a bill of attainder if Danby should not surrender by 1 May. On 15 April Charles persuaded Danby to give himself up, and the next day the Lords committed him to the Tower. Parliament could now turn its attention to the Exclusion crisis.

Danby spent five years in the Tower. He waged a vigorous campaign to persuade Charles to dissolve Parliament, call another one outside London, and ensure for himself full control of the Army and Navy. Charles chose his own course during the crisis. Danby made repeated efforts to persuade the House of Lords or the judges to order his release. Only in 1684, when it became clear that Charles was not going to summon another parliament, did he secure his own release, although French influence at Court prevented him from regaining significance there.

It says something for his commitment to an Anglican policy that he spoke openly against James's demand to appoint Catholic officers in the Army in November 1685. From then on he was clearly in opposition to the King, and by early 1687 was in contact with William's envoys to England. His presence at the Seven Bishops' Trial boosted the number of leading politicians there who thus showed their support for the Church of England, and also enabled him to meet with those planning the invitation to William, joining with six others in signing it on the night of the bishops' acquittal.

VI

In all probability, Danby envisaged a much more important role for himself in the events of 1688–9 than circumstances actually allowed him to play. His was by far the most significant Tory name in the invitation to William of Orange, and in the autumn of 1688 he took the major part in securing the North, and in particular York, against James's supporters. After ten years in the political wilderness Danby could perhaps look forward to being chief adviser to William and Mary in a possible regency. He could not, however, have foreseen the dramatic collapse of James's cause. The fact that William arrived not in the north but in the south-west and with a very large army meant that Danby could be practically ignored. Further, James's flight to France left the English leadership with no option but to turn to William. There was only one possible way out for Danby – for Mary to be given the throne alone. This would have salved his Tory conscience and maybe increased his influence, but Mary would have none of it and made this abundantly clear to him.

The formal accession of William and Mary in February 1689 left Danby then, with some hopes of office but nothing like as close to the new king as he had hoped. It was his rival, Halifax, who for the moment had William's attention, and instead of being made Lord Treasurer he was only to have the prestigious but far less powerful (and, worse still, not very profitable) post of Lord President of the Council. Promotion to the marquisate of Carmarthen in April 1689 can have done little to satisfy his ambition. Nevertheless, if the fluid political situation had its difficulties both for Carmarthen and for the very survival of the regime, it also had its possibilities. The Ministry which William appointed was a coalition of Whigs and Tories and there was no co-operation between its members. Halifax and Carmarthen hated one another; the Whigs hated both for their activities in the two previous reigns. On 1 June 1689, for example, there was an attempt at all-out attack when it was debated in the Commons that there should be an address to the King to remove from his Council such as had been impeached by Parliament. The targets were Carmarthen and Halifax, but this was aiming at far too much, for they were the two chief props of William's government.

It was in fact Whig extremism in the Convention Parliament which was to give Carmarthen his chance.[11] William's aim in taking the crown was to bring England into the coming war with France. He looked for national unity and a generous supply of money from Parliament. What he got from the Whigs in 1689 was constant attacks on his Tory ministers, caused largely by an understandable desire for revenge for past wrongs suffered under Charles and James, and a settlement of the Crown's revenue for one year only rather than the usual settlement for the life of the sovereign. The Tory party, on the other hand, was fearful of Whig vengeance and desperately anxious for the future of the Church of England, even though all that had been achieved for dissenters in 1689 was a very limited Toleration Act. By January 1690 William was totally exasperated with the party quarrels of the Convention Parliament. Although it was finally defeated, the Whig-inspired Sacheverell Clause was the final blow. This would have banned from municipal office for seven years all those who had helped in the surrender of borough charters and was a naked attempt to purge Tories from their local power bases. Clearly then, the 'trimming' policies supported by Halifax had failed to produce political stability and a co-operative Parliament. The best alternative seemed to be a dissolution and a new, remodelled ministry largely made up of Tories and led by Carmarthen.

The election of 1690 produced some Tory gains. However, lack of party discipline together with the novelty of the issues – in particular, how to wage and pay for a war of unprecedented dimensions – made it impossible to be sure of the attitude of wayward backbench MPs. And of course this was also true of members of the House of Lords. There were some changes in the ministry. Halifax resigned and the Treasury and Admiralty commissions were altered, but some Whigs, inevitably furious at the turn of events, were left in office. Further, while Carmarthen himself was the most important member of the government, he had nothing like the influence over either his colleagues or the King that he had possessed in the 1670s. He also lacked the political and administrative base that the lord treasurership would have given him.

In these circumstances Carmarthen demonstrated his lack of flexibility and real political insight. No one was better able to manipulate all the various strands of patronage to his own and his family's advantage, but this would help him little in his dealings with Parliament in the new post-revolutionary era. Carmarthen had learnt little from his failures in the 1670s, for he still believed that a ministry satisfactory to the Church party, pursuing a sound Protestant foreign policy, would succeed in carrying Parliament with it, and if there were any problems from recalcitrant MPs or peers they could be solved by judicious use of patronage and informal pressure. This approach had two drawbacks. In the first place, William's policy of vigorous war against France could not, in the end, be supported by the Tories, and, secondly, use of office-holders in Parliament to support government policy produced a sharp counter-reaction. The issue of bought votes became one of the major causes of concern in the period after 1689, as it had been in the 1670s.

Thus, while the new Tory-inclined ministry set up in 1690 had its successes, especially at first, it soon ran into serious problems. Unprecedented sums of money – £4 million in the autumn of that year – were voted for the armed forces. The crisis caused by the naval defeat at Beachy Head was surmounted, Whig attacks on Carmarthen in both Houses in December 1690 collapsed and he played the major role in exposing Lord Preston's plot to restore James II. None the less, as time went on and the expensive and apparently futile war continued, Carmarthen's position began to weaken. Broadly, three lines of attack on the ministry developed. The first was largely financial and centred around the inquiries of the parliamentary commission for examining the public accounts, created in 1690. The MPs elected to it provided a focus for discontent and were, naturally, the likeliest critics of government spending. Secondly, attacks on the conduct of government continued in both Houses, fuelled by the failure to achieve any substantial success in the war. Even the naval victory of La Hogue in 1692, for instance, was a disappointment, because it was not followed up. Thirdly, backbenchers of both parties demanded constitutional reforms, such as a Place Act to prevent office-holders from being MPs and a Triennial Act to write the need for frequent parliaments into law.

In the spring of 1692 William responded to these pressures by a further lurch towards the Tories. Lord Rochester was appointed to the Privy Council and Sir Edward Seymour was given a place on the Treasury Commission. These changes did not help the ministry or indeed Carmarthen's position within it. He had little in common with either of these men; his ideal was a moderate Tory government containing also those Whigs who would support it, and his relations with the Secretary of State, Nottingham, were poor. The plain fact was that a Tory ministry would not support the war as William conceived of it, demanding large British forces on the continent of Europe. What Rochester suggested instead was a primarily naval contribution.

The failure of Carmarthen's approach was clear in the events of 1693. That it had lost control of Parliament became evident in March, when William was forced to the final expedient of vetoing a Triennial Bill. Further, the vital ideas for increasing government revenue were coming not from the former Lord Treasurer, but from a newly appointed Treasury Commissioner, the dedicated Whig, Charles Montagu. But it was the disaster at sea, the destruction of the Smyrna Convoy, for which Carmarthen could not personally be held responsible, that finally destroyed the ministry. By this stage William had found a new political adviser, the formidable Earl of Sunderland, who successfully preached the need for a Whig administration. 1693–4 saw a whole crop of Whig appointments and Nottingham's dismissal; but, shorn of real political influence, Carmarthen nevertheless survived and indeed prospered. He was allowed to remain Lord President (the King could not afford to offend the Tory party completely) and in May 1694 he was created Duke of Leeds. But his position was inevitably one of isolation and vulnerability. Sooner or later the Whigs would seek to bring him down. Their opportunity to do so came during a parliamentary investigation of bribery which was to involve not only Leeds (which we have now, confusingly, to call him) but also the Speaker of the House of Commons. Although his guilt was never proved, it appeared that Leeds had been paid by the East India Company for his help in defending its charter from those who sought to set up a new company. The principal witness, the

Duke's servant John Robart, disappeared, so that his impeachment for high crimes and misdemeanours could not be carried but his reputation was finally blasted.

Leeds was to remain in office until 1699, but he never again actually appeared in Council during William's reign. His day was over and, while he had friends and associates among the Tories, he was probably out of sympathy with the increasingly 'country' opposition trend the party followed in the later 1690s. Although he lived until 1712, his great age meant he could play little part in the ferocious party strife of Anne's reign.

The last phase of his political life, then, was primarily one of disappointment. He performed a valuable role in helping to secure national unity in the dangerous period after 1689. Undoubtedly his adhesion to the Revolution and his moderation thereafter strengthened the new regime. Nor was it his selfishness or cupidity which fatally undermined him – in these he did not differ greatly from the majority of his contemporaries. But he had little idea of how to operate in the new circumstances of the 1690s – little understanding, in other words, of the constitutional, political and economic implications of the Revolution and, more especially, of the vast war in which England then found herself engaged.

VII

This gradual fading into insignificance in a political situation he failed to understand forms a suitable epitaph for Danby's career. On every significant occasion in his career from 1673 onwards, he had a clearly formulated political programme which he confidently asserted would resolve the King's difficulties, so also securing himself the high office which he craved and financially needed. Yet on each occasion he had misjudged contemporary circumstances. In the 1670s the country (particularly MPs) was increasingly resentful of Court influence and intrigue, and the role of Anglicanism as a bulwark against nonconformity and republicanism no longer seemed so vital. In the 1690s party organisation was emerging in a different format, with new sources he had not expected. In both periods his suggestions harked back to a previous decade. Since his administrative and financial actions also broke little new ground, it is surely necessary to see him as a hard-working, intelligent and loyal if greedy minister in a somewhat old-fashioned mode rather than as a proponent of new political responses. The solutions to the financial and parliamentary problems of the Stuarts were to emerge along lines very different from those envisaged by Danby, whose significance must therefore be seen in terms of short-term political survival rather than far-sighted reform.

As a personality he equally fails to make any great impact. Like Clarendon he did not fit into the easy and indolent cynicism of Charles II's court; unlike Clarendon he lacked the polish of being a literate, cultured and self-confident gentleman. He could not share Charles's enthusiasms for the racecourse, the theatre or the boudoir. He was a conscientious and extremely persevering politician and bureaucrat, but little more. The demands of his family encouraged his appetite for work, since he needed the fruits of office more than most. Yet his apparently inexhaustible demand for and later expectation of office has something attractive about it, if only humorously so. Despite his rough experiences in early 1679, he continually plagued Charles for five years with both requests for release and political advice. The manipulator of Parliament in the 1670s, and probable proponent of absolutism in 1678, could bounce back in 1688 as one of the signatories on the invitation to William, and could confidently proclaim his indispensability in the much-changed post-Revolution world of politics. Not for first time he was wrong.

Bluntly it must be said that Danby was not a particularly interesting or congenial person. Ultimately it must be admitted that his political achievements were short-lived and of limited significance. Ironically, perhaps his greatest contributions to English government were, in his first period of office, to provoke Shaftesbury into forming the first effective political party and, in his second, to help provoke the Whig junto into establishing the principle of one-party government.

10. Robert Spencer, Earl of Sunderland

ROD MARTIN

ROBERT Spencer, second Earl of Sunderland, was the politician's politician – he has no other claim on the historian's respect or sympathy. Though he was a man of considerable intelligence and cultivation, he was devoid of principles and sheer physical courage, utterly unscrupulous and inordinately ambitious. In a period often dominated by religious issues Sunderland stood almost alone in a cynical, disbelieving detachment, quite prepared when necessary to use the deepest beliefs of others as a weapon to increase his own power. Only towards the end of his life, under the influence of his wife, did he perhaps develop any genuine religious feelings; and at the same time the shattering effect of the Glorious Revolution taught him the only real political ethics he ever had, based largely on gratitude to William III. On the other hand, as a political manipulator he was unequalled in seventeenth-century England. Further, in the 1690s Sunderland showed himself capable of a constructive statesmanship which was to have profound effects on British political history.

Whatever the internal consistencies of particular periods of Sunderland's career, taken as a whole it has only one persistent theme: a desire to possess as much power as possible. Money seems to have meant little to him in itself: he used it to pay off gambling debts – his one vice – and to support a lavish patronage of the arts, notably a constantly growing collection of paintings. But a brief summary of his political life demonstrates, if nothing else, an astonishing capacity to survive. Sunderland supported the exclusion from the throne of James Duke of York in 1680 and lost office when Charles II began to strike back at his opponents in 1681. Changing tack completely, he worked his way back into Charles's favour, out-manoeuvring rivals to become in James's reign the dedicated instrument of royal power.

Inevitably overwhelmed by the Glorious Revolution, he none the less became, in the 1690s, William III's chief political adviser. Then, at first without office, Sunderland wielded ironically his most important influence, and he used it in 1693 to bring the Whigs to office, creating in the process the first working relationship between Crown and Parliament since the end of the sixteenth century.

I

Sunderland was born in 1641, the son of a moderate royalist who two years later got himself killed at the First Battle of Newbury. He was, however, more fortunate in his other relatives for they brought valuable connections. Sunderland's mother was a member of the Sydney family, the daughter of the Earl of Leicester. His sister Dorothy married Sir George Savile, later Marquis of Halifax. Little is known of Sunderland's early years, but the events which led to his marriage to Anne Digby, daughter of the Earl of Bristol, in 1665 display his impetuosity (and possibly his lack of courage!). On the eve of their wedding, scheduled for June 1663, the bridegroom slipped away, eventually to leave for a tour of the continent. The fact that despite this insult the marriage did take place was important for the help the Countess's friends, such as John Evelyn, provided when his prospects looked ruined in 1688–9.

Having made an eminently suitable marriage, the next essential step for a young aristocrat in this period was to establish a position at Court. This was true even for those without active political ambition, for the Court was the centre of social prestige and, more concretely, the source of money in the form of pensions, sinecures and lucrative offices. A man who wished to live in style, and Sunderland certainly did – witness his vast improvements to his seat at Althorp in Northamptonshire – needed this 'aristocratic dole' to supplement the inadequate income provided by his rents.

In the 1670s, therefore, Sunderland served his political apprenticeship in a number of diplomatic posts, including visits to Madrid and to Paris. But by 1678 he had made little progress. The only asset he possessed, apart from his family connections, was a wide circle of friends, including the Earl of Shaftesbury and, possibly more importantly, Charles II's mistress Louise de Kéroualle, Duchess of Portsmouth. However, he had one crucial advantage: his career so far had not firmly linked him either with Danby or with the leaders of the country opposition. The desperate clash between the latter and Charles in the fevered circumstances of the Popish Plot made Sunderland an ideal compromise candidate for one of the two secretaryships of state in place of the unpopular Williamson. The job was a valuable one but it was a risky gamble in February 1679 with anti-Catholic hysteria turning against James. It was also an expensive one. Sunderland had to pay £6000 to his predecessor for the post, and as usual his financial situation left a lot to be desired.

This, to modern eyes, curious custom of paying for a job in government explains much of Sunderland's – and indeed all Stuart politicians' – attitude to office. An important post such as Secretary of State or, more powerful still, Lord Treasurer might carry great influence with the king, or it might not. Policy-making was very much the prerogative of the Crown and it was quite possible for the king to ignore much of the advice which his ministers gave him. The ministers for their part carried out the royal wishes and made money from their jobs. The concept of a minister's resignation in face of a policy decision with which he profoundly disagreed was alien to the period, as was its concomitant, a united Cabinet. This is why Charles II's 'ministries' saw a constant squabbling over policies and the key positions in government. No minister in this situation was indispensable, as Sunderland recognised when he remarked on the new Privy Council of 1679 in his affected nasal drawl, 'Whaat . . . if his Majesty tuarn out fuarty of us, may not he have fuarty athors to saarve him as well? And whaat maaters who saarves his Majesty, so lang as his Majesty is saarved?'[1] Curiously, it was Sunderland who would in the 1690s change this situation when he organised a united government based on party strength in Parliament.

The Exclusion crisis was doubly important for Sunderland's career. In the first place it made him one of the major figures in English politics; and in the second place the failure of the Whigs to exclude James from the throne led him to draw the wrong conclusions from the events of 1679–81. His actual influence on this great political struggle was, however, very limited. It was Shaftesbury and his supporters who made the running and it was Charles himself who in the end out-manoeuvred them, rejecting in the process Sunderland's view that James should be excluded in favour of William of Orange. Initially he had shown support for James, with whom he was also on friendly terms, and the failure of Charles's attempts to compromise with Shaftesbury had led to the opposition's removal from the Privy Council and the formation of a ministry of courtiers, nicknamed the 'Chits', consisting of Sunderland, Lawrence Hyde and Godolphin. But, as it became clear that the Whigs were not going to abandon Exclusion, Sunderland's reaction was to see if an anti-French policy might make the government more popular. A defensive treaty was signed with Spain in June 1680 and an attempt was made to bring in Holland and other Protestant states, such as Brandenburg and Denmark. However, this was far too ambitious to have any chance of success and in any case the parliamentary opposition was, in comparison with its desperate concern with Exclusion, uninterested in foreign policy.

The trouble was that the logical end of an anti-French foreign policy was in fact support for Exclusion. From the Crown's point of view either the Whigs must be conciliated or Parliament neutralised by French financial support. At the same time, Shaftesbury's staggering impudence in June 1680 in presenting James as a Popish recusant and the Duchess of Portsmouth as a common whore before the Grand Jury of Middlesex, demonstrated the fixed purpose of the Whigs. It seemed to Sunderland that the time had come for Charles to ditch his brother as heir to the throne and replace him with William, who should come over to England as soon as possible to safeguard his wife's rights to the throne against the possibility of Monmouth's succeeding. But William was rightly very wary of being used by English politicians against Charles and James, and the Whigs were by no means united in support of Monmouth – indeed, the second Exclusion Bill was amended on 8 November 1680 so that the Crown would go to Mary, and Sunderland's influence may have had something to do with this.

Of course, it was Charles's attitude to Exclusion that mattered. Logically it may have seemed that the King, who had shown himself so far in his reign to be highly flexible, changing policies and dropping ministers as necessary, would be quite prepared to sacrifice his brother. Sunderland certainly thought so. But, while Charles had little confidence in his brother's ability to govern England, he saw Exclusion as an attack on the basic principle of monarchy, on all that his father had stood for, and he would not move. He was prepared only to offer 'Limitations' on a Catholic successor, but these the opposition dismissed as unrealistic. Thus, from the moment Sunderland voted for Exclusion on 15 November 1680 he was doomed. The

Bill itself was thrown out by the Lords, largely owing to Charles's personal influence. Sunderland, like many of his contemporaries, had misjudged his man. On 18 January Charles dissolved his fourth parliament. Six days later Sunderland was dismissed and the King refused to allow Lord Conway, who succeeded him, to reimburse the £6000 he had paid for the office of Secretary of State.

II

The failure of the Whigs was owing to a variety of factors: their own internal divisions, especially on the question of who was to succeed Charles; their dependence on Parliament's sitting; and, most important, the conservative nature of the landed classes and their fear of another civil war. The King had fought a long delaying action, and the inability of the opposition to force through their policy of Exclusion considerably strengthened the Crown's position. Without any need in the last four years of his reign to call Parliament, Charles could strike at his enemies. Shaftesbury was driven into exile and the Rye House Plot disposed of Essex, Russell and Algernon Sidney. He could also undermine the sources of Whig electoral strength by purging the corporations. By 1685, then, the monarchy seemed very strong; it needed extreme political incompetence over the next three years to dissipate this strength. The 'natural tendency' of English history in the 1680s might well be regarded as leading ultimately towards a stronger monarchy rather than, as the Whig historians saw it, the inevitable triumph of Parliament. This was certainly Sunderland's conclusion based on the experience of the Exclusion crisis. By no stretch of the imagination could the 1688 Revolution have been foreseen by English politicians. Outside intervention leading to a change of régime in Britain had been unknown since 1485 – as Sunderland with suitably apologetic hyperbole wrote in 1689 in his defence of his conduct in James's reign:

the Prince [of Orange]'s designs . . . were not then looked on as they have proved, nobody foreseeing the miracles he has done by his wonderful prudence, conduct and courage; for the greatest thing which has been undertaken these thousand years . . . could not be effected without virtues hardly to be imagined till seen nearer hand.

The proper course for an ambitious politician in the 1680s was, it seemed, to behave as submissively as possible to the royal will, and Sunderland went overboard in his desire to do just that. Admitting his past errors, he worked his way back into royal favour through the Duchess of Portsmouth and in January 1683 was reappointed as Secretary of State largely because of his knowledge and experience in the field of foreign affairs. The next five and a half years were to see Sunderland reaching the heights of political office in England. At times, such as in the last months of Charles II's reign and more especially under James after the dismissal of the Hyde brothers – the earls of Clarendon and Rochester – at the beginning of 1687, he possessed a near-monopoly of ministerial influence. His success was partly owing to the weaknesses of his rivals for office. Sunderland was utterly unscrupulous in his willingness to implement the royal wishes. Halifax with his nagging constitutionalism and the devotedly Anglican Hydes were not. But they also lacked, and so for that matter did that indispensable man of business Sidney Godolphin, Sunderland's driving ambition and manipulative skill.

The death of Charles in February 1685 was a severe blow, for it destroyed the influence of Sunderland's great ally, the Duchess of Portsmouth. It also gave Rochester the paramount office of Lord Treasurer which he craved. James had much reason to support the brother of his first wife, who had never wavered in his allegiance to the principle of legitimate monarchy, rather than Sunderland, who had voted for Exclusion and almost succeeded in 1684 in despatching his rival to the outer darkness of Ireland. Sunderland survived by his willingness to agree with James's ultimate aims.

James's policy was to restore the Roman Catholic Church in England: to secure complete toleration (that is to say, civil equality for Catholics) and to reconcile England with Rome. Specifically he wanted to remove the penal laws and Test Acts. It does not necessarily follow that he sought to impose Catholicism on his subjects. With all the enthusiasm of a convert James was in all probability naïve enough to believe that, once his religion was given equality, its divine truth would convert large numbers of people. But in fact, since the vast majority of Englishmen were highly bigoted Protestants, the achievement even of this goal would inevitably have necessitated the rigid subordination of Parliament and a tight control over the localities. Given James's obstinacy and political incompetence, as well as his age – he was very much an 'old man in a hurry' – it is difficult to believe that he had much chance of success. But this highlights Sunderland's dilemma. In order to remove Rochester, indeed in order to have much influence at all, he needed to outflank him by supporting James's Catholic policy – something Rochester could never countenance. In this way, close to the King, he could also draw on the support of Catholic courtiers such as the Jesuit Edward Petre and Richard Talbot, Earl of Tyrconnel. He dominated these men in the informal Catholic Council which James had set up to advise him and which Sunderland now used to increase his power. He was also able to play on Queen Mary and make use of whatever influence she possessed.

But this tactic had two, ultimately fatal, drawbacks. In his turn Sunderland could be outflanked, for he was very vulnerable to the pressures of Catholic extremists who wanted to go much farther and faster than was remotely politically possible and could accuse him, when he advised caution, of cowardice in the great cause. Eventually, in 1688, the increasing influence of these extremists, such as John Drummond, Earl of Melfort, undermined Sunderland's position. His very caution, when contrasted with the advice offered James by the extremists, demonstrates the second drawback. Sunderland was burning his bridges and he knew it. His links with the Catholics tended to isolate him from almost everyone else – except other time-servers such as the Lord Chancellor, Jeffreys.

All this brings into question exactly what Sunderland hoped to achieve in this period. The assumption must be that during James's reign he intended simply to be rich and powerful and that he did not care one way or the other about James's religious aims except in so far as they affected his political career. But it is also probably true that Sunderland expected James's reign to come to a fairly speedy end when he would be succeeded, as things stood until the summer of 1688, by his Protestant daughter Mary and her formidable husband, William of Orange. If he played his cards carefully, he might hope to survive into the new régime – as indeed he did, even after the disaster of the Revolution. This view would explain his disinclination to take the step of public conversion to Catholicism which, while it carried immense political advantages – the King would be overjoyed – was also irrevocable, or so it seemed. Instead, he flirted with conversion for at least eighteen months until, undermined by the Catholic extremists, he sought to recover his position by announcing his change of faith days after the birth of the Prince of Wales, when in fact it was too late to help him and his room for manoeuvre had gone. He was driven to the extremity of pinning his hopes, in the event of James's death, on the unlikely survival of the Catholic cause with Mary of Modena as regent for her son. So, as James's position deteriorated in the last year of his reign, Sunderland's support of the régime reduced him to the position of Mr Micawber, desperately hoping that something would turn up.

Having examined Sunderland's attitudes in the 1680s, it remains to assess his impact on policy. The successful out-manoeuvring of opponents at Court and the possession of the highest offices of state did not necessarily mean, as we shall see, that his influence over policy was correspondingly great. He was, however, in an excellent position to exert influence in certain fields. For one thing he had considerable expertise in foreign affairs and was by no means as insular as most of his contemporaries. He also spoke fluently the language of diplomacy, French, a by-no-means common accomplishment among the English upper class at this time.

In the final years of Charles II, when he was clearly a Francophile, the policy of the King was in any case friendship with France. Under James, foreign affairs continued to be bound up with domestic necessities. If the rivalry between the French and the Dutch turned into war, England would be hard pressed to stand aside. That would mean asking Parliament for funds and Parliament would almost certainly put a stop to James's Catholic policies. Alliance with France, the destruction of the Dutch and the alteration of the succession to exclude Mary was the policy of the Catholic extremists embodied in 1686 in a remonstrance to the King which rapidly became public knowledge. James would have nothing to do with this policy. In fact he persistently refused to identify himself wholly with Louis, but his intentions were misunderstood. The large army he was building up and the expansion in the Royal Navy might well be directed against his own subjects and, in alliance with France, against the Dutch.

Sunderland's advice did nothing to aid his master. While working to keep the peace in Europe, he helped to worsen relations with the Dutch and increased their suspicion of the English government. In 1687, hoping to improve his position with the King and increase the pension of about £7000 a year he was already receiving from Louis XIV, he supported the advice of the Catholic extremists to recall the English and Scots regiments from Holland. This would strengthen

James's beloved Army and the King agreed, but in the early spring of 1688 the States General refused to let them go. James was furious but there was little he could do and he had added fuel to Dutch fears of a secret Anglo-French alliance, thus nerving the States General to support William of Orange's invasion. English foreign policy was inept but Sunderland cannot be held totally responsible. First Charles II and later James II had since the 1660s wavered between supporting one or other of their neighbours while leaning on the whole towards France. Besides this, domestic issues – the need to impress Parliament or as in 1681–5 and 1686–8 the desire to do without Parliament – had often determined foreign relations. Sunderland lacked both the strength and the determination to break this pattern. Not until William of Orange took the throne was the choice to be finally made and a policy of opposition to France followed. Then the complete reverse happened: the needs of the war came to dominate everything else.

Sunderland's impact on domestic policy, however, is far more open to criticism, for, whatever the merits of James's intentions, the unwise advice he received from his minister bolstered his self-confidence so that, by the time Sunderland realised that he had gone too far, it was too late. His primary concern was in the key area of relations with Parliament. Sunderland had played little part in the purging of corporations in the early 1680s that was intended to put them into the hands of loyal Tories. On the other hand, in the 1685 election he was ultimately in charge of wielding government influence wherever possible through the usual channels of the lords lieutenant of counties and those landowners amenable to pressure from above. The result of this influence plus the remodelling of corporation charters, as well as a swing in opinion in favour of the Crown since 1681, was the election of the most tractable House of Commons of the century. But, when, in November 1685, James demanded money to support a large standing army and the approval of Parliament for the employment of Catholic officers, he found to his intense anger that there were limits to this docility. If complete equality for Roman Catholics could not be brought about by alliance with the loyalist Tories, that left only two alternatives: settle for less, which was Rochester's attitude, or, as Sunderland argued, attempt a more drastic solution. This would take the form of a purge of all office-holders who would not support James's policy (including, of course, Rochester). Such a policy would appeal to the self-interest of peers and MPs who stood to lose their lucrative posts and the fact that James's large revenue enabled him to do without Parliament would frighten them into obedience. All of this was designed specifically to pander to James's authoritarian instincts and he responded in December 1685 by appointing Sunderland to the highly prestigious post of Lord President of the Council while retaining him as principal Secretary of State.

The trouble was that the policy did not work, even when backed up with the personal interviews of members of both Houses with the King ('closeting'). They would not agree to commit themselves to repeal the penal laws and Test Acts. In the meantime office-holders and JPs were sacked and often replaced by Catholics. And, in the spring of 1687, the Anglican Church was attacked directly when the King tried to force Magdalen College, Oxford, to accept as President Anthony Farmer, a debauched crypto-Catholic. Sunderland afterwards claimed to have defended the College – he may well have done so, for the affair was at best a major political blunder. He was certainly fearful of the consequences when the King, disillusioned in his hopes of persuading Parliament to see the wisdom of his ideas, dissolved it in July 1687. But it was partly Sunderland's fault that James was rapidly going to extremes, and he could hardly advise caution now without admitting that his previous advice had been mistaken.

The failure to force Parliament to be amenable left the government with only one alternative short of using military force: a thorough manipulation of elections so that those groups who might be supposed to favour toleration – Catholics, dissenters and miscellaneous hacks – would be able to elect a subservient majority when a new parliament was called. James saw the Queen's pregnancy in the late autumn of 1687 as the divine blessing on his work. Sunderland recognised all too well that such a project would need time and he also saw that the nonconformists hated Catholics quite as much as the Anglicans did. Thus, while he was forced, if he wanted to stay in office, to be a leading organiser in the campaign to get the right men elected, his basic tactic during the autumn and spring of 1687–8 was to prevent the calling of a parliament before its success could be guaranteed.

It is difficult to estimate the success of the campaign. Agents were appointed to report in the borough constituencies and the opinions of lords lieutenant and JPs canvassed, but the right time to call Parliament never came. Sunderland and Penn, the dissenting leader, argued that some sort of compromise ought to be offered – say the repeal of the Test Acts but Catholics to be excluded from the House of Commons. In any case, caution and moderation on the part of the government was essential. Instead, James plunged into disaster by trying for seditious libel seven bishops who petitioned him in May 1688 against the order to read in church the reissue of the Edict of Toleration.

Sunderland was appalled, especially when he saw the spontaneous outburst of joy which accompanied the bishops' acquittal. He was called to give evidence and could hardly fail to be affected by the scorn with which he was received by the public. Sunderland's policy was in ruins, the Catholic extremists were getting the upper hand at Court, and on the horizon loomed the spectre of William of Orange. Yet neither James nor his minister could really believe until early September 1688 that invasion was near. And, if William did try it, his chances of success were surely remote against James's naval and land forces. The final recognition in the middle of the month that the Dutch were coming broke Sunderland's nerve. Thoroughly panic-stricken and fearful for his life, he recommended immediate and far reaching concessions. He was accused by the extreme Catholics of cowardice and even treason; but there is no evidence for the particular myth, fostered later by the Jacobites and seemingly supported by Sunderland's renewed influence in the 1690s, that he was in league with William and sought from the first to ruin James.

In late October came the news that the Dutch fleet had been driven back by a storm – as it turned out only temporarily – and James, disgusted by Sunderland's personal collapse, finally dismissed him. It was now only a matter of personal safety. Clearly, fighting by James's side was hardly his métier and Louis was not likely to look kindly on a deserter whose activity had been at least partly responsible for the catastrophe. Sometime early in December, therefore, Sunderland and his wife left England for Rotterdam, his political career apparently totally wrecked. Had he died at this point his career could easily be regarded as utterly devoid of principle and barren of achievement.

III

After the Revolution we inhabit a different political world. There were of course considerable elements of continuity – Parliament, for instance, continued to be made up of the same sort of people, landowners, as before – but the conditions in which politicians operated were fundamentally different. For one thing the monarchy's position was considerably weakened. Not by the Bill of Rights as such, for the Crown's theoretical power was much the same in 1690 as it had been in 1687. The decisive factor was William III's determination to fight France. Parliament had to be called every year to vote taxes. Inevitably it became more assertive, demanding both reforms such as the Triennial Act and a greater influence on the conduct of government. While it is completely misguided to underestimate the importance of Queen Anne or of her Hanoverian successors, it is also true that William III was the last English king to control broad policy at home and abroad and its detailed implementation. Fortunately he was by far the most competent English monarch since 1603.

The long war with France, which lasted, with one interval, from 1689 to 1713, had an enormous impact. Apart from its revolutionary effect on foreign policy and on finance it eventually crystallised the party battle which was the central feature of English political life from the early 1690s into the reign of George I. This did not seem to be the case at first, for the war and the succession of William III cut across traditional party boundaries. Whigs could hardly insist on limitations on the power of the monarch when the king in question was firmly for the Protestant cause and might well be the only barrier against the wrath of their enemies or, even worse, of a returning James II. The Tories were in the same boat though for different reasons. They could not support William III's just prerogatives when they were not altogether sure that they were just. By what right was William King? It took time for the parties to reorient themselves round the new issues of the 1690s: how to fight and finance a war of unprecedented dimensions, and the extent to which it was necessary to curb the power of the executive, the monarchy, after the experience of the last thirty years.

Not surprisingly therefore, the years of William's reign were a period of considerable political factionalism, made worse by the King's personal unpopularity. Cosmopolitan, reserved, utterly uninterested in the pomp and ceremony of kingship and profoundly distrustful of party politicians, William was not a man with much in common with the English upper classes. It took him some time to understand the political situation with which he was faced. His first reaction in 1689 was to appoint a balanced group of Whigs and Tories. But the behaviour of the Whigs in the Convention Parliament of 1689–90 was tactless in the extreme. They sought to punish those responsible for their miseries in the previous reigns; they attacked the King's Tory ministers, such as the Earl of Nottingham and the Marquis of Carmarthen; and they showed insensitivity to William's financial needs. This was not the unity William desired in order to fight France, and in the early months of 1690 he turned to their opponents and created a ministry biased towards the Tories under Carmarthen. This survived for three years but can hardly be described as a success. The war on the continent went badly. Mons fell in 1691, William's army was mauled at Steenkirk in July 1692 and the Army and Navy estimates rapidly rose to over £4 million per year. The only bright spot was the naval victory at La Hogue in May 1692, which balanced defeat at Beachy Head two years earlier. However, this did not strengthen the government, because Russell, the Whig Admiral, did not follow up his success and soon fell to arguing with the Tory Secretary of State, Nottingham.

At home the ministers faced a highly critical Parliament where, although the Tories were probably in a majority in the Lower House, this was little help, for many Tory backbenchers, such as Sir Thomas Clarges and Sir Christopher Musgrave, were highly critical of the war as it was being fought. As for the Whigs, though they persistently attacked Tory ministers, that did not stop them allying with Tory backbenchers to demand constitutional reform, especially a Triennial Act. And they were now beginning to be led by a new generation of able parliamentarians all of whom held junior office. These were the men who were to dominate the party until the Hanoverian succession: Thomas Wharton, an outstanding electioneer, John Somers with his massive legal prestige, Admiral Edward Russell and the financial expert Charles Montagu. Later they were to be called the Junto.

The parliamentary session of 1692–3 demonstrated convincingly the extent to which the government had lost control. It proved very difficult to squeeze adequate supply out of the Commons; there was considerable criticism of the employment of foreign officers in the Army; and Nottingham and Russell were at open war. Ominously, in December 1692 the House of Lords considered the drastic step of proposing to the Commons a Committee of Both Houses to consider the state of the nation. This could have led to a straight fight for control with the King. The idea was defeated by only twelve votes. Worse still, although the Court just managed to defeat a Place Bill which would have deprived the government of much of its influence in the Commons, the ministers could not stop the passing of a Triennial Bill. William hesitated, but after over a month's consideration he vetoed it. This was clearly the last resort: he wished to defend the royal prerogative but he was more anxious still to fight the war. By the spring of 1693 it was not clear that he would be able to do either for much longer.

IV

What was needed was a hard look at the way in which the government was organised. Since William was absent for months on end fighting the war, he needed a manager – as it turned out, the first of that series of men transitional between the Stuart favourite/minister and the Hanoverian prime minister – who could organise and discipline the supporters of the government in parliament. The problem was, who was available? Carmarthen had proved a failure; the Tories could not be harnessed to the war effort – the last three years had shown that. The Earl of Shrewsbury, nominal leader of the Whigs, lacked political stamina. But there was another possibility.

William's indifference to past crimes, his concern only with present usefulness, had meant that after a brief sojourn in a Dutch prison Sunderland was allowed to return home to England. He was well connected – for example, his uncle Henry Sidney was high in William's confidence – and he had not been associated with the fate of the Whig martyrs of Charles's reign which so occupied the attention of the Convention Parliament. Of course, Sunderland was excluded from William's Act of Grace in 1690, but clearly his life and estates were secure. It goes without saying that he rapidly abandoned his Roman Catholicism. On the positive side he had a number of advantages from William's point of view. First, his boats were thoroughly burnt – he was also excepted from James II's proclamation of pardon in April 1692 (the only person to manage both exceptions). Secondly, his experience meant that more than almost any of his contemporaries he could understand and appreciate the King's foreign policy. Thirdly, he had been involved in the details of parliamentary management.

Sunderland's advice when he was first received by William in the spring of 1691 was unpalatable, but two years later the King's range of options had narrowed. As Sunderland recognised, after the

Revolution, given that England was involved in a highly expensive war, the King could not hope to control the Lords and Commons as his predecessors had done. However useful place and patronage were to influence peers and MPs, they were utterly inadequate as a means by which the government could get its way in Parliament. Further, the Commons especially were bound to use the fact that they had to be called every year to vote massive sums of money to restrict further the King's prerogative power. Into this vacuum, as it were, between the needs of the executive and the power of the legislature Sunderland proposed to insert party. Thirty years later, when the long war had increased the number of offices available for distribution, another great politician, Sir Robert Walpole, used place to ensure that the King's government would be carred on with the support of Parliament.

Next, if party was to be used in this way, it had to be the Whig party. In his famous letter to the Earl of Portland in 1694 Sunderland wrote,

> I have so often repeated my opinion concerning the Whig party and the Tory party . . . but I must however say that the great mistake that has been made for five years together has been to think that they were equal in relation to this government, since the whole of one may be made for it and not a quarter of the other ever can. Whenever the government has leaned to the Whigs it has been strong, whenever the other has prevailed it has been despised.[2]

He repeated the same theme, more succinctly, in a reputed reply to William himself, who distrusted the Whig party's anti-monarchical principles: 'It was very true, that the Tories were better friends to monarchy than the Whigs were, but then his Majesty was to consider, he was not their Monarch.'[3]

Finally, it was no use having a ministry made up largely of Whigs but with some important posts held by Tories. William's balancing between parties would have to stop. In Sunderland's own words, there should be no 'patching', but a 'thorough good administration and employing men firm to this government, and thought to be so'.[4] Moreover, party government implies that those in power will stand together against outside opposition. In the circumstances of the 1690s it meant mutual ministerial co-operation, but, above all, support of the King's policies. Sunderland was consistent in his recognition of the importance of unity among those in office, a concept as novel for the period as his use of party, or as significant as his insistence on a small, powerful Cabinet. 'A Cabinet Council of twelve or thirteen men of which no-one takes himself to be particularly concerned in the general conduct of affairs, where there is neither secrecy, despatch or credit is a monstrous thing.'⁵ In all these views lies the germ for the development of that most vital of British political institutions, the Cabinet, which binds together party, administration and Parliament.

Sunderland's advice, then, was little short of revolutionary in its implications and William found it difficult to accept wholeheartedly. In the spring of 1693 he appointed Somers Lord Keeper and another leading Whig, Sir John Trenchard, Secretary of State, but the Tories Carmarthen and Nottingham remained in office. Nevertheless it was Sunderland who was constructing a new, largely Whig, party of Court supporters in Parliament. He spent the early summer analysing which MPs and peers could be bought off and with what, and he wrote a remonstrance to the King's factotum, the Earl of Portland, in June about the mistakes in the 1692–3 session of Parliament and complaining of the folly of doing things by halves. Several meetings took place involving Sunderland and leading politicians, culminating in a conference in late August at Althorp attended by the chiefs of the Whig party, the earls of Shrewsbury and Devonshire, and Montagu, Admiral Russell and Wharton, as well as the non-party man of business, Godolphin. By then, the disaster which befell the Smyrna Convoy in June had destroyed Nottingham's chances of remaining in office. Whoever was at fault, he and the Tory admirals were widely blamed.

The parliamentary session in the winter of 1693–4 proved Sunderland's advice right. True, a Place Bill had to be vetoed, but against this there was no trouble over the enormous estimates for the fleet, amounting to £2.5 million, and the Commons agreed to an increase in the number of troops for the coming year. Of more lasting significance was the scheme piloted through the Commons by Charles Montagu for the creation of the Bank of England. The success of the session was signalised by the promotion of more Whigs to office – for example, Russell became First Lord of the Admiralty and the great Whig aristocrats, the earls of Bedford, Clare, Devonshire and Shrewsbury, were all made dukes. The only cloud on the Whig horizon – the initial refusal of William to pass a Triennial Bill, which prevented Shrewsbury from taking office – was dispelled when the King gave the requisite promise. In March 1694 Shrewsbury accepted the seals of Secretary of State, and the following December a bill to secure triennial parliaments became law.

One group of Whigs could not, however, be satisfied. Small in number but highly vociferous, based on the Welsh-border connections of the Harley and Foley families, they demanded more constitutional reform and a cutback in military expenditure, which they saw as primarily benefiting foreigners. Office-holding was anathema to them and Sunderland could not buy their support, though his close friend and ally, Henry Guy, maintained contacts with Paul Foley when the latter was elected Speaker in the spring of 1695.

Indeed, Sunderland's very success was a potential source of weakness. The embryonic Junto were ambitious party politicans who resented his closeness to the King and his control over patronage. Sunderland himself could not take office – his reputation was still too bad for that and he was forced to rely on a partnership with Shrewsbury in his control over the Whig ministers. The early spring of 1695 saw a determined attempt by the Junto to undermine him by destroying his closest allies in the Commons. Henry Guy and Speaker Trevor were driven from office by a corruption inquiry, but when, in April, Sir John Trenchard died he was replaced as Secretary not by Wharton but by Sunderland's candidate, Sir William Trumbull. The Whig ministers' recognition that they were still dependent on Sunderland enabled him to force them back into line in the summer of 1695, an achievement which, as Guy wrote, 'was and is a matter of that difficulty, that I will boldly say, no man in England but himself could have done it'.[6]

Yet, while Sunderland's official position as the King's political manager was publicly demonstrated when William stayed at Althorp in October 1695 during the general election, it could only be a matter of time before the Junto turned on him again. As long as the war continued, the government's main strength would have to come from the Whigs. As it turned out, the party was not as strong in the 1695–8 Parliament as its members had hoped. Indeed, their control might well have slipped decisively had it not been for the Assassination Plot of February 1696, which allowed them to play the loyalty card against the Tories. Sunderland's position was strengthened when one of those involved in the Plot, Sir John Fenwick, accused Russell and Shrewsbury as well as Godolphin and Marlborough of conspiring with James II. They certainly had maintained contacts – a useful insurance policy – but it did not mean, as William himself fully realised, that their loyalty to the present government was seriously in doubt. The Junto got rid of Fenwick by Act of Attainder, but Shrewsbury had collapsed under the nervous strain and that left them in the hands of Sunderland.

The year 1697 saw the status quo destroyed. William insisted on appointing Sunderland to office in April, first as Lord Chamberlain and then as one of the Lord Justices of the Realm during his absence abroad. This reappointment to high office had a disastrous effect on public opinion. Even more serious in the long run was the Peace of Ryswick in September. There seemed now, to both Whig and Tory backbenchers, no reason why the Army should not be reduced to peacetime establishment. Country prejudice against the war, the ministers, the King and his Dutch favourites could be allowed full rein. The ministry itself was deeply divided by the resignation of Sir William Trumbull, for he was succeeded by James Vernon – Wharton had been rejected again.

The result was that, when Sunderland was attacked by MPs in December 1697, Whigs did nothing to defend him. Whether or not he would have been used as a whipping-boy for the Commons' discontent, Sunderland had had enough. He was all too aware of the vulnerability of his record at a time of massive criticism of the government, and he resigned at Christmas, much to William's annonyance – directed largely at the Junto. This was simply the prelude to a series of blows which fell upon the Whig party – defeat at the general election of 1698, loss of office, the attempted impeachment of its leaders in 1701, and finally the accession of Anne, who at first favoured the Tories.

If the Whigs lived to fight another day, Sunderland's life was drawing to a close. His last years recorded one outstanding domestic success when, in 1700, his son Charles married Lady Anne Churchill, daughter of the Duke of Marlborough, which eventually brought her father's title into the Spencer family. But a return to power was impossible without Shrewsbury's help and Shrewsbury was, intermittently, seriously ill. In 1700 Sunderland did help in the formation of a Tory ministry under Robert Harley and Godolphin which was designed to secure the succession and by passing the Act of Settlement duly did so. Conversely, when that ministry proved unable to bring the Commons to a sense of the danger posed by Louis XIV's acceptance of Carlos II's will, he successfully advised the return of the Whigs. But the death of William III in March 1702 finally ended Sunderland's political career, and his own death followed at Althorp six months later, on 28 September.

V

Sunderland's career is full of ironies and contradictions. For some years he was the supporter of Stuart despotism and a pro-French policy but later did more than anyone to reconcile responsible parliamentary party government with a powerful executive monarchy at a time when the defeat of France necessitated a close partnership. He wielded most influence when he was in fact out of office. Lord Macaulay, the great Whig historian, said of him, 'The art in which he surpassed all men was the art of whispering . . . his caressing manners, his power of insinuation and above all his apparent frankness made him irresistible in private conversation.' But, on the contrary, as his biographer J. P. Kenyon has made clear, 'The emotion Sunderland aroused in all his contemporaries was quite simply, fear. . . .'[7] His strength lay in his force of personality and his sheer self-confidence. These were the qualities which appealed to James II and William III – these and his considerable expertise especially in foreign policy, which he understood far better than his often xenophobic contemporaries. In addition, no one so excelled in the ability to manage men, to play on their susceptibilities and their ambitions. Finally, he was of course highly skilled in the business of seventeenth-century politics, the manipulations and manoeuvres that anyone had to be master of to achieve office under the Stuarts. He made mistakes. He backed the wrong horse in the Exclusion crisis and he totally miscalculated the chances of success of James's policies. Even so, it is difficult to believe that many could have foreseen the success of William's invasion in 1688. Against these errors can be placed Sunderland's undoubted success in recognising the changed political situation of the 1690s.

His significance in the history of later Stuart England is dependent on this last point. Sunderland's career before 1688 was surely devoid of any lasting result: he did not ruin James; James did that himself. But Sunderland's advice may well have saved William in 1693–4 from being forced into a disadvantageous peace. Only the Whigs could provide the parliamentary support essential to continuing the war as William fought it, with a large and highly expensive English land contingent. And the Whigs needed skilled management. Linked with this was Sunderland's understanding of the importance of a small efficient Cabinet which could command support in Parliament.

There is one more point which is often missed in the confusion which surrounds parties in the 1690s. By harnessing the Whigs to the war effort, by making them a party of government rather than of opposition, Sunderland gave their leaders experience of office and the chance to recognise the importance of staying united in the face of opponents' criticism, and the party as a whole the chance to get rid of some of its embarrassing radical country leftovers from the 1670s and 1680s. The Whig party reoriented itself in the 1690s and became the party which demanded firm opposition to Louis XIV and forged close links with the world of commerce and finance. To the extent that the long Whig supremacy in the eighteenth century, years of moderate constitutional government in partnership with the Crown, was the result of this reorientation, it was the most important legacy of Robert Spencer, second Earl of Sunderland.

Bibliography

Note: the place of publication is London unless otherwise stated.

1. LIONEL CRANFIELD, EARL OF MIDDLESEX

There are two impressive, scholarly and stylish biographies of Cranfield: R. H. Tawney, *Business and Politics under James I: Lionel Cranfield as Merchant and Minister* (Cambridge, 1958); and the longer study by Menna Prestwich, *Cranfield: Politics and Profits under the Early Stuarts* (Oxford, 1966). Tawney is more sympathetic in his treatment of Cranfield, but Prestwich has a wealth of factual detail, lucid explanations of the tortuous financial deals, and useful examinations of Cranfield's private fortune and the defence of it after his fall. She has summarised her views in 'English Politics and Administration, 1603–1625' in *The Reign of James VI and I*, ed. A. G. R. Smith (1973). In a short review article, 'The Political Morality of Early Stuart Statesmen', in *History* 1971, reprinted in his *Freedom, Corruption and Government in Elizabethan England* (1973), Joel Hurstfield provides a corrective to Prestwich's view of Cranfield's corruption. A clear account of royal finance under James I is in David Thomas's essay 'Financial and Administrative Developments' in *Before the English Civil War*, ed. H. Tomlinson (1983); other useful sources are R. Ashton, *The Crown and the Money Market 1603–1640* (Oxford, 1960); and F. C. Dietz, *English Public Finance 1558–1641* (London and New York, 1932). For Cranfield's relations with Parliament, see R. E. Zaller, *The Parliament of 1621* (Berkeley, Calif., 1971); R. E. Ruigh, *The Parliament of 1624* (Cambridge, Mass., and Oxford, 1971); and C. Russell, *Parliaments and English Politics 1621–1629* (Oxford, 1979). His relations with Buckingham and the Court are covered by Roger Lockyer in *Buckingham: The Life and Political Career of George Villiers, First Duke of Buckingham, 1592–1628* (1981). Cranfield's views on foreign policy are discussed by S. L. Adams in 'Foreign Policy and the Parliaments of 1621 and 1624' in *Faction and Parliament*, ed. K. Sharpe (Oxford, 1978).

2. GEORGE VILLIERS, DUKE OF BUCKINGHAM

The essential starting-point for work on Buckingham is R. Lockyer, *Buckingham: The Life and Political Career of George Villiers, First Duke of Buckingham, 1592—1628* (1981). My essay relies very heavily on this work. The political background of Buckingham's career can be followed in C. Russell, *Parliaments and English Politics, 1621–1629* (Oxford, 1979); and *Faction and Parliament: Essays on Early Stuart History*, ed. K. Sharpe (Oxford, 1978), in which the essays by Sharpe, Hirst and Adams are particularly useful. D. Hirst, *The*

Representative of the People? Voters and Voting under the Early Stuarts (Cambridge, 1975), explains why MPs were becoming more accountable to their constituents. Biographies of other leading figures at Court also provide useful information on Buckingham. One of the best is M. Prestwich, *Cranfield: Politics and Profit under the Early Stuarts* (Oxford, 1966). Of older works, S. R. Gardiner, *History of England from the Accession of James I to the Outbreak of the Civil War, 1603–1642* (10 vols, 1883–4) is still, despite its age, very readable and exceptionally accurate. Buckingham's career can be followed in vols II to VI, and vol. x contains a very detailed and helpful index. G. Parry, *The Golden Age Restor'd: The Culture of the Stuart Court, 1603—1642* (Manchester, 1981), provides an introduction to the cultural history of the time, and contains a chapter on Buckingham.

As judgements about Buckingham depend very much on one's views of the political developments of the Jacobean and early Caroline periods, the following articles are useful for the arguments they pursue. D. Hirst, 'Parliament, Law and War in the 1620s', *Historical Journal*, XXIII (1980) 455–61, and 'Revisionism Revised: The Place of Principle', *Past and Present*, XCIV (1981) 79–99, have important criticisms of some features of the 'revisionist' approach to early Stuart history. J. A. Guy, 'The Origins of the Petition of Right Reconsidered', *Historical Journal*, XXV (1982) 289–312, illuminates the duplicity of the Crown in the aftermath of the forced loan. J. Wormald, 'James VI and I: Two Kings or One?', *History*, LXVIII (1983) 187–209, offers a suggestive reinterpretation of James I's kingship. Finally, K. Sharpe, 'Faction at the Early Stuart Court', *History Today*, XXXIII (Oct 1983) 39–46, places Buckingham in context in developments in faction at the Jacobean and Caroline Courts.

3.   WILLIAM LAUD, ARCHBISHOP OF CANTERBURY

H. R. Trevor-Roper, *Archbishop Laud 1573–1645* (1962), is by far the most useful biography of Laud and one of the best written on any seventeenth-century figure. H. G. Alexander, *Religion in England* (1968), is a useful survey of religious developments from the Elizabethan Settlement to the Restoration. Two books by Christopher Hill do much to make sense of the religious complexities of the early seventeenth century: *The Economic Problems of the Church* (Oxford, 1956), and *Society and Puritanism in Pre-Revolutionary England* (1964).

Other helpful works covering the Laudian period include Edward Hyde, Earl of Clarendon, *History of the Rebellion and Civil Wars in England* I (Oxford, 1888); M. Van Cleave Alexander, *Charles I's Lord Treasurer, Sir Richard Weston* (1975), M. Havran, *The Catholics in Caroline England* (Oxford, 1962), and *Caroline Courtier: The Life of Lord Cottington* (1973); C. Carlton, *Charles I: the Personal Monarch* (1983); M. Tolmie, *The Triumph of the Saints: The Separate Churches of London 1616–49* (Cambridge, 1977); P. Seaver, *The Puritan Lectureships: The Politics of Religious Dissent 1560–1662* (Stanford, Calif., 1970); E. R. Adair, 'Laud and the Church of England', *Church History*, 1936; R. M. Smuts, 'The Puritan Followers of Henrietta Maria', *English Historical Review*, Jan 1978; O. U. Kalu, 'Continuity and Change, Bishops of London and Religious Dissent in Early Stuart England', *Journal of British Studies*, XVIII (1979).

Lastly, there is no substitute, of course, for reading Laud's own works, especially his diary, and interested students should visit the Library of St John's College, Oxford, where there is a fine collection of Laudiana. The author is grateful to the President of St John's for permission to use the Laudian library in the preparation of this chapter.

4.   THOMAS WENTWORTH, EARL OF STRAFFORD

The fullest biography of Wentworth is by C. V. Wedgwood, *Thomas Wentworth, First Earl of Strafford, 1593–1641: A Revaluation* (1961), an expanded and revised edition of the volume originally published in 1935. S. P. Salt's article 'Sir Thomas Wentworth and the Parliamentary Representation of Yorkshire, 1614–1628', in *Northern History*, 1980, contains much useful information on Wentworth's early career in its county context, while C. Russell, *Parliaments and English Politics, 1621–29* (Oxford, 1979), details his career at Westminster. J. P. Cooper's edition of *The Wentworth Papers 1597–1628* (Camden Society, 1973) provides essential source material, and his article 'The Fortune of Sir Thomas Wentworth Earl of Strafford', *Economic History Review*, 1958, gives insight into Wentworth's personal finances. J. T. Cliffe, *The Yorkshire Gentry*, (1969) illustrates Wentworth's activities with the Council of the North and his relations with fellow Yorkshire landowners. For Wentworth in Ireland, the standard work is H. F. Kearney, *Strafford in Ireland* (Manchester, 1959), and there is good material in the chapters by Aidan Clarke in *The Cambridge New History of Ireland*, III (1976). T. Ranger has added to Kearney's account in 'Strafford in Ireland: A Revaluation', in *Past and Present*, 1961, reprinted in *Crisis in Europe 1560–1660*, ed. T. Aston (1965). Wentworth's dealings with the Long Parliament, his impeachment and attainder are all covered by Anthony Fletcher in *The Outbreak of the English Civil War* (1981).

5.   JOHN PYM

There is no good biography of Pym. The article by Gardiner in the *Dictionary of National Biography* provides the best introduction, along with the general accounts by I. Roots in *The Great Rebellion* (1966) and P. Zagorin in *The Court and the Country* (1969). For the 1620s an invaluable source of information and ideas is Conrad Russell's essay 'The Parliamentary Career of John Pym, 1621–29', in *The English Commonwealth 1547–1640: Essays in Politics and Society Presented to Joel Hurstfield* (Leicester, 1979), and further detail is contained in Russell's *Parliaments and English Politics 1621–29* (Oxford, 1979). For the development of Arminianism and religious ideas in the 1620s see the essay by Nicholas Tyacke, 'Puritanism, Arminianism and Counter-revolution', in *The Origins of the English Civil War*, ed. C. Russell (1973), and Peter White's 'The Rise of Arminianism Reconsidered', *Past and Present*, 1983. The only useful material on the 1630s is in J. H. Hexter, *The Reign of King Pym* (Cambridge, Mass., 1941), which also discusses the politics and management of the Middle Group in the Long Parliament. Pym's relations with London are mentioned in V. Pearl, *London and the Outbreak of the Puritan Revolution* (Oxford, 1961). Anthony Fletcher's detailed study, *The Outbreak of the English Civil War* (1981) gives a full account of Pym's activities in the early days of the Long Parliament. His financial programme is covered in Russell's essay 'Parliament and the King's Finances', in *Origins of the English Civil War*. Pym's role as a parliamentary manager and committee man are dealt with in three articles by L. Glow: 'Pym and Parliament', *Journal of Modern History*, 1964; 'The Committee Men in the Long Parliament', *Historical Journal*, 1965; and 'The Committee of Safety', *English Historical Review*, 1965. J. S. Morrill's *The Revolt of the Provinces* (1976) contains details of the parliamentary war machine on the local level. Articles in the *Journal of Modern*

History, 1977, provide some interesting comments on the Long Parliament and Pym's role.

6. SIR HENRY VANE THE YOUNGER

The best study of Vane's career is V. A. Rowe, *Sir Henry Vane the Younger* (1970), which is a thorough and precise survey of his politics and administrative work. Further biographical detail is available in J. H. Adamson and H. F. Folland, *Sir Harry Vane* (1973), which is perhaps more readable but is more superficial and discursive. For understanding the political developments from 1647–53, both D. Underdown, *Pride's Purge* (Oxford, 1971), and B. Worden, *The Rump Parliament* (Cambridge, 1974), are essential reading. Useful information can also be found in *The Interregnum*, ed. G. E. Aylmer (1972), especially on the events of 1659. For an understanding of radical religious attitudes and behaviour, the most accessible and valuable surveys are C. Hill, *The World Turned Upside Down* (1975) and W. Lamont, *Godly Rule* (1969), although neither deals in particular detail with Vane himself. The most useful summary of the whole period appears in I. Roots, *The Great Rebellion* (1966). See also L. Glow, 'Political Affiliations in the House of Commons after Pym's Death', *Bulletin of the Institute of Historical Research*, XXXVIII (1965).

7. EDWARD HYDE, EARL OF CLARENDON

The fullest biography of Clarendon is still T. H. Lister, *Life of Clarendon* (1837–8), not accessible to most readers. R. W. Harris, *Clarendon and the English Revolution* (1983) appeared in print only after this essay was completed. It does not produce anything very new in material or analysis, but it will obviously become the main source for those wishing to study Hyde's career in greater depth, although it devotes almost as much space to 'relating the developments of the age' as to examining his life. In many respects the best modern study is still B. H. G. Wormald, *Clarendon: Politics, History and Religion 1640–1660* (Cambridge, 1951), a brilliant and illuminating insight into his ideas, but its title makes clear its limitations as a biographical work. Well worth reading, for its style as well as its content, is, of course, Clarendon's own *History of the Rebellion and Civil Wars* and *Life by Himself*, but their accuracy must not be taken for granted; the best modern edition of extracts is edited by H. Trevor-Roper (Oxford, 1978), whose lecture *Clarendon* (1975), is a useful summary of his career.

Other works which impinge on his career and deserve study are A. Fletcher, *The Outbreak of the English Civil War* (1981) for the years 1640–2, and R. Ashton, *The English Civil War* (1978). For the Restoration, see *The Restoration*, ed. J. Thirsk (1976). For the religious restoration, the most useful guide is R. A. Beddard, 'The Restoration Church', in *The Restored Monarchy*, ed. J. R. Jones (1979), but also see the volumes and articles listed in note 10 to this chapter. For Clarendon's ideas on government after 1660, see E. I. Carlyle, 'Clarendon and the Privy Council', *English Historical Review*, XXVII (1912). Also useful are J. R. Jones, 'Political Groups in the Convention of 1660', *Historical Journal*, XI (1963); and C. Roberts, 'The Impeachment of the Earl of Clarendon', *Cambridge Historical Journal*, 1957. For both a genuine feel of the atmosphere in London during the years of the Restoration period, and for comments on the various personalities at Court, *The Diary of Samuel Pepys*, ed. R. Latham and W. Matthews, 11 vols (1970–83), provides fascinating reading.

8. ANTHONY ASHLEY COOPER, EARL OF SHAFTESBURY

A meticulous and thorough account of Shaftesbury's life and career is provided in K. H. D. Haley, *The First Earl of Shaftesbury* (Oxford, 1968). The best study of the development of the Whig party is in J. R. Jones, *The First Whigs* (Oxford, 1961), and details of their methods and electioneering-techniques can be discovered in D. George, 'Elections and Electioneering 1679–81', *English Historical Review*, 1930; E. R. Lipson, 'Elections to the Exclusion Parliaments 1679–81', *English Historical Review*, 1913; and J. R. Jones, 'The Green Ribbon Club', *Durham University Journal*, XLIX (1956). The hysteria of the Exclusion crisis is best seen in J. P. Kenyon, *The Popish Plot* (1972). A useful summary of politics in this period appears in J. R. Jones, 'Parties and Parliament', in *The Restored Monarchy*, ed. J. R. Jones (1979). Other useful material will be found in C. Roberts, *The Growth of Responsible Government in England* (Cambridge, 1966); B. Behrens, 'The Whig Theory of the Constitution in the Reign of Charles II', *Cambridge Historical Journal*, 1941; and O. W. Furley, 'The Whig Exclusionists: Pamphlet Literature in the Exclusion Campaign, 1679–81', *Cambridge Historical Journal*, 1957.

9. THOMAS OSBORNE, EARL OF DANBY

The standard and complete biography is A. Browning, *Thomas Osborne, Earl of Danby*, 3 vols (Glasgow, 1944–51). The third volume consists of a selection of papers and letters by Danby. Little work has been done since then specifically on Danby, but K. Feiling, *A History of the Tory Party, 1640–1714* (Oxford, 1924), contains valuable material on this period, as does D. T. Witcombe, *Charles II and the Cavalier House of Commons* (Manchester, 1966). A useful summary of party organisation appears in A. Browning, 'Parties and Party Organisation in the Reign of Charles II', *Transactions of the Royal Historical Society*, XXX (1948). For both details and understanding of Danby's financial administration, reference must be made to C. D. Chandaman, *The English Public Revenue 1660–1688* (Oxford, 1975). There are also useful summaries of his party management in J. R. Jones, 'Parties and Parliament', and of his financial work in H. Tomlinson, 'Financial and Administrative Developments in England, 1660–88', both in *The Restored Monarchy*, ed. J. R. Jones (1979). Useful summaries of his years in office will be found in D. Ogg, *England in the Reign of Charles II* (Oxford, 1934), and J. R. Jones, *Country and Court* (1978).

10. ROBERT SPENCER, EARL OF SUNDERLAND

There is, fortunately, an outstanding biography of Sunderland: J. P. Kenyon, *Robert Spencer, Earl of Sunderland 1641–1702* (1958). Recent research has done little to modify the views expressed in this work. See also J. P. Kenyon, 'The Earl of Sunderland and the King's Administration 1693–5', *English Historical Review*, LXXI (1956).

For Sunderland and James II see J. Miller, *James II – a Study in Kingship* (Hove,

1977), and 'The Earl of Sunderland's Letter to a Friend', in *Parliamentary History*, v: *1688–1702*, ed. W. Cobbett (1809) Appendixes, iii, xiii–xviii.

The reign of William III has not always been well served by historians. H. Horwitz, *Parliament, Policy and Politics in the Reign of William III* (Manchester, 1977) is the most scholarly work, but the detail often obscures the interpretation of events. Still very useful is S. B. Baxter, *William III* (1966), while the most helpful book for students is *Britain after the Glorious Revolution*, ed. G. Holmes (1969). D. Rubini, *Court and Country* (1968), is very misleading.

Finally, the Portland MSS in Nottingham University Library contains an invaluable series of letters of the 1690s.

Notes and References

INTRODUCTION *Timothy Eustace*

1. See the development of this argument in C. Russell, 'Parliamentary History in Perspective, 1604–29', *History*, LXI, no. 20 (1976) 1–27.
2. A. Fletcher, *The Outbreak of the English Civil War* (1981).
3. C. D. Chandaman, *The English Public Revenue 1660–88* (Oxford, 1975) pp. 203–8.
4. J. Morrill, 'The Church in England, 1642–49', in *Reactions to the English Civil War, 1642–49*, ed. J. Morrill (1982).
5. K. Thomas, *Religion and the Decline of Magic* (1971).

1. LIONEL CRANFIELD, EARL OF MIDDLESEX   *Jonathan Watts*

1. M. Prestwich, *Cranfield: Politics and Profits under the Early Stuarts* (Oxford, 1966) p. 66.
2. Ibid. p. 72.
3. R. H. Tawney, *Business and Politics under James I: Lionel Cranfield as Merchant and Minister* (Cambridge, 1958) p. 92.
4. D. Thomas, 'Financial and Administrative Developments', in *Before the English Civil War*, ed. H. Tomlinson (1983) p. 104.
5. J. Hurstfield, 'The Political Morality of Early Stuart Statesmen', *History*, 1971, p. 240.
6. Tawney, *Business and Politics*, p. 147.
7. R. Lockyer, *Buckingham: The Life and Political Career of George Villiers, First Duke of Buckingham, 1592–1628* (1981) p. 61.
8. Ibid. p. 74.
9. Ibid. p. 49.
10. Ibid. p. 48.
11. Ibid. p. 72.
12. Tawney, *Business and Politics*, p. 147.
13. R. E. Zaller, *The Parliament of 1621* (Berkeley, Calif., 1971) p. 51.
14. Prestwich, *Cranfield*, p. 250.
15. Tawney, *Business and Politics*, p. 161.
16. Ibid. p. 167.
17. Prestwich, 'English Politics and Administration 1603–1625', in *The Reign of James VI and I*, ed. A. G. R. Smith (1973).
18. Prestwich, *Cranfield*, p. 328.
19. Zaller, *The Parliament of 1621*, p. 50.

20. Prestwich, *Cranfield*, p. 340.
21. Tawney, *Business and Politics*, p. 197.
22. Lockyer, *Buckingham*, p. 193.
23. Prestwich, *Cranfield*, p. 448.
24. Lockyer, *Buckingham*, p. 37.
25. Prestwich, in *The Reign of James VI and I*, p. 142.

2. GEORGE VILLIERS, DUKE OF BUCKINGHAM
Donald Wilkinson

1. S. R. Gardiner, *History of England from the Accession of James I to the Outbreak of the Civil War, 1603–1642* (1883–4) VI, 358.

2. H. R. Trevor-Roper, *Archbishop Laud*, 2nd edn (1965) p. 51.

3. C. Roberts, *The Growth of Responsible Government in Stuart England* (Cambridge, 1966) p. 54.

4. C. Russell, *Parliaments and English Politics, 1621–1629* (Oxford, 1979) p. 10.

5. Edward Hyde, Earl of Clarendon, *The History of the Rebellion and Civil Wars in England*, ed. W. D. Macray (Oxford, 1888) I, 10.

6. *The Autobiography and Correspondence of Sir Simonds D'Ewes*, ed. J. O. Halliwell (1845) I, 166.

7. R. Ashton, *James I by his Contemporaries* (1969) p. 127.

8. Historical Manuscripts Commission, *Calendar of the MSS of the Marquis of Bath* (1907) II, 71.

9. Gardiner, *History*, III, 98.

10. Clarendon, *History of the Rebellion*, I, 42.

11. Ashton, *James I by his Contemporaries*, p. 124.

12. Clarendon, *History of the Rebellion*, I, 38.

13. Historical Manuscripts Commission, *Supplementary Report on the MSS of the Earl of Mar and Kellie* (1930) p. 129.

14. *Calendar of the State Papers Domestic, 1619–1623*, p. 257.

15. *Autobiography of Sir Simonds D'Ewes*, I, 368.

16. *Journal of the House of Lords*, III, 663.

17. *Journal of the House of Commons*, I, 911.

18. J. Rushworth, *Historical Collections* (1721) I, 355.

19. R. Lockyer, *Buckingham: The Life and Political Career of George Villiers, First Duke of Buckingham, 1592–1628* (1981) p. 458.

20. J. P. Cooper, 'The Fall of the Stuart Monarchy', in *The New Cambridge Modern History*, IV: *The Decline of Spain and the Thirty Years War, 1609–1648/59*, ed. J. P. Cooper (Cambridge, 1970) p. 541.

21. Trevor-Roper, *Laud*, p. 456.

22. *Lords' Journal*, III, 666.

3. WILLIAM LAUD, ARCHBISHOP OF CANTERBURY
Jeremy Ward

1. See A. Wood, *Annals* (1606).
2. C. Charlton, *Charles I: The Personal Monarch* (1983) p. 162.
3. There is some disagreement among historians as to how anti-Puritan Laud was. He was more concerned about Puritan practices of worship, especially where they deviated from orthodox Anglicanism as he saw it. He was less concerned with Puritan theology, for Laud took little interest in theological matters and even at his trial was not accused of 'Arminian' views. For the most recent opinions see N. Tyacke, 'Puritanism, Arminianism and Counter-Revolution', in *The Origins of the English Civil War*, ed. C. Russell (1973); H. Schwartz, 'Arminianism and the English Parliament 1624–29', *Journal of British Studies*, XII (1973); and P. White, 'The Rise of Arminianism Reconsidered', *Past and Present*, Nov 1983.
4. Lecturers were employed by local groups of laity such as a town corporation to preach sermons on fixed days, usually market day. They were paid from a fund set up for the purpose and therefore owed no direct loyalty to a bishop. Many of the lecturers were Puritans.
5. P. Seaver, *The Puritan Lectureships, the Politics of Religious Dissent, 1560–1662* (Stanford, Calif., 1970).
6. Laud won a test case concerning the position of the altar at St Gregory's Church, London, in 1633.
7. Although it is often supposed that most cases were heard in the Court of High Commission, only 5 per cent of that court's cases were brought by the authorities. Most of the other cases were private prosecutions. Laud's most important cases – Leighton, Prynne, Burton, Bastwick for example – were all heard in the Star Chamber.
8. M. Havran, *The Catholics in Caroline England* (Oxford, 1962) p. 149.
9. Quoted in Allen Birchler, 'Archbishop John Spottiswoode: Chancellor of Scotland 1635–38', *Church History*, 1970, p. 317.
10. C. Hill, *The Economic Problems of the Church* (Oxford, 1956) p. 344.
11. H. R. Trevor-Roper, *Archbishop Laud* (1962) p. 119.

4. THOMAS WENTWORTH, EARL OF STRAFFORD
Jonathan Watts

1. S. R. Gardiner, *Constitutional Documents of the Puritan Revolution* (Oxford, 1906) pp. 156–7
2. *The Wentworth Papers 1597–1628*, ed. J. P. Cooper (Camden Society, 1973) Introduction.
3. C. Russell, *Parliaments and English Politics, 1621–29* (Oxford, 1979) p. 258.
4. C. V. Wedgwood, *Thomas Wentworth, First Earl of Strafford: A Revaluation* (1961) p. 57.
5. Ibid., p. 64.
6. J. T. Cliffe, *The Yorkshire Gentry* (1969) p. 295.
7. J. P. Kenyon, *The Stuart Constitution* (Cambridge, 1966) pp. 18–19.

8. Ibid., p. 212.

9. Cliffe, *Yorkshire Gentry*, p. 301.

10. J. P. Cooper, 'The Fortune of Thomas Wentworth, Earl of Strafford', *Economic History Review*, 1958, p. 234.

11. T. Ranger, 'Richard Boyle and the Making of an Irish Fortune', *Irish Historical Studies*, 1957.

12. H. F. Kearney, *Strafford in Ireland* (Manchester, 1959) p. 60.

13. Wedgwood, *Wentworth*, p. 259.

14. Ibid., p. 345.

15. Ibid., p. 310.

16. A. Fletcher, *The Outbreak of the English Civil War* (1981) p. 9.

17. P. Christianson, 'The Obliterated Portions of the House of Lords Journal Dealing with the Attainder of Strafford 1641', *English Historical Review*, 1980, p. 346.

5.   JOHN PYM   *Jonathan Watts*

1. C. Russell, 'The Parliamentary Career of John Pym 1621–29', in *The English Commonwealth: Essays in Politics and Society Presented to Joel Hurstfield* (Leicester, 1979) p. 164.

2. V. Pearl, *London and the Outbreak of the Puritan Revolution* (Oxford, 1961) p. 1.

3. A. Fletcher, *The Outbreak of the English Civil War* (1981) p. 26.

4. Ibid., p. 43.

5. Ibid., p. 106.

6. J. H. Hexter, *The Reign of King Pym* (Cambridge, Mass., 1941) p. 196.

7. Ibid., p. 1.

6.   SIR HENRY VANE THE YOUNGER
Timothy Eustace

1. Quoted in D. Underdown, *Pride's Purge* (Oxford, 1971) p. 17.

2. J. H. Adamson and H. F. Folland, *Sir Harry Vane* (1973) p. 238.

3. See M. A. Kishlansky, 'The Case of the Army Truly Stated: The Creation of the New Model Army', *Past and Present*, LXXXI (1978) 51–74.

4. M. A. Kishlansky, 'The Army and the Levellers: The Road to Putney', *Historical Journal*, XXII (1979) 795–824.

5. V. A. Rowe, *Sir Henry Vane the Younger* (1970) p. 1.

6. Ibid., p. 97.

7. B. Worden, *The Rump Parliament* (Cambridge, 1974) p. 26.

8. Rowe, *Sir Henry Vane*, p. 134.

9. Adamson and Folland, *Sir Harry Vane*, p. 466.

10. Ibid., p. 448.

7. EDWARD HYDE, EARL OF CLARENDON
Timothy Eustace

1. Edward Hyde, Earl of Clarendon, *The Life of Edward, Earl of Clarendon* (Oxford, 1827) I, 34.
2. T. H. Lister, *Life of Clarendon* (1837) I, 90.
3. *Dictionary of National Biography* (1891) XXVIII, 372.
4. Lister, *Life of Clarendon*, I, 167.
5. B. H. G. Wormald, *Clarendon: Politics, History and Religion 1640–1660* (Cambridge, 1951) p. 173.
6. Ibid., p. 238.
7. J. R. Jones, 'Political Groups and Tactics in the Convention of 1660', *Historical Journal*, XI (1963) 159–77.
8. *DNB*, XXVIII, 377.
9. E. I. Carlyle, 'Clarendon and the Privy Council, 1660–7', *English Historical Review*, XXVII (1912) 251.
10. R. S. Bosher, *The Making of the Restoration Settlement, 1649–1662* (1951); G. R. Abernathy, 'English Presbyterians and the Stuart Restoration, 1648–1663', *Transactions of the American Philosophical Society*, 1965, pp. 50–93, and 'Clarendon and the Declaration of Indulgence, *Journal of Ecclesiastical History*, XI (1960) 55–73; I. M. Green, *The Re-establishment of the Church of England 1660—1663* (Oxford, 1978); D. Witcombe, *Charles II and the Cavalier House of Commons* (Manchester, 1966) pp. 8–9, 211.
11. Bosher, *Making of the Restoration Settlement*, p. 165.
12. R. A. Beddard, 'The Restoration Church', in *The Restored Monarchy*, ed. J. R. Jones (1979) p. 167.
13. Lister, *Life of Clarendon*, II, 83.
14. C. D. Chandaman, *The English Public Revenue 1660–88* (Oxford, 1975) pp. 262–8.
15. Lister, *Life of Clarendon*, III, 120.
16. *DNB*, XXVIII, 382–83.

8. ANTHONY ASHLEY COOPER, EARL OF SHAFTESBURY
Timothy Eustace

1. C. Roberts, *The Growth of Responsible Government in Stuart England* (Cambridge, 1966) p. 206.
2. S. Pepys, *Diary*, ed. R. Latham and W. Matthews (1970–6) VI, 13.
3. K. H. D. Haley, *The First Earl of Shaftesbury* (Oxford, 1968) p. 312.
4. Ibid., p. 316.
5. Ibid., p. 343.
6. Ibid., p. 355.
7. For details see below, pp. 205–6.
8. Haley, op. cit., p. 390.
9. For more details of the Green Ribbon Club, see J. R. Jones, 'The Green Ribbon Club', *Durham University Journal*, XLIX (1956) 17–20.
10. F. S. Ronalds, 'The Attempted Whig Revolution of 1678–81', *University of Illinois Bulletin*, XXI (1937) p. 75.

11. Haley, *The First Earl of Shaftesbury*, p. 462.

12. J. R. Jones, *The First Whigs* (Oxford, 1961) p. 59.

9.   THOMAS OSBORNE, EARL OF DANBY
Timothy Eustace and Rod Martin

1. A. Browning, *Thomas Osborne, Earl of Danby*, 3 vols (Glasgow, 1951) I, 109.

2. Ibid., I, 156.

3. See above, p. 188.

4. For details of Danby's financial work, see C. D. Chandaman, *The English Public Revenue 1660–88* (Oxford, 1975) esp. pp. 231–47.

5. Ibid., p. 235.

6. Ibid., p. 278.

7. D. Ogg, *England in the Reign of Charles II*, 2 vols (Oxford, 1934) II, 529.

8. See above, p. 189.

9. Browning, *Osborne*, II, 68.

10. Ibid., I, 291.

11. For an explanation of the changed political circumstances post-1688, see below, pp. 233–4.

10.   ROBERT SPENCER, EARL OF SUNDERLAND
Rod Martin

1. Quoted in J. P. Kenyon, *Robert Spencer, Earl of Sunderland* (1958) p. 330.

2. Quoted in *The Divided Society*, ed. G. Holmes and W. Speck (1967) pp. 11–12.

3. G. Burnet, *History of his Own Time* (Oxford, 1823) IV, 5 (Onslow's note).

4. Nottingham University Library, Portland MSS PWA 1229: Sunderland to Earl of Portland, 14 Aug 1693.

5. Ibid., PWA 1218: Sunderland to Portland, 27 June 1695. For more of Sunderland's views on the Cabinet, see ibid., PWA 1238, 1240: Sunderland to Portland, 13 July, 5 Aug 1694.

6. Ibid., PWA 511: Henry Guy to Portland, 6 Aug 1695.

7. J. P. Kenyon, *Spencer*, pp. 331–2.

Notes on Contributors

TIMOTHY EUSTACE is a member of the History department at the Manchester Grammar School, having previously taught at Eton College and Malvern College. He was an undergraduate at Magdalene College, Cambridge.

ROD MARTIN is Head of Politics and a member of the History department at the Manchester Grammar School. He studied history at Cardiff University and went on to do research at Lancaster University, writing his thesis on the Whig party in the 1690s.

JEREMY WARD is Head of Arts and a member of the History department at the Manchester Grammar School. He was previously Head of History at Eastbourne College. He was an undergraduate at Fitzwilliam College, Cambridge, and then studied at Indiana University.

JONATHAN WATTS is Head of History at Birkenhead School, having previously taught at the Manchester Grammar School and then spent four years as Head of History at Ashville College, Harrogate. He was an undergraduate at the Queen's College, Oxford, and then did research at York University.

DONALD WILKINSON is Head of History at Oakham School, having previously taught at the Manchester Grammar School. He was an undergraduate and graduate student at Keeble College, Oxford, where he did research into the Justices of the Peace and their work in early Stuart Lancashire.

Index

256